Human Resource Management in the Hospitality Industry

FIFTH EDITION

Previously called *Personnel Management in the Hotel and Catering Industry*, then *Human Resource Management in the Hotel and Catering Industry*

M. J. Boella, MA, MHCIMA, MIPM, MIMC.

Stanley Thornes (Publishers) Ltd

First published by Barrie & Jenkins 1974
Second edition published by Hutchinson 1980
Reprinted with amendments 1981
Third edition 1983
Reprinted 1983
Fourth edition 1987
Reprinted 1988

Fifth edition published by Stanley Thornes (Publishers) Ltd 1992
© M. J. Boella 1974, 1980, 1983, 1987, 1988, 1992

British Library Cataloguing in Publication Data
Boella, M. J.
  Human resource management in the hospitality
  industry. – 5th ed.
  I. Title
  647.068

  ISBN 0-7487-0567-8

Photoset in Linotron Plantin by
Northern Phototypesetting Co. Ltd, Bolton

Printed and bound in Great Britain at
The Bath Press, Avon

Contents

List of figures

Foreword

The ultimate test of hospitality management occurs at the point of contact between service staff and the customer. But this also depends on the quality and consistency of work performed by production staff. The co-ordination of efforts made by these working groups will determine the degree of satisfaction experienced by the customer, whether it is in a hotel, restaurant or institutional operation.

It seems self-evident to me that the standards achieved must depend on the system of recruitment, selection and training in any particular enterprise. Sophisticated techniques of marketing, planning, food and beverage control or computer application may be used in a business, and these are important, but the extent to which employees can successfully cope with their job will determine the level of 'service', so often stated as being our basic endeavour. Human resource management is concerned with how people cope with their jobs; in retrospect it seems puzzling that it took until 1974 for the first edition, the first on the subject, to be published. It gives me great pleasure to introduce the fifth edition of this book. That it has reached this stage is a testimonial to the contribution which earlier editions have made to our industry. Michael Boella has incorporated new material, in the light of his experience, which the contemporary hospitality manager now needs to know. At the same time, emphasis has been maintained on the responsibility of line managers for the human resource under their command.

Human Resource Management is not, therefore, a text for personnel managers, although such specialists will find the contents of interest and benefit; it is essentially concerned with presenting the information required by a line manager to complement his or her technical knowledge. *Human Resource Management in the Hospitality Industry* has its origins in the series of short courses for managers which I organized in the early 1960s. I had great difficulty in collecting suitable case material from the industry and was heavily dependent on a small number of enlightened personnel managers. The lack of a suitable text was strongly felt and Michael Boella, one of the students, vowed to remedy this when he had gained experience in his newly chosen career. After nine years of dealing with just about every facet of personnel and training work with Forte's and Bass Charrington, he finally undertook the task. But the book was only completed after he had gained a wider experience, as a consultant dealing with problems of several large organizations, as well as many smaller ones. Subsequent experience as Principal Lecturer and Course Director for hotel and catering courses at Brighton Polytechnic has provided an opportunity of sharing his knowledge with a new generation of managers as well as to extend his consultancy work in more specialized areas.

Effective staff, committed to company objectives, confident of their skills and deriving satisfaction from their work will not result from reading this or any other text. Nor will it happen overnight; a good standard of human resource management can only be evolved over a lengthy period of co-operative effort between line managers and specialists. In order to achieve this a shared understanding of the processes involved is requisite, and *Human Resource Management* provides this in relation to recruitment, selection and maintenance of staff, together with the associated techniques. As such, it can be useful to the practising manager as well as being a starting point for the potential manager. But this book will also be a valuable source to that jack-of-all-trades of our industry, the predominating small-unit operator.

Philip Nailon, BSc., MPhil., FHICMA
Professor of Hotel and Catering Management
Department of Management Studies
for Tourism and Hotel Industries
University of Surrey

Preface to the fifth edition

It is only three years since the fourth edition of this book was published but already many changes have taken place which have made the production of a fifth edition desirable, if not essential.

Of outstanding importance to me appears to be the increasing awareness of the differences between personnel management and human resource management and I have attempted to face up to this issue by including new chapters on Managing People, Customer Care, and Managing in an International Context which may appear more at home in an operations management text rather than a personnel text. This probably highlights what human resource management is as opposed to personnel management. It is essentially what all managers should be concerned with in order to achieve their business objectives.

Another key issue affecting the industry is the increasing concentration of ownership both at the domestic level and at the international level. Some observers of the industry predict that by the mid-nineties there may well be only eight key international hotel operators. This increasing internationalism is being accelerated by a number of different forces including the Single Europe Act, which means that by 1993 most barriers to cross border trade in Europe will have been lifted. The 'marketization' of Eastern Europe also means that opportunities will develop both for those countries to develop their own domestic tourist industries, but also for many different operators to develop new markets.

On the domestic front the development of compulsory competitive tendering has meant massive changes in the ways in which the many different public sector catering and leisure services are delivered to the consumer.

Of major concern to the industry over the next few years must be the question of hygiene and food safety. There have been such dramatic changes to the food chain that new methods of control and better staff training are going to be essential for the future. The industry's managers and proprietors need to be much more cautious about the use of equipment and ingredients – the common use of domestic microwave ovens in many catering situations is just one such example which can lead to serious risks of food poisoning.

Finally I would like to thank those managers who have assisted by meeting with me to discuss the contents and by providing examples of their documentation which have been included in this text book. These include Trusthouse Forte Hotels UK Ltd, Crest Hotels (since acquired by THF),

Marriott Hotels USA, Sheraton and many others as well. In addition I have been able to continue to make use of my recent consultancy experience which has included work in competitive tendering, customer care and also with Continental companies such as SNCF Sealink Ferries.

I would also like to thank the many colleagues who have helped by providing suggestions and material for this text. These include Pam Carter, Chris Hampshire and Lorraine Worland of Brighton Polytechnic's Learning Resources, Bob Sang, Clifford Goodwin and Peter Jones, of Brighton Polytechnic.

Finally a word to colleague lecturers in other colleges. I have tried very hard to keep the readers of this book very much in mind. These are the practitioners and the students, the future practitioners. I have not written this book for colleague lecturers therefore I can be accused by them of over-simplifications, ommissions and minimal use of references. For this I do not apologize. I have set out, more than anything else, to make the book readable. I believe also that there is a tendency to over-complicate much of management and the study of management. It is my belief that the principles of management essentially are very simple to understand – it is the achievement of an organization's aims and objectives, particularly quality objectives, which is very difficult. I hope that this latest edition of my book will contribute in some small way to this end.

Michael J. Boella MA, MHCIMA, MIPM
September 1990

'Customer satisfaction begins not with the customer, but in the relations between those who manage and those who are managed, so one must start right at the top and ensure that company policy about personnel management is clear and unmistakable.'

LORD ROBENS, Sir Julian Salmon Lecture, 28 October 1976

'In a service industry the most important ingredient in the product is people. The quality of our people determines the quality of the service we give to customers and thus our success in the market place. Not surprisingly almost every discussion we have in the company starts or finishes with personnel matters. We recognise that we can only continue to exist by attracting, training and motivating good people. Doing that successfully means having a caring and efficient personnel function to assist line managers in what is one of their primary responsibilities.'

ROCCO FORTE, *Personnel Management*, August 1982

chapter 1

A background to the industry's workforce

Over the last fifty years or so, in spite of economic ups and downs, the advanced nations of the world have seen many important changes. The major one, with little doubt, is almost certainly the considerable improvement in the standard of living of the vast majority of people, involving increased leisure and travel, accompanied by a redistribution of the work force away from manufacturing to the service industries. These improvements have come about as a result of many different factors including technological advances in industry and commerce, the increased role of the media, heightened and changed expectations of the majority of the populations, pressure from working people and changes in approaches to management.

The contributions made by the hotel and catering industry to this general rise in standard of living are considerable and varied, providing essential and leisure services, employment and wealth creation. Tourism, of which the hotel and catering industry is a principal element, is now claimed to be the country's fastest growing industry and also one of the leading earners of foreign currency. Tourism now contributes around 3% of total national output and contributes around £7.5 billion from incoming tourism. The fact that millions of people eat meals at or near their places of work or study, rather than at home, would not be possible without restaurants, cafés, public houses, fast food and take-away establishments, and 'in-house' catering facilities. Furthermore the improved standard of living enjoyed by most people has resulted in many more ordinary people being able to 'enjoy a meal out' for pleasure rather than necessity, and in spite of a very persistent poor reputation many more school children, students and hospital patients, enjoy a better standard of catering than ever before. This is partly as a direct response to the demands for improved quality but also because of a more efficient and professional body of catering managers. Even so there is little room for complacency – there are still many examples of poor catering in both the private and the public sectors.

Yet in spite of improvements to the standard of living for the majority of the country's population, and the technical improvements within the hotel and catering industry itself, the conditions of employment of large numbers of the industry's staff have not kept pace with those enjoyed by working people elsewhere. As the British Hotels Restaurants and Caterers Association reported in January 1990 the industry's manual workers are paid around £6,000 per annum or 28% less on average than the national average for all manual workers. Catering managers are little better off – their annual average wage is 27% less than the national average for non-manual workers (British Hotels Restaurants and Caterers Association, *Wages Survey 1989*). Admittedly at the top of the scale craftsmen, such as chefs who are in short supply, can command very high incomes, but at the other end of the scale kitchen porters, for example, may be lucky to earn a third of what they would earn for broadly similar work in many offices, factories and warehouses. The situation is even worse when women's rates of pay are compared with men's rates.

Whilst conditions in the industry may have improved over what they were in the past the relative position of the industry as an employer, compared with other employers, has not improved. This is in spite of efforts being made by some of the larger companies in the industry to improve conditions. Amongst the reasons must be the fact that the labour cost is always a significant proportion of a hotel or catering operation, ranging from around 10% to 40% of revenue, and with few exceptions catering services, as yet, do not lend themselves easily to mechanization, although there are now signs that significant changes in productivity may be forthcoming in the future.

The reasons for the slow rate of improvement in the industry's conditions of employment are considerable including an understandable reluctance on the part of many proprietors and managers to be among the first to charge higher prices for their services, particularly when Britain is reported to be already among the most expensive of tourist destinations. Another reason, however, is probably that the trade union movement exerts little influence in most sectors of the industry and the wages council have certainly not been a substitute. A third reason is that the industry's workforce consists largely of people drawn from the 'secondary' labour market, i.e. those people who use the industry on a short-term basis (such as students, housewives, school leavers) and who are prepared to accept low pay as they may not be the primary 'bread winner'. Because of low pay, low union presence and the high proportion of staff drawn from the secondary labour market the industry has its own less obvious but costly labour problems, including such things as a high labour turnover rate 'institutionalized pilfering' and low standards in many establishments.

It is, of course, to be expected that some aspects of working in the hotel and catering industry are unattractive. There are the intrinsic problems which are unavoidable such as having to work evenings, weekends and bank holidays. Other problems, however, can certainly be reduced or eliminated by determined management action. These problems include unnecessary 'split shift' working, staff reliance on tips, ignorance of methods of calculating pay and distributing service charges, and management's reluctance to 'involve' staff in matters that affect their working lives. A number of reports have highlighted these difficulties which, together with management attitudes, undoubtedly cause much of the industry's labour difficulties. Even today for example many employers and managers expect their ordinary employees to be dedicated to their jobs, to have a 'vocational' attitude to their work, to sacrifice leisure time for pay that is not high by most standards. This attitude is not confined to the commercial and more entrepreneurial sectors of the industry but is found as a discordant element in many organizations. These same employers and managers fail to recognize that their own motivation to work is usually completely different from that of their staff, and that many work people throughout the community are becoming less work-orientated for various reasons. Employers in industry must reconcile themselves rapidly to the fact that the majority of potential staff are less likely to be vocationally committed unless ways and means are found to harness what some researchers claim is a natural motivation to work. And employers in the hotel and catering industry must recognize that. Instead, staff, if they are to stay, expect competitive conditions of employment and leisure, and unless these are offered the industry's staffing problems will persist.

Even in the midst of high unemployment and a significant drop in labour turnover, many employers claimed that they were unable to attract and retain competent and committed staff and they must ask themselves 'why?' It is interesting to note that the major sector in the industry, where there are the least, and in many cases no staff problems, is the institutional and industrial catering sector where leisure time and other conditions are generally more attractive than in many other sectors.

The hotel and catering industry and the British economy

The hotel and catering industry (see Figure 1.2) employs in excess of two million people, and in 1985 Britain was reported to be earning £20 billion in the hotel and catering industry (HCTB – Catering for Employment Seminar 1986). To do this owners, local authorities, management and employees within the industry provided for the needs of millions, including working people, holidaymakers, business travellers, schoolchildren, students and hospital patients. The industry is now a vital part of our economy and over the last ten years has slowly but increasingly been recognized as such. In recognition of this importance, Mrs Sally Oppenheim, Minister responsible for tourism in 1981 said, ' . . . tourism must be accorded to its full status as an industry of absolutely major importance' (*British Travel News*, 1981). Five years later Lord Young, Employment Minister, said '. . . tourism is already one of our largest employers . . . I therefore, want tourism to have a high profile' (reported in *Tourism in Action* 1986). By 1989 the Government's view seemed to accept that tourism was now a key part of the economy and emphasized the need for quality in our tourism product. Mr John Lee, Tourism Minister, said 'We have such a lot to offer in this country. It is clear that emphasis on quality and standards, and current levels of investment in the tourism, leisure and hospitality industry, are helping to keep Britain in the forefront of world tourism' (reported in *Tourism in Action 1989*).

Tourism and travel

Between 1970 and 1987 tourism into Britain increased by 23% and London alone experienced a 4% increase between 1987 and 1988. In the 1990s a further but slower growth approaching 50% for the decade is anticipated (Kleinwort Grieveson Research 1988). They also predict a significant growth in the domestic tourism market, specifically the long break market, with the development of resort holidays such as Centre Parcs. The short break holiday growth trend is also predicted to continue (*ibid*).

This increased demand for tourism and international travel services is a worldwide development and one consequence is the internationalization of many of the leading hotel companies. Twenty-four of the world's leading hotel operators on average each operate hotels in seventeen countries and 40% of the bedrooms they own are in countries other than their own (Kleinwort Grieveson Research 1988). One consequence for the British hospitality industry's employers is that many potential employees now look to overseas for employment.

The growth in demand for business travel, conferences, exhibitions and short courses

An important feature of technologically advanced societies is the need for business people, professionals, administrators and others to travel and to meet. In Britain at the end of the 1980s this market was estimated to be around 18.5 million room nights, having grown over the decade by 120%. This market is anticipated to grow to about 20 million room nights by the year 2000.

This overall growth in tourism creates demands for additional jobs. In the Department of Employment's report 'Tourism '88' the increased number of jobs were estimated at around 50,000 per year. Professor Medlik, on the other hand, writing in *Hospitality* (October 1988), challenges these figures and estimates that new jobs are likely to be nearer 23,000 than the 50,000 estimated by the Department of Employment.

Social and demographic changes

The industry is, of course, responding to major changes in the 'demand' side of the industry, i.e. the consumer side. Demographic changes alone, such as the increased proportion and number of older people, have created demands for more products catering for their needs, and the reduced number of young people (see Figure 1.1) is creating both demand and labour market problems. Amongst the younger population changes in eating habits, a shift to 'grazing' for example, has created opportunities for many different types of fast food outlets. The move to 'healthy eating' too is responsible for a range of new products and a related growth in vegetarianism.

A breakdown in the traditional socio-economic usage of different catering products is probably of significance. No longer are most different products used exclusively by particular socio-economic groups. Instead the use of catering products, to a greater extent than previously, is determined by the *occasion* (*behaviourly determined*) rather than merely by the socio-economic group.

Figure 1.1   *Trends and projections of the number of school leavers*

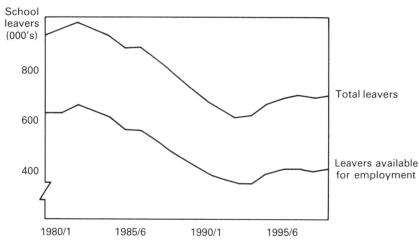

Source: Central Statistical Office

The changing hotel and catering industry

Within the hotel and catering industry itself there are important developments which have long-term implications for the industry.

First, as hotel and catering groups become larger, and also as individual establishments become larger and more complex, there has been an expansion in the junior and middle management cadres.

Also during recent years hotel and catering organizations have become more market oriented. This has led to increased market segmentation. These developments have led to many of the larger companies establishing specialist subsidiary companies, which are concerned with a range of highly specialized products. This has involved, in some cases, considerable changes in products and managements, or the negotiation of franchise-type agreement with international branded names such as Wendy's, Huckleberry's and Dayvilles.

This last development is associated with the rapid growth of fast food outlets in Britain and elsewhere in Europe. The nature of such operations, dependent as they are on the maintenance of rigorous operational and quality standards, has altered the face of British popular catering and is putting many of the traditional operators in jeopardy.

Popular catering is still a relatively easy and inexpensive field to enter but nowadays success demands considerable expertise and promotional effort, which are increasingly becoming beyond the resources of the independent. The franchise side of the industry is growing therefore along with franchising generally.

Growth of the industry, however, has not been regularly distributed across the various sectors of the industry. Contract catering, for example, declined considerably losing over 100,000 employees between 1974 and 1982. However, as a consequence of compulsory competitive tendering, contract catering is seeing growth again, to some extent at a cost to the traditional 'in-house' caterers.

Restaurants and cafés also suffered a decline. On the other hand the fast food sector is now providing more opportunities for employment and rapid promotion. In particular it is providing openings for young people, with a significant proportion of the workforce aged under 21.

While the industry has established its importance from an economic point of view, it could be hoped that those employed in the industry would be reaping rewards that echo this increased importance. In many cases this may well be so with key people such as chefs and waiters at leading restaurants, and good managers, earning high rewards.

Having said this, a variety of reports from organizations such as the Low Pay Unit, The New Earning Survey and the Labour Research Unit put the industry's workers amongst the lowest paid in the country. The Labour Research Unit's 'Bargaining Report' in 1984 reported that hotel and catering workers were among those receiving the lowest basic pay in the country, working longer than average hours and receiving less than average holiday entitlement. The report placed the Licensed Residential Wages Council minimum pay agreement at 389 out of 392 agreements listed, the Unlicensed Residential at 342. As reported above, the industry's own trade association, the British Hotels Restaurants and Caterers Association, reported in January 1990 that the industry's manual workers are paid around £6,000 per annum or 28% less on average than the national average for all manual workers. Catering managers are little better off – their annual average wage is 27% less than the national average for non-manual workers (British Hotels Restaurants and Caterers Association, Wages Survey 1989). This question of low pay is discussed later in the book, because it is not as simple a matter as outside observers appear to think. The value of tips, food, accommodation, laundry and savings on fuel and fares all have to be taken into account so that anyone 'living in' has been largely protected against the worst of recent inflation. Also it must be borne in mind that a very large proportion of the industry's workforce is drawn from a 'secondary labour market'. Because of this many work people may not have high value skills to offer, or alternatively their motives to work may put a premium on the convenience of their work (location, hours) for which they will sacrifice higher incomes.

Undoubtedly, low pay in the industry exists, but it is not something that can be put right overnight. Britain's hotels and restaurants are already reported to be amongst the most expensive in the world, so increases to tariffs are not the answer. Instead, a thorough reappraisal of the services offered and the consequent manning levels and staff training may lead to greater productivity. In this field, strides have been made; capital investment is made to replace the most menial tasks, and efforts are made to improve the standard of training. However, increased productivity in service industries is not as easy to achieve as in many other industries without making radical changes to the nature of the service itself. To some extent this is happening particularly by increasing the amount of customer participation, whether this be by buffet style breakfasts or by automated check-in procedures as being developed by *Formule 1*, the budget division of the French Accor group. The subject of productivity is discussed more fully in Chapter 19.

Most improvements and efforts seem to be made at the tip of the iceberg, mainly amongst the larger companies. The remaining 80–90 per cent of the

Figure 1.2 *Structure of the industry*

Accommodation	Hotels and motels	21,000	
	Bed and breakfast, farm houses	18,600	
	Holiday camps, camping and holiday caravan sites	1,600	
	Licensed private hotels and guest houses	4,500	
Meals	Unlicensed restaurants	14,590	
	Licensed restaurants	12,750	
	Department store catering	4,000	
Public houses and clubs	Public houses	76,250	
	Clubs	35,000	
Tourism and travel	Historic buildings, etc. (with catering)	700	
	Railway stations	370	
	Motorway services	42	
	Airports	66	
	Trains	420 per day	
	Ferries	40	
	Cruise ships	12	
Industrial	Factories and offices (with catering)	22,000	(35% are run by contract caterers)
Public services	Education	35,700	
	Hospitals, homes, etc.	11,500	
	Total:	259,140	

Source: HCTB. *Statistical review of the Hotel and Catering Industry, 1984*

industry is made up of smaller employers who each employ a few staff only and who for a variety of reasons are not able or prepared to evaluate their own business methods as rigorously as is required in today's aggressive business climate. One consequence is the growth of the larger companies, at the expense of smaller companies, which is a phenomenon not confined to the hotel and catering industry, but is a general phenomenon of industrialized societies.

Changing working patterns

In 1986 the National Economic Development Office (NEDO) published its report 'Changing Working Patterns' which identified major changes that have taken place in recent years regarding working patterns.

The report came to a number of conclusions. Firstly it was found that firms were aware of the need to alter working practices. The awareness varied according to the impact of recession on sectors so that manufacturing firms were much more aware of the need for change than service sector firms. One concomitant of these changes was an increased level of communication with the work force and a decline in union opposition to change.

The second major finding was that the main constraints to more flexibility were inadequate skill levels and training resources and also status differences due to staff/manual differentiation and union membership. These constraints were less important in the service sector.

The third finding was that 'distancing', the process by which employers use contractors, agents, etc. to replace employees, had been confined mainly to ancillary or support services such as catering, cleaning, security and transport.

Fourthly it was found that peripheral forms of employment had grown since 1980. Such employment tended to lack continuity and security and such workers enjoyed substantially worse non-pay benefits. The work tended to require low level skills and peripheral status tended to inhibit investment in training and consequently advancement opportunities were limited. Any claimed benefits flowing from peripheral employment were limited to a small number of freelance professionals in shortage occupations.

Finally it was concluded that there had been a growth in 'segmentation' of the labour market and 'this seemed likely to increase the volatility of employment patterns, giving rise to more short-term, interrupted employment while at the same time reducing access to core status'. In addition, NEDO expected firms to shift their recruitment orientation to workers not aspiring to core status, particularly if service sector employment continued to grow. This finding of NEDO has since been reinforced by the statement made by the Institute of Directors which proposed that the government take measures to break traditional work patterns and encourage self-employment, part-time jobs and working from home (Institute of Directors, 24 June 1987). This is in contradiction to the proposed European Economic Community 'Social Charter' which would aim to increase rather than reduce protection of employees.

Such changes in the structure of the labour market and the workforce have not finished by any means yet. They appear to be following Engel's law which states that there 'is an increasing demand for the more sophisticated final service functions' (quoted from Gershuny and Miles 1983). It is predicted by many that the proportion employed in manufacturing will continue to decline because of the ease with which manufacturing can be mechanized, robotized and computerized.

In essence therefore major structural changes are taking place in the workforce, and in methods and organization of work. These can be summarized as follows:

1   Employment in manufacturing is declining as productivity is improved through automation.
2   Employment in 'personal' services is increasing.
3   There will be fewer full time jobs for men.
4   There will be more part-time jobs for women.
5   There will be growth in the secondary labour market and a decline in the primary labour market.

6 There will be an increase in white collar employment.
7 There will be a decline in manual employment.
8 There will be a decline in full time work, with more people doing more than one job.
9 There will be a reduction in job security.
10 Technological change causes re-distribution and re-organization of work.

These trends were summarized by Charles Handy, who wrote that the full-employment society was becoming the part-employment society, that the one-organization career was becoming rarer and that sexual stereo-typing at work was no longer so rigid.

The industry's workforce

In 1985 the Hotel and Catering Industry Training Board (HCITB) published its report *Hotel and Catering Manpower in Britain 1984*. The principal findings are illustrated in Figures 1.3 to 1.7 (reproduced by courtesy of HCTC).

Figure 1.3 *Estimate of the numbers employed in hotel and catering occupations, 1984*

	Numbers	Proportion of full-time employees
MAIN ACTIVITY SECTORS		
Hotels, guesthouses and other tourist accommodation	375	59%
Restaurants, cafés and snackbars	304	58%
Public houses and bars	373	32%
Nightclubs and licensed clubs	155	20%
Canteens and messes (contract catering)	117	52%
Others (self-employed)	9	—
All main activity sectors	1,332	45%
SUBSIDIARY ACTIVITY SECTORS		
Tourism and travel catering:		
Recreational and cultural services	211	N/a
Travel	24	N/a
Public services catering:		
Education	294	N/a
Medical and other health services	190	N/a
Public administration and national defence	48	N/a
Retail distribution	33	N/a
Personal and domestic services	73	N/a
Industrial and office catering (i.e. all other industries and services)	126	N/a
All subsidiary activity sectors	998	38%
All hotel and catering	**2,330**	**42%**

Notes
A 'main activity' sector is one where the main business of the enterprise is catering or the provision of accommodation.
A 'subsidiary activity' sector is one where the main business of the enterprise is something other than catering or the provision of accommodation. This distinction is reflected in statistics published in the *Employment Gazette* which only identifies hotel and catering employees for the main activity sectors.

Figure 1.4   *Numbers employed in hotel and catering by sex and full-*
or part-time working, 1984

	Men		Women		Total	
	Nos.	%	Nos.	%	Nos.	%
MAIN ACTIVITY SECTORS[1]						
Full-time	301	60	301	36	602	45
Part-time	200	40	530	64	730	55
Total	501	100	831	100	1,332	100
SUBSIDIARY ACTIVITY SECTORS[1]						
Full-time	80	93	297	33	377	38
Part-time	6	7	615	67	621	62
Total	86	100	912	100	998	100
ALL INDUSTRY						
Full-time	381	65	598	34	979	42
Part-time	206	35	1,145	66	1,351	58
Total	**587**	**100**	**1,743**	**100**	**2,330**	**100**

Note
1   See note to Figure 1.3

The main points to be drawn from *Hotel and Catering Manpower in Britain 1984* are:

1   The hotel and catering industry employs in excess of 2.3 million. This represents nearly 11% of the total working population. (These figures include the self-employed.)
2   1.3 million are employed in establishments where catering and hotel services are the main activity. One million are employed in sectors such as offices, banks, hospitals, etc., where catering is subsidiary to the main activity.
3   Just under 1 million are full-time workers; 1.7 million are women, i.e. nearly 75% of the workforce.
4   The workforce of the industry has grown by 4% since 1981.
5   Hotels and guest houses have shown the greatest growth, 16%. Restaurants, cafés and industrial catering showed a slight decline. Recreation and cultural services catering showed a growth of 6%.

(In order to follow some of the changes that have occurred since 1978 reference can be made to Chapter 1 of the third edition of this book or the HCITB report *Manpower in the Hotel and Catering Industry*, 1978.)

One important fact to bear in mind is that whilst the industry is described as the hotel and catering industry, it does in fact consist of a number of separate sectors. To what extent each sector is a discrete labour market, still has to be determined. Without a doubt, however, there is movement between sectors and chefs are probably a prime example of this.

Figure 1.5 *Changes in the size of the hotel and catering workforce between 1981 and 1984*

	Nos. of employees 1981	Nos. of employees 1984	Growth/decline Nos.	Growth/decline %
MAIN ACTIVITY SECTORS				
Hotels, guesthouses and other tourist accommodation	324	375	+51	+16%
Restaurants, cafés and snackbars	307	304	−3	−1%
Public houses and bars	351	373	+22	+6%
Nightclubs and licensed clubs	150	155	+5	+3%
Canteens and messes (contract catering)	114	117	+3	+3%
Others (self-employed)	9	9	—	—
All main activity sectors	1,255	1,333	+78	+6%
SUBSIDIARY ACTIVITY SECTORS				
Recreation and cultural services	200	211	+11	+6%
Travel	27	24	−3	−11%
Education	294	294	—	—
Medical and other health services	190	190	—	—
Public administration and national defence	49	48	−1	−2%
Retail distribution	32	33	+1	+3%
Personal and domestic services	72	73	+1	+1%
Industrial and office catering (i.e. all other industries and services)	133	126	−7	−5%
All subsidiary activity sectors	996	998	+2	*
All hotel and catering	**2,251**	**2,330**	**+79**	**+4%**

∗ rounds down to zero

Figure 1.6 *Main activity sectors: breakdown of occupations by sex and full- or part-time working, September 1984*

	Men	Women	Full-time	Part-time	Total
Self-employed working proprietors	77.7	52.7	130.4	—	130.4
Employed managers	146.6	60.9	199.0	8.5	207.5
Supervisors	20.9	29.2	40.2	9.9	50.1
Chefs/cooks	72.0	62.7	56.2	78.5	134.7
Waiters/ waitresses	32.1	75.8	31.8	76.1	107.9
Barmen/barmaids	30.7	123.7	24.0	130.4	154.4
Hotel porters	8.8	0.7	3.7	5.8	9.5
Kitchen porters/hands	21.9	122.4	23.9	120.4	144.3
Counter hands/assistants	4.0	71.7	14.4	60.7	75.1
Domestic staff	2.3	78.8	9.3	71.8	81.1
Butchers/bakers	0.8	0.4	0.4	0.8	1.2
Receptionists	2.0	25.4	14.7	12.7	27.4
Self-employed non-managerial staff	6.1	3.3	9.4	—	9.4
Others (in non-catering occupations)	75.4	123.7	45.5	153.6	199.1
Total	**500.8**	**831.4**	**602.0**	**730.4**	**1,332.2**

Notes
This table is primarily based on the figures for employees in employment for September 1984 in the *Employment Gazette*, divided between occupations in the same proportions as in the Census of Population 1981.

Figures for self-employed are taken from the Census of Population 1981. A figure of 180,000 has also been added to the *Employment Gazette* figures to allow for employees of self-employed working proprietors. This is equal to twice the estimated number of establishments run by a self-employed working proprietor. The figures in other tables have been calculated in a similar manner.

Figure 1.7   *Subsidiary activity sectors: breakdown of occupations by sex and full- or part-time working, September 1984*

	Men	Women	Full-time	Part-time	Total
Employed managers	10.7	15.9	23.6	2.9	26.5
Supervisors	10.3	26.1	29.9	6.5	36.5
Chefs/cooks	18.8	81.1	63.5	36.4	99.9
Waiters/waitresses	3.9	9.9	7.7	6.1	13.6
Barmen/barmaids	3.8	15.5	5.7	13.6	19.4
Counter hands/assistants	5.0	196.0	69.8	131.2	200.9
Kitchen porters/hands	7.4	52.2	18.7	40.9	59.7
Domestic staff and school helpers	5.9	407.7	85.9	327.7	413.6
Hospital ward orderlies	10.0	88.5	52.8	45.7	98.5
Travel stewards and attendants	8.8	17.6	17.7	8.7	26.4
Butchers/bakers	1.5	0.4	2.0	—	2.0
Others			Not available		
Total	**86.1**	**912.8**	**377.3**	**620.7**	**998.2**

Labour turnover and employment

The industry has, for many years, had a reputation for a very high level of labour turnover. In 1984 the HCITB published its report *Manpower Flows in the Hotel and Catering Industry*. The report predicted that there would be in the region of 1.4 million vacancies per annum, 3 per cent arising from growth, 2 per cent from retirements, the remaining 95 per cent from staff turnover. It found the following gross turnover rates: managers 19 per cent; supervisors 94 per cent; craftspeople 55 per cent; operatives 65 per cent. Cafés and public houses had the highest rates of losses to the industry, caused largely by young people using the industry as an interlude between school or college and full-time career.

While some reports categorize the industry's problems very much in statistical terms, it is possible to illustrate some of the problems in more human terms. These range right through the employment process from the initial selection to the termination of employment. All of these aspects will be discussed at more length later, but it is important to see some of the industry's practices in terms that are related to the employee – the individual – who is subject to an employer's employment practices.

Initial selection

At one end of the scale, there are employers who use only expert techniques including group selection procedures and psychological tests. In addition, many companies and the HCTC are now training their managers in most of the skills of management, such as interviewing techniques. At the other end of the scale, however, are many employers who do not even acknowledge receipt of application forms. One manager applied to over fifty employers and received less than twenty acknowledgements. Another employer uses box numbers for the express purpose of avoiding the need to acknowledge applications. On the other hand many employers are frustrated by the casual approach to employment of employees – with many just not turning up for a prearranged interview.

Induction and training

This is an area that has shown considerable improvements in the last few years because of HCTB pressure. However, there are still serious problems which are completely ignored by many managers; for example, some managers or supervisors do not have the empathy to recognize that skills such as laying a table formally, making a bed correctly, using telephones, which are second nature to themselves, may be worrying to some, such as a middle-aged housewife who has come out to work for the first time.

A related problem is the large number of small and medium-sized employers, and large company managers, who continue to insist upon 'experience' rather than being prepared to recruit and train staff, in spite of the fact that about 80 per cent of the industry's workforce does not need other than ordinary 'life and social' skills.

In a more general sense, there is still the argument that because of tight staff budgets, there is no time to train, so to acquire training skills is not worthwhile. Some managers are persuaded, however, that even with understaffing or reduced staffing, training does take place somehow and that training skills become *more* not *less* necessary as staff levels are reduced.

Pay

While there are many instances of high rates of pay in the industry, its image overall is not good.

The reliance, in some sectors, on tipping still exists to a greater extent than some consider desirable. The practice of paying employees the basic or near basic wage and also putting notices on tariffs that service charges are included, has had the effect of diverting guests' tips into company revenue. In many cases this practice has had an adverse effect on net earnings. First, all of the service charge may not be distributed to the staff, and second, income from such a source is taxed, which it was not previously. In spite of this it is to be hoped that the practice of 'all inclusive pricing' (including service charge and VAT) will become common practice in Britain, as it is in some other European countries. However, this practice will have to be linked to a fair system of distribution and the establishment of realistic minimum rates.

In these circumstances, where low pay and distrust of the employer's wages practices exist, it is to be expected that pilfering on a significant scale takes place. A report based upon an Open University case study *Room for Reform* claims that pilfering appears to be an institutionalized part of wage bargaining in hotels. Management often recognizes it as a way to boost inadequate pay.

'Fiddles' range from straightforward short-measuring and short-changing of customers to supplying one's own household with cleaning materials, toilet paper, light bulbs, crockery, cutlery and even towels and other linen. Some 'fiddles' are quite sophisticated and at quite high levels. It has been known for managers to redecorate their own homes at their employer's expense, or for a manager to deduct 'the cost of grass cutting' from the hotel's petty cash and to arrange for a farmer to pay the manager for some acres of hay taken from the same land. In a recent spot survey not one industrial release student questioned had *not* witnessed pilfering.

Such practices, however, must be seen in proper perspective, bearing in mind that some other industries, trades and professions provide vastly more lucrative opportunities than those provided in the hotel and catering industry.

Women

Women, according to the HCTC statistics, make up 1.7 million or 75% of the industry's workforce. This figure represents 17% or nearly one in five of all female employment in Britain. Most women employed in catering are employed in operative or sub-craft level jobs, although women's proportion of management jobs is substantial, 47%. This is the highest proportion of women managers in all of Britain's industries. This may be one explanation of the relatively low rate of pay of the industry's managers (see above).

About 75% of women's jobs in the commercial sector are part-time. Around 830,000 are employed in the main commercial sectors whilst another million are employed in the subsidiary sectors of the industry, i.e. those where catering is an ancillary rather than the main service such as schools and hospitals. One explanation of this concentration in part-time work is that this enables women to combine work with their family responsibilities. Figure 1.7 shows the industry's occupational groups by sex.

Personnel management in the hospitality industry

Until the early 1960s personnel management as a specialist function in the hotel and catering industry was almost non-existent. Where it did exist, it was devoted to small elements of personnel management, such as recruitment and training. It was not until the introduction of employment legislation, such as the Contracts of Employment Act 1964, and the establishment of the Industrial Training Board, that personnel managers began to appear in the industry in any numbers. Today all of the larger companies now employ personnel specialists and personnel management is seen as an essential part of the organization. There is still, however, too little regard paid to it by many employers where personnel managers are frequently junior managers 'learning the ropes' at the staff's expense. As Kelliher and Johnson found, 'the personnel function is not given enough time or consideration for it to be taken seriously'. The overall performance of personnel activities within small hotels was found to be simple and unsophisticated and conducted in the former 'hire and fire' era of personnel work (*International Journal of Hospitality Management*, Volume 6, No. 2, 1987).

Within larger hotels and at senior level in the larger companies personnel work appears to be taken more seriously. Even so the determining factor appears to be more one of attitude to human resource issues rather than size in itself. Where personnel professionals are employed 'the scope of personnel has become more sophisticated, particularly in the areas of industrial relations and employee development' (Kelliher and Johnson *ibid*). In other cases, and increasingly so, the value of professional personnel managers is being recognized and they are increasingly joining management teams at senior level.

The development of personnel management in the industry is examined in much greater detail in a paper published in the *International Journal of Hospitality Management* in 1986 (see Appendix 1).

Further reading

Gershuny, J. and Miles, I., *The New Service Economy*, London, Frances Pinter, 1983

Handy, C., *The Future of Work*, London, Blackwell, 1984

Hotel and Catering Training Company Publications

    Manpower Changes in the Hotel and Catering Industry, London: 1983

    Manpower Flows in the Hotel and Catering Industry, London: 1984

    Hotel and Catering Manpower in Britain, London: 1984

    Statistical Review of the Hotel and Catering Industry, London: 1984

Mars, G. and Mitchell, P., *Manpower Problems in the Hotel and Catering Industry*, London: Heinemann, 1979

Medlik, S., *The Business of Hotels*, London: Heinemann, 1989

Questions

These questions have been designed so that the first question in every case can be answered from material in the preceding chapter or chapters. Subsequent questions may need reference to the books contained in the reading list and maybe to other sources as well, such as the *Employment Gazette*. The last question, in most cases, requires knowledge and experience of the industry, acquired, for example, through normal employment, holiday work or industrial placement.

1 Describe the size and nature of the hotel and catering industry's workforce. What are the outstanding features?

2 Describe the size and nature of the hotel and catering industry's workforce relative to the UK's total workforce.

3 What factors are likely to influence the hotel and catering industry's workforce in the future?

chapter 2

Human resource management

Virtually every management decision affects, to a greater or lesser extent, the people working in the organization. Most decisions are made within an organization's policy framework, explicit or implicit. Policies represent the aims, purposes, principles or intentions of an organization and provide the framework or guidelines for management decisions. Policies, sometimes referred to as 'mission statements', may be written down, as is the case with many larger organizations. Alternatively they may be merely inferred by decisions taken. Some companies within the hotel and catering industry, such as McDonalds, have a policy to operate within a narrow market sector. Other companies, such as Trusthouse Forte, have a policy to operate within many market sectors. These policies provide management with the framework within which they make their decisions; for example, where to expand what to divest, etc.

Human resource policies are normally a part of an organization's overall policy which will consist of a number of components. The extent to which they are a 'sub-policy' or an essential component of the overall policy is a key indicator of how an organization values its human assets.

Figure 2.1 *The components of an organization's policy*

Currently there is a big debate concerning the differences between *human resource management* and *personnel management*. Some hold the view that human resource management is merely a new name for personnel management whilst others consider it to be a new and different view of the way human resources are managed by the enterprise.

David Guest of the London School of Economics writes (*Personnel Management*, January 1989) that there are probably three popular approaches to defining 'human resource management'. The first is merely a re-titling of personnel management, the second approach emphasizes the strategic aspects of managing human resources and the third approach suggests that 'human resource management' is 'distinctively different' from personnel management. He proposes a theory of human resource management, the principal elements of which are shown in Figure 2.2 below.

Figure 2.2 *A theory of human resource management*
(after David Guest, *Personnel Management*, January 1989)

Human resource policy goals

Strategic integration; this is concerned with ensuring that human resource issues are totally integrated into strategic planning and the related organizational structures, etc.

Commitment; this is concerned with binding employees to the organization and obtaining commitment to high performance.

Flexibility/adaptability; this is concerned with ensuring that the organization and the workforce are adaptive and responsive to change.

Quality; this is concerned with ensuring that quality pervades all activities including the production of goods or services, the processes of management and the staff themselves.

Policies

In order to achieve these policy goals certain 'personnel' policies are needed. However, rather than being concerned merely with 'good' personnel practice these are concerned with achieving the goals listed above. These include:

Job design, management of change, recruitment, selection and induction/orientation, appraisal, training, development, reward systems and communication systems.

Cement

In order that integration really takes place the following are also necessary:

Support from key leadership, a powerful sponsor/patron of human resource management, a conscious strategy to pursue success through the proper use of human resources.

Organizational outcomes

These include high job performance, high ability to innovate, change and to solve problems, high cost-effectiveness, low staff turnover, absenteeism and grievances.

The theory contains four main components; human resource policy goals, human resource policies, a 'cement' which binds the system, and organizational outcomes.

From this brief description of human resource management by one writer it is apparent that good human resource management should be the responsibility of all managers – not just personnel managers. And if the Institute of Personnel Management's (IPM) definition of personnel management is examined it is apparent that there are strong similarities.

> Personnel management is a responsibility of all those who manage people, as well as being a description of the work of those who are employed as specialists. It is that part of management which is concerned with people at work and with their relationships within an enterprise. It applies not only to industry and commerce but to all fields of employment.
>
> Personnel management aims to achieve both efficiency and justice, neither of which can be pursued successfully without the other. It seeks to bring together and develop into an effective organization the men and women who make up an enterprise, enabling each to make his own best contribution to its success both as an individual and as a member of a working group. It seeks to provide fair terms and conditions of employment, and satisfying work for those employed.

The main distinction is that the IPM's definition is rather general and 'pluralist' (i.e. it indicates a balancing of the employer's and employees' interests) whereas the definition put forward by David Guest is more concerned with organizational outcomes (a unitarist approach) and resourcing so that the organization's desired outcomes are achieved.

For the purpose of this book human resource management is to be defined along the lines of David Guest's proposition, i.e. the concern of all managers, whilst personnel management is to be discussed as the activities of specialist personnel managers. For this reason this book contains chapters on groups and customer care (being concerned with quality) all concerns of line management.

Human resource and personnel policies should embrace a number of different but interrelated issues. The first may be to do with deciding to be a 'leader' or 'follower' on the terms and conditions offered. A second may be concerned with human resource policies such as career prospects and to what extent an employer sets out to offer long-term secure careers to a significant proportion of the workforce. A third may deal with employee involvement and management style. To what extent do senior management really want to involve staff in decisions? Interestingly one general feature of the top US companies identified by *In Search of Excellence* has been a statement of company credo, and in particular, the emphasis this has put on policy towards employees. Maybe it is this third type of concern which distinguishes human resource management from personnel management.

Personnel management, as a distinct specialization of management, is relatively new and consequently its specialist role and definition varies much more than is the case with older established specializations such as management accounting. In addition, because it leans heavily on the social sciences, its definitions and duties are more fluid. Hence there are many definitions of the role of personnel management, but probably a suitable one is that adopted by the Institute of Personnel Management in 1963 (see above).

Personnel management as a specialist function

To some, personnel management is seen as no more than the welfare branch of the company – concerned with looking after individual employees when in need. In 1986 two writers suggested that the personnel function could be described in one of three ways; clerk of works, contracts manager or architect (Tyson, S. and Fell, A., *Evaluating the Personnel Function*, Hutchinson, London 1989). In 1989 Nick Georgiades, at the European Association for Personnel Management conference, suggested other roles; administrative handmaiden, policeman, toilet flusher, sanitary engineer. To others, it is the 'in-house staff agency', whilst in other cases the personnel management function is integrated completely into the whole company activity. It is concerned with assisting in the harnessing of the employees' energies, in order that the enterprise operates efficiently, and it is also concerned with ensuring that the enterprise meets fully its social responsibilities to every employee.

This is no easy role, and frequently the personnel manager is seen, particularly in the private sector, as no more than a 'cost centre', or the company's 'social conscience', by those managers who have to 'make the profits'. This should not be the case, because it must be recognized that for every organization there are two major functions. One is to achieve the 'group goals' such as increased sales or profits or, in the public sector, to provide services. The other is 'group maintenance', that is, the role of creating and maintaining the group so that it can achieve its goals. Personnel management is concerned primarily with this latter role and in carrying it out should assist line managers to achieve their objectives in the most effective manner by ensuring conditions of employment that attract, retain and motivate the appropriate labour force. Personnel managers assist management to find the best possible candidates and provide training for the successful applicants. Effective personnel management requires imagination in obtaining a fair share of the available labour. Consequently, good personnel policies can make considerable contributions to the success of an undertaking, and although their efforts frequently cannot be measured accurately in monetary terms, management should not be able to visualize doing its job effectively without the support of such policies. Figure 2.3 shows the main functions and responsibilities normally covered under personnel management.

Human resource policies

Human resource policies do not develop in a vacuum, however. They are, as said earlier, an expression of the 'style of management' of an organization, an expression of its values. Personnel policies should be dynamic, both changing with and bringing about changes in the behaviour of the workforce and the organization. The part a personnel department should play in assisting to formulate human resource policies will depend crucially on its current standing in the organization. However, the importance can be estimated probably by looking at the levels of risk with which the department is involved. Figure 2.4 illustrates the different levels of risk with which an organization's personnel department can be associated.

Figure 2.3   *The personnel function*

In order to arrive at a clearer understanding of the relationship between human resource policies and the style of management of an organization, it is necessary for managers and students of management to look at the findings of those who have studied the behaviour of people at work.

One of the problems in attempting such a task is the amount of published work available and also the wide variety of opinions. As a result only what are considered (by the author) to be the most important points have been selected. (Anyone wishing to study the subject should refer, as a starting point, to the reading list at the end of this chapter.)

People at work

The study of people at work falls within the province of the social sciences which are concerned with studying the relationship between individuals,

Figure 2.4   *The level of personnel work*

Source: Personnel Management, February 1990

groups of individuals and their environment. The knowledge obtained can be used in two principal ways, namely to understand and predict changes and also to bring about changes. The fundamental conclusion to be drawn from the work of recent behavioural scientists, and Abraham Maslow in particular, is that man is a satisfaction-seeking animal motivated primarily by his biological needs. Hotel and catering managers should be more conscious of the truth of this than most others. In addition, and unlike most other animals, once man's biological needs are satisfied further needs emerge – mainly of a social nature. This manifests itself in the pursuit of power, status, security and other outward signs of 'success'. Most people are not conscious of these needs which drive or motivate them. If, however, management can recognize them, they can take appropriate steps to ensure that these driving forces can be used to the advantage of both the organization and the individual.

The first need, the need for bodily comfort, is satisfied relatively simply by adequate meals and housing. The welfare state, recognizing that the satisfaction of this need is essential to the survival of individuals and of society ensures by and large that no one needs to go without food and shelter. Individuals in our society, therefore, no longer accept that working merely for food and shelter is an end in itself. There are many cases where people are financially better off unemployed rather than employed, and consequently they choose to remain unemployed. A recent report indicated that whilst pay is the single most important aspiration of unemployed people, satisfying and stimulating work and good relations with colleagues and managers are also regarded as being important (Mike Hall, *Great Expectations*, Brighton Polytechnic, 1989). Most people expect much more from their employment than being able merely to purchase food and shelter.

Physical security is also these days very largely assured by the State. Regulations designed to protect the community and the individual from injury or disease penetrate every aspect of our daily lives, ranging from traffic to hygiene regulations. Even after this, if a man does fall ill or suffer injury, the State cares for him so that he need not fear the financial consequences to the same extent that he may have done a few years ago or that he might do today in many other countries. Therefore, seeking employment with low physical risk or with benevolent employers is no longer as important as it may have been a hundred or even fifty years ago. Consequently, because our biological needs are now largely guaranteed by the State, they no longer provide the motivation that they once did. Instead, other and much more complex needs – the social needs – have emerged.

Satisfactory relationships with other people are among the highest of our needs. To work with and for people we get on with is something most of us like to do, and it is no doubt a major force attracting many people into the hotel and catering industry. In looking at staff turnover it should be noted that the greatest numbers leave in the earliest days of employment – the period when relationships have not developed. On the other hand, one of the main reasons why people stay in their jobs, when all other conditions should encourage them to leave, is because of their relationship with those at work, including colleagues, bosses, subordinates and customers.

In our society another aspect of our relationship with others which plays a significant part is our need for social acceptance. Frequently this depends on our job and our way of living. By certain indications society locates us on the social ladder but many people not content with their position attempt to move up. Social mobility has increased considerably even in the last thirty years and the main evidence is change of occupational status, type of housing, earning more money, obtaining a variety of other status symbols such as motor cars, longer holidays, thicker carpet in the office, etc., or even by changing from one occupation or employer to another with a higher social standing. This fact unfortunately deters many people from working in the hotel and catering industry because many jobs, in spite of being highly skilled, are not awarded the status awarded to other jobs demanding the same or maybe less skill. It is within this field that the industry's trade and professional bodies need to do a great deal more work. This problem is not unique to Britain. At the International Hotels' Association Conference in Geneva in 1985 the delegates resolved that national bodies worldwide needed to put greater effort into improving the perceived standing of hotel and catering work.

Next on the list of human needs comes the need to satisfy one's own ambitions and aspirations. This usually means making the maximum use of one's intellectual, social and manual skills. It may include the desire to be a company chairman or, more modestly, the wish to produce a satisfactory piece of workmanship. Today with the undoubted economic need for mass production and consequent simplification, whether it be the production of 'in-flight' meals or motor cars, a person's need for this satisfaction is con-stantly overridden. It is one of the strongest needs of working people and one for which they often make considerable sacrifices. People will put in long hours in difficult conditions even for low pay when intrinsic job satisfaction is high.

Finally – having satisfied all these needs – security of their continuing satisfaction is itself another and, these days, a growing need. Mergers and acquisitions along with automation now threaten many more people than ever before, and even those who a few years ago could feel secure no longer do so. The current trend to 'distancing', i.e. employing people on short contracts, through agencies, etc., whilst increasing an employer's flexibility, reduces job security (see also Chapter 1). Seeking this security now plays an impor-tant part in employment relations and many people leave insecure employ-ment for what they believe to be a secure alternative position. It is usually found that where job security is higher, such as in banking or insurance, labour turnover is lower – completely unlike the rate of labour turnover in some sectors of the hotel and catering industry, where job tenure is often short and notoriously precarious. Job security normally leads to a stable and skilled labour force with many of the consequent efficiencies. On the other hand, job security can be such that it can work against the best interests of the organization with abuse abounding, such as excessive absenteeism and the protection of the grossly inefficient.

When all these needs are satisfied, it is argued that an employee is more likely to offer stable and competent service, but, if any one of these needs remains unsatisfied, he or she will almost certainly behave in one of a variety of ways, some of which are contrary to the business interest.

First, he may seek employment elsewhere which offers more likelihood of a satisfying job. Second, he may seek other compensations, such as extra money or more time off. If he has leadership qualities, he may become the focus for group, rather than individual, dissatisfaction or aspirations and this may lead him to play an active part in trade union affairs or other similar activities. Third, he may just opt out and seek his satisfaction outside work, for example, at home or in club activities. This last is unfortunately not often the case, since evidence indicates that those who obtain most satisfaction at work also play the biggest part in social or community affairs. In between these three distinct patterns of behaviour there are many degrees that most managers will recognize, including absenteeism, lateness, waste, pilferage and, of course, lack of co-operation or even sheer obstructionism, not all of which can be laid at the door of management.

The behavioural scientist F. Herzberg developed a theory that suggests two largely independent sets of factors which influence work behaviour. One set of factors, the 'hygiene' factors (such as work conditions), influences mainly the level of dissatisfaction. Improving the hygiene factors only removes causes of dissatisfaction without motivating the worker. Room tem-perature illustrates the point: ideal temperature goes unnoticed and does not motivate a person; a temperature which is too hot or too cold creates discomfort and demotivates.

The other set of factors are known as motivators (achievement, praise, work itself). These actually make people feel positive about their work and have to be built into work in order to motivate the workforce. Ideally the hygiene factors should be put right at the same time.

Some alternative models of excellence in human resource management

Some recent research conducted by the London School of Economics (see David Guest, January 1989) identified a number of different approaches to personnel management. These are:

A paternalist welfare model   This approach emphasizes the need to look after employees as a means to the employees, in turn, looking after customers. One example is Marks and Spencer. Both the quotations on page 13 indicate such an approach.

A production model   The principal role of the personnel department is to support continuity of production by ensuring a proper supply of human resources, properly regulated through clear and consistent industrial relations guidelines. The Ford Motor Company is cited as an example.

A professional model   This model is based upon demonstrated and acknowledged competence of the personnel department in such technical areas as selection, training, pay and industrial relations. Examples include Shell and ICI.

A human resource model   This reflects a people-oriented focus throughout the organization, including respect for the individual, full utilization of individual abilities and sophisticated policies for employee involvement. An example of such a company is IBM.

Modern-day Taylorism   A variant of the production model, found in parts of the service sector. An example is McDonald's.

Which approach for which organization?

Most organizations will have to pay much closer attention to their human resource policies as labour markets become tighter and working people's expectations and aspirations become heightened. Which of the above models or variants on these models will be the most suitable depends upon a whole range of different influences. The five different models above suggest that there are different solutions for different product markets and different technologies.

Human resource management and styles of leadership

A finding of considerable importance, highlighted by Douglas McGregor in his book *The Human Side of Enterprise*, is that most people behave in the way expected of them and consequently 'live up' or 'down to' their superiors' expectations. Therefore the relationship between employee and boss can be described as a dynamic one – the higher the expectations made (within reason) of an employee, the higher the performance, and consequently even higher expectations can and will be made of and met by him or her in the future.

The 'style' of management is therefore of vital importance in an organization because this determines to a large extent whether employees obtain satisfaction from their jobs and whether managers will achieve their business objectives.

The 'authoritarian' manager generally manages by issuing orders and instructions leaving little or no opportunity for discussion or even explanation. Very similar to this style is the 'unitarist' style which is based on a reliance on traditional market forces and hierarchical systems with a clear split between the responsibilities of management and those of the workforce.

There are also the 'democratic' managers, who recognize that they are not only leading, but are also part of a team and that this requires the others in the team – the staff – to be involved in decisions through discussion and explanation. The expression 'pluralist' is often used nowadays to describe such a style of management which recognizes that the aspirations of all sections of the workforce are to be taken into account in the decision-making process.

The third manager, the *laissez-faire* type, abdicates responsibility – leaving his or her staff to face the problems that are rightly the manager's. The staff are left to face complaints from customers without the authority to rectify or overcome causes of disruption.

These three very simplified descriptions of styles of management have been included to illustrate that there are several different ways of managing which are complex interactions between the individuals, the tasks and the environment which usually determines a particular style of management.

There also exist different attitudes or orientations towards the workforce. Amitai Etzioni has produced a useful classification of the power used by managers to ensure compliance, and as with McGregor's theory, it can be shown that particular styles have particular effects. Etzioni states that there are three principal management orientations to workers.

First, there is the *coercive* power used by managers in which fear of the consequences is the main motivator. Those managers who bewail the passing of the 'divine right of dismissal' most probably fall into this category. The second category is the *utilitarian* use of power. This depends upon the manipulation of material rewards, such as wages, and is commonly seen in large manufacturing industries where the only reward for work done is money. It is also seen in the hotel and catering industry, particularly in the way seasonal and casual workers are employed. Etzioni's third category is *normative* power. This rests largely upon the use of prestige, esteem and social acceptance. The managers of many organizations are motivated very much in this way, seeking titles, bigger cars, admission to prestige-carrying committees, etc.

Etzioni goes on to argue that each management type has an appropriate worker involvement. First, there is an *alienative* involvement which signifies that the employee has strong negative attitudes towards the employer. Normally, this would probably persist only where no reasonable employment alternatives exist, but such an attitude would be manifested probably by various forms of sabotage, theft, or worst of all, arson (which does occur in hotels). Second, Etzioni identifies a *calculative* involvement which is based on money or material exchange. Casual workers in catering are very likely to have

Figure 2.5   *Ten management theorists of crucial importance to the development of manpower policies*

1841–1925	Henri Fayol (France)	Claimed to be the earliest known proponent of a theoretical analysis of managerial activities. He defined management as having five functions:

to forecast
to organize
to command
to co-ordinate
to control

1856–1915	Frederick W. Taylor (U S A)	The founder of the movement known as 'scientific management'. He proposed four 'great underlying principles':

The development of a true science of work
The scientific selection and progressive development of the workman
The bringing together of the science of work and the scientifically selected and trained man
The constant and intimate co-operation of management and men

1868–1924	Frank Gilbreth (U S A)	Followers of F.W. Taylor, whose combined work emphasized that in applying scientific management principles it is essential first to understand the needs and personalities of workers
1879–1972	Lillian Gilbreth (U S A)	

1880–1949	Elton Mayo (U S A)	Often referred to as the founder of the Human Relations movement. His work demonstrated the importance of groups in affecting the behaviour of individuals at work. He is most famous for the Hawthorne investigations which led to a fuller understanding of the 'human factor' at work

1903–1981	Rensis Likert (U S A)	Showed that effective supervisors and managers tended to be 'employee centred' rather than 'job centred'. Likert distinguished four systems of management:

exploitive/authoratitive
benevolent/authoratitive
consultative
participative

He favoured the participative system although other systems could also produce high productivity

1906–1964	Douglas McGregor (U S A)	Famous for theories X and Y. In theory X people are assumed to dislike work and need direction and control. In theory Y people are assumed to enjoy work and external control is not necessary. Managers' assumptions about their subordinates shape their behaviour

	Frederick Herzberg (U S A)	Famous for demonstrating that factors which led to dissatisfaction ('hygiene' factors) were quite different from those that led to satisfaction (motivators).

Determinants of job satisfaction	*Determinants of dissatisfaction*
Achievement	Company policy and administration
Recognition	Supervision
Work itself	Salary
Responsibility	Interpersonal relations
Advancement	Working conditions

	Abraham Maslow (U S A)	Maslow saw human needs in a form of hierarchy, for which he is famous; as one set of needs was satisfied another emerged. Their order is:

physiological needs
security and safety needs
affiliation, or acceptance needs
esteem needs
self-actualization

	Peter Drucker (U S A)	Famous for developing the concept of Management by Objectives (MbO). When used properly MbO harnesses the aspirations and energies of managers in striving to meet the aims of the employing organizations.

this attitude towards their employers. Third, there is a *moral* involvement which signifies that the employee identifies closely with the employer's and colleagues' values and objectives. He or she will carry out their work because they value the objectives of the work. Many hotel and catering staff will hold this attitude to their work because they believe that it is worthwhile to make people comfortable and to help them enjoy themselves.

There is, of course, one other crucial perspective which needs to be considered – the Marxist one. Professor V. L. Allen, of Leeds University, wrote in *Personnel Management* (December 1976) that both the unitarist and the pluralist relationships are 'protective of the status quo' (the capitalist system). He went on to write that Marxism provides the alternative form of analysis of industrial relations and that the industrial relationship is one of permanent conflict between the buyers and sellers of labour power. He wrote, 'The conflict . . . is permanent . . . it is pervasive and influences every aspect of people's lives', and he suggested that in accepting such a perspective social relationships will be better understood. In considering such statements of course it is vital to be clear that in the case of Marx there is still considerable debate as to whether it is a scientific method or an ideology.

Having given these brief outlines of some important contributions to our understanding of work people's behaviour, it must be emphasized that there are many other important contributions which, perforce, have had to be omitted. The purpose, however, is to show that there are different, often mutually supporting, explanations of behaviour which state that different styles of management engender different worker attitudes.

Associated research also demonstrates that there is no such thing as a universal leadership or management quality. Instead, successful management and leadership is dependent, or contingent, upon the interaction of a whole variety of factors, of which the nature of the goods and services being offered and the market itself are vital. A steady, non-seasonal trade, as encountered in much industrial catering, will call for a style of management very different from that required by a busy seasonal hotel. Circumstances and time, therefore, can make a manager who would have been a failure in one situation, a success in another. See also Chapter 21.

Further reading

Armstrong, M., *A Handbook of Human Resource Management*, London: Kogan Page, 1988

Etzioni, A., *Modern Organization*, Englewood Cliffs, N.J.: Prentice-Hall, 1980

Handy, C., *Understanding Organizations*, London: Penguin, 1985

Koontz, H., and Weirich, H., *Management*, New York: McGraw Hill, 1988

McGregor, D., *The Human Side of Enterprise*, New York: McGraw Hill, 1960

Pratt, K. J., and Bennett, S. C., *Elements of Personnel Management*, 3rd ed., Wokingham: GEE, 1989,

Pugh, D. S., and Hickson, D. J., *Writers on Organisations*, 4th ed. London: Penguin, 1989

Rothwell, S., In Search of Excellence, *Personnel Management*, London: 1984

Sisson K., (ed), *Personnel Management in Britain*, Oxford: Blackwell, 1989
Thomason, G., *Textbook of Human Resource Management*, London: Institute of Personnel Management, 1988
Torrington, D. and Hall, L., *Personnel Management – A New Approach*, London: Prentice Hall, 1987

Questions

1 Describe the alternative types of human resource policies which can be adopted by employing organizations.

2 Using an employer from the private (commercial) sector and another from the public sector, compare and contrast their approaches to human resource management.

3 Discuss the nature of human resource policies which are likely to be necessary in the future to attract, retain and motivate staff. (Divide staff into a number of different categories, e.g. full-time, part-time, casual, management, supervisory, operative, craft, unskilled, male, female.)

4 Using an employer you know well, evaluate their human resource policies.

chapter 3

Job design

Although the term *management* (in its abstract sense) has almost as many definitions as there are managers, it is generally understood to refer to the art or skill of achieving required results through the efforts of others. There is today, however, considerable debate regarding what precisely it is that motivates people to achieve the results required of them. On the one hand there are those of the scientific school of management (see Chapter 2), who believe that all that is necessary is to select the right people, give clear directions and enough money and the required results will be achieved. On the other hand there are those from the human relations school (see Chapter 2) who believe that organizational objectives will only be achieved by recognizing to the full the needs and expectations of working people. Whichever view prevails, however, it is generally held that people produce their best performances when they know clearly what is expected of them. Consequently if an undertaking's objectives are to be achieved it follows that all its managers and work people must know clearly the results they are expected to produce. Such a statement of an organization's expectations of its employees can be made either orally or in writing, but experience proves that the written word is less likely to be misunderstood and that the need to think carefully before putting words to paper generally produces more logical and effective results than oral statements.

It is for such reasons that clear, precise job descriptions are given to people at work, because once a job is clearly described on paper there should be little room for subsequent misunderstandings. As a result a job should be performed more efficiently. Having said this, in this industry with the large number of small establishments, there are many work people who do not have or need job descriptions. Furthermore there is a view that job descriptions and the related hierarchies merely serve to slow down effective communication. Tom Peters, author of *In Search of Excellence*, says that the only way to compete in an ever faster world . . . is for 'a revolution in structure to create a world with no barriers between functions' (*The Financial Times*, 23 February 1990).

However before producing job descriptions it is essential to realize that the job description should be the result of a process referred to as job design.

In the past job design was seen as the process by which the employer set out to maximize the output of the workforce – a scientific school of management approach. For many employers this remains the sole objective. However, there is an increasing recognition that if job design is to be effective, the resulting jobs must satisfy the individual worker's needs also.

This second approach recognizes Drucker's view that it is important to distinguish between efficiency and effectiveness. Designing jobs for short-term efficiency may result, for example, in high labour turnover with a drop in customer satisfaction and hence in long-term effectiveness.

Figure 3.1   *Aspects of job design*

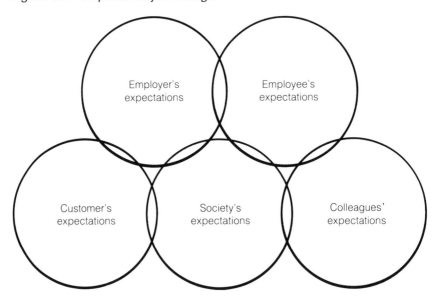

Third, of course, job design must result in customer satisfaction. Fourth, most people work in teams or groups, so colleagues' expectations have to be considered. And, finally, the job must be designed in such a way that society's expectations (e.g. health and safety) are satisfied.

Approaches to job design

In setting out to design any job therefore it is essential to recognize the expectations of everyone involved. The actual approach adopted will depend on the amalgam of these sets of expectations; for example where customers and employers want fast service, with minimum personalized contact, such as in many fast food operations, the resultant job may emphasize speed at the cost of job satisfaction. The consequence will be a high labour turnover, which may well be acceptable, even desirable, to the employer where there is a steady supply of replacement labour.

Job specialization

This approach to organizing work has been around for thousands of years and has led to civilization as we know it today. However, as an approach to organizing modern industrial production it was developed by a number of practitioners and theorists including F. W. Taylor, the founder of scentific management. Major principles resulting from the scientific management approach are as follows.

> *Science of work* The need for scientific methods of observing, measuring and analysing work activities to replace existing unsystematic approaches.
> *Standardization* Using the resulting knowledge, efficient working methods and performance levels can be set for work.
> *Selection* Systematic and scientific approaches to selecting workers with relevant qualities and abilities, together with planned training for the work involved.
> *Specialization* Both management and workers should concentrate upon specific functional activities, involving a limited range of tasks for which the individual's abilities and training enable expert performance. (Reproduced from Torrington and Chapman 1983.)

There have been two main consequences of the application of these ideas. First, areas of expertise and responsibility have become much more specialized, particularly in the management areas. There are now many more specialists in management than there were fifty years ago, even ten years ago. The hotel and catering industry has been no exception to this trend with a considerable recent growth in the range and numbers of those involved in middle and senior management. Second, and particularly at an operative level, job content is simplified by reducing the number of tasks each operative performs to a very limited number so that the need for skill and training is minimized.

The apparent benefits of job simplification, however, were accompanied by many problems, such as industrial strife, the causes being put down to that same job simplification. In contrast, the findings of behavioural scientists were showing that work people could not be treated as mere components of machines: instead they had a range of needs to be met by the work they performed. As a consequence other approaches to job design became necessary.

Job rotation

One reaction to job simplification was job rotation. This provides individuals with some variety in either the working conditions (i.e. where or when the basic job is done) or in the actual tasks performed. The jobs, however, remain simple, provide little stimulation and do not satisfy esteem needs.

Job enlargement

Job enlargement, in contrast, extends the range of tasks performed and is aimed at reducing boredom, increasing interest in work and increasing self-esteem. Job enlargement, however, brings about the very problems that work simplification sets out to eliminate, such as the need for greater knowledge, skill and training.

Job enrichment

Job enlargement extends 'horizontally' the range of tasks to be performed by an individual by adding tasks of a similar nature. It does not, however, meet the more complex expectations such as the need for autonomy. Job enrichment instead extends 'vertically' the range of tasks by increasing an individual's responsibility and autonomy through adding elements of the job which may have been the responsibility of supervisors or management, such as planning, organization and control.

Sociotechnical systems

This approach to job design sets out to bring together an employer's technical system (e.g. buildings and equipment) and the social system comprising the work people. This is because the scientific school aimed to maximize the technical system, seeing the work people as components. In contrast, the human relations theorists concentrated on maximizing the satisfaction of human needs. These two approaches can be seen to be incompatible. It is necessary to look at an organization as a sociotechnical system which compromises between technical efficiency and group needs.

In the sociotechnical system of job design three major factors are considered. These are: first, the need to recognize the needs that are met by formal and informal groups; second, work is allocated to groups who are able to identify clearly with the work; third, the group is given a high degree of autonomy over its work.

Quality circles

Quality circles trace their origin to post-war Japan and the Japanese concern with the desire to change the image of Japanese products as cheap imitations of Western products. They evolved as a result of an increasingly literate workforce being able to participate in problem solving. The quality circles movement spread from Japan to the United States in the 1970s and to the UK in the late 1970s.

The principles of quality circles (QC) are:

QCs should be introduced in a totally voluntary way and should only grow as and when volunteers wish to join

QCs are based on a McGregor Theory Y (see Chapter 2) concept of working people; i.e. they are willing and able to participate in solving problems which affect them

QCs should be unbureaucratic and need only brief action notes following each meeting

QCs, as with any other crucial approach to management, need middle and senior management commitment

QCs focus problem solving at the point at which problems occur, and therefore release middle and senior management time.

Quality circles are based upon the working group. Groups of about four to ten *volunteers* who work for the same supervisor meet about once a week, for about an hour, to identify, analyse and solve their own work-related problems. Discussions should be free from hierarchical restraints. Members take ownership of departmental issues and no longer see problems as other people's problems. QC members will need some training in appropriate techniques such as brain-storming, used to identify and suggest solutions. In addition they will need to be trained in problem-solving techniques which include; check sheets, cause and effect charts, stratification, 80/20 diagrams, scatter diagrams, histograms, control charts (see Chapter 20, Murphy, J. *Quality in Practice*, Gill and Macmillan, Dublin 1986).

The benefits of QCs are at least threefold: firstly, problems are solved; secondly, attitudes which identify with the organization's goals are developed, and thirdly, the quality of supervision and communications is improved.

Obviously it can be seen that if QCs are developed and operated effectively their influence on job design can be very significant. In particular, job design becomes a dynamic process with the possibility that jobs could be constantly changing in detail.

Job design, therefore, is the process which sets out to harness the energies of the human resource in order to achieve an organization's objectives. In turn job descriptions are the written results of the process of job design.

In some cases, particularly in the industry's smallest establishments, written job descriptions are not used and may even be too formal and rigid, in other situations brief descriptions only may be sufficient, whereas in others quite detailed and complex documents are called for. The degree of detail needed in describing the various elements of a job varies from job to job and from organization to organization. There are, however, two main documents: job descriptions and job specifications. Job analysis is also sometimes considered to be a document describing a job in detail, but it is more commonly used when referring to the technique of examining jobs in depth. Job descriptions and job specifications are described below. In addition a brief description of Management by Objectives is included in this chapter because it describes a methodical and systematic approach to the design and description of jobs and setting of objectives.

Job descriptions

Job descriptions are a broad statement of the scope, purpose, duties and responsibilities involved in a job. Their main purposes are to:

1 Give employees an understanding of their jobs and standards of performance.
2 Clarify duties, responsibilities and authority in order to design the organization structure.
3 Assist in assessing employees' performance.
4 Assist in the recruitment and placement of employees.
5 Assist in the induction of new employees.
6 Evaluate jobs for grading and salary administration.
7 Provide information for training and management development.

Figure 3.2 *Job descriptions: the 'hub' of personnel management*

There are two distinct but equally important parts to the full description of jobs. The first is the statement of conditions for which employees contract to do work; some time ago in the United Kingdom it was recognized that the clear definition of conditions was not generally adequate, with the result that the Contracts of Employment Act became law in 1963. Now the 1978 Employment

Protection (Consolidation) Act requires that certain information regarding conditions of employment, such as hours of work, job title and length of notice, be given to employees. This subject, together with other legal reasons for producing and issuing comprehensive job descriptions, will be dealt with in subsequent chapters.

The second part of describing jobs requires the provision of information to employees which specifies clearly what results are expected of them and indicates how their performance will be measured.

Job descriptions should contain the following main elements:

Job identification   This section identifies the job by title, department, level in the hierarchy.
Scope of job   A brief description of the scope of a job.
Content   This section is a detailed statement and normally includes a list of duties and how these are performed, and what standard of performance is required.
Conditions   This section describes any particular conditions which make the

Figure 3.3   *Job description for a chef*

Title	Chef
Department	Food and Beverage
Scope	All hotel food preparation operations
Responsible to	Food and Beverage Manager
Responsible for	1 Personnel: all kitchen staff including kitchen manual staff 2 Equipment: all kitchen fixed and removable equipment and kitchen utensils
Lateral communication	Restaurant Manager, Front Office Manager, Head Housekeeper
Main responsibilities	The planning, organization and supervision of food preparation in the hotel including: 1 Menu compilation according to agreed costed recipes 2 Purchasing of foodstuffs, kitchen materials and equipment from nominated suppliers within agreed budget levels 3 Portion and waste control 4 Control of labour and other variable costs within budget levels 5 Arrangement of staff rosters 6 Training of new staff 7 Hygiene and cleanliness 8 Fire precautions 9 Security of all kitchen supplies, equipment, utensils and silverware
Limits of authority	1 Engagement and suspension of all subordinates until circumstances can be reported to the Food and Beverage Manager
Hours of work	As agreed with Food and Beverage Manager

job more or less difficult; for example, if a public house is situated in a rough area, this will need to be highlighted.

Authority   This section describes any limits to his or her authority such as: cash limits; authority to make contracts on behalf of the employer; authority to engage or dismiss subordinates.

Figure 3.3 shows a typical job description for a chef and Figure 3.4 shows one for a counter assistant.

Job specifications

In many cases more detail than is normally contained in a brief job description may be necessary for a job to be performed satisfactorily. A detailed statement of the job may be required specifying the precise skills and knowledge needed to carry out the various component tasks of a job. This information may be contained in a document often referred to as a job specification. Alternatively, the information may be contained in such documents as manuals of operation, operating instructions and the like. Extracts from a job specification for a waitress are shown in Figure 3.5.

Within the last few years job descriptions and specifications have become much more highly developed in the hotel and catering industry.

Figure 3.4   *Job description for a counter assistant*

Title	Counter Assistant
Department	Depot Restaurant
Scope	To assist in the preparation of meals, to keep the kitchen and dining areas in a clean and tidy state and to serve customers
Responsible to	Assistant Manageress
Responsible for	No subordinate staff
Lateral communication	Cashier, cooks
Main responsibilities	1 Prepare foodstuffs according to directions 2 Clean and lay up canteen dining area 3 Stock up and replenish service points as necessary 4 Serve customers during service periods 5 Clear away used plates, utensils, trays, and wipe down tables and working surfaces during and after the service period 6 Clean and polish service equipment and kitchen areas after service periods 7 Comply with company standards and statutory hygiene regulations
Limits of authority	No authority to authorize or make expenditure No authority over other staff
Hours of work	08.00 to 16.00, 45 minute lunch break

Figure 3.5 *Extracts from a job specification for a waitress*

Duties	Knowledge	Skill	Social skills
1 Preparation			
1.3 Preparation of butter, cruets and accompaniments	1 Correct accompaniments for the dishes on the day's menu	Operation of butter pat maker. Preparation of sauces, e.g. vinaigrette	
3 Service of customers			
3.3 Taking orders	1 Procedures for taking wine and food orders 2 Menu and dish composition 3 Procedure for taking requisitions to kitchen, bar dispense and cashier		1 Assisting customers with selection in order to maximize sales 2 Informing customers of composition of dishes
8 Wine dispense	Product knowledge 1 Suitable wines for dishes on the menu 2 Suitable glasses for different wines 3 Correct temperatures for red, white and rosé Licensing law 1 Young persons 2 Drinking up time	1 Presenting bottle 2 Opening bottle 3 Pouring wine	1 Assisting customers with selection 2 Dealing with complaints
11 Preparation for cleaners after last customers have left			1 Refusing service 2 Asking people to 'drink up'
11.3 Stripping tables	1 Safe disposal of ash tray contents 2 Disposal of cutlery, crockery, linen, cruets		

Several companies are now using training booklets which serve several important purposes, including the provision of:

Job descriptions
Trainers' programme
Trainees' aide-mémoires
List of duties
List of tasks
Standards of performance
Interviewing attainments checklist
Training checklist.

Not only are these booklets very useful for selection, induction and training purposes, they are also useful from a discipline point of view. If someone has been trained to do something, and the fact is recorded, then certain standards can be expected.

Preparation of job descriptions and job specifications

Some managers like to prepare job descriptions and other such documents with the employees concerned, and generally speaking this is by far the best approach. Frequently, however, this principle can only apply to supervisory and management grades because the jobs of operative grades are often so clearly defined that discussion, apart from explanation, would only raise hopes that would be disappointed when it became apparent that no changes were forthcoming. Furthermore, it is not always possible to involve the employee concerned because the need for job descriptions often does not make itself apparent until a person has to be recruited. Even so, with the increasing development of participative approaches such as quality circles, it is very likely that the involvement of operative staff in the design of their own jobs will increase in the industry as it is in other sectors.

The preparation of job specifications normally requires a more skilled approach than that needed for the preparation of job descriptions. The uses to which such documents are to be put should determine who prepares them; for example, if job specifications are to be used for training purposes, they should be prepared by training specialists and the line management concerned. On the other hand, if they are to be used as a basis for work measurement, work study specialists should work with line management.

Whatever form the description of jobs takes, however, vague terms such as 'satisfactory levels of gross profit' should be avoided and, instead, actual quantities or levels should be specified, such as 'a gross profit of 65 per cent is to be obtained'. It is good practice also to incorporate budgets and forecasts into job descriptions as it sets specific and quantified targets. Additionally, documents such as manuals of operation or training booklets may be directly related to job descriptions.

Because of the vital part played by job descriptions and specifications, particularly in such things as induction, training, job evaluation and perform-ance appraisal, their preparation should be monitored by one person or department to ensure consistency. They should be regularly updated and a copy held by the job holder, by his or her superior, sometimes by the superior's boss as well, and, of course, by the personnel department, where one exists.

Some job design tools

Job design, as indicated above, can involve a number of different skills and techniques. These can include:

Work study; this is divided into method study and work measurement.

Method study; a part of work study concerned with recording and analyzing methods and proposed methods of work, the purpose being to develop more effective ways of doing things.

Work measurement; a technique used to measure the time an experienced worker will take to perform a task or job to a pre-determined standard. Measurement may be carried out by direct observation, by sampling or by using 'synthetic' values, i.e. times determined for particular movements.

Ergonomics; the study of the relationship between a worker and his or her work equipment and environment. In particular it is concerned with the application of anatomical, physiological and psychological knowledge to working situations. The aim of ergonomics is to produce safe and effective equipment for working people using physical and psychological knowledge.

Management by Objectives (MbO)

Management by objectives is an approach to management which, if operated effectively, influences all levels and activities of an organization. By concept it is typical of a *democratic* style of management although, in practice, it is often introduced by other types of manager. It usually relies heavily on specially designed job descriptions and similar documents. MbO seeks to integrate all of an organization's principal targets with the individual managers' own aspirations.

MbO requires the establishment of an undertaking's objectives, the development of plans to achieve these objectives, and the methods for monitoring progress. At the same time each manager must be personally involved in the preparation of his or her own department's targets and in the means of achieving these targets. Objectives should not be handed down by superior to subordinate, but should be agreed between the two after all factors have been considered.

The critical areas only (key result areas) of each manager's job are defined, the objectives where possible are quantified, the means of checking results, or identifying obstacles and of achieving objectives are developed. Planning and improvement goes on continuously through review meetings being held at regular intervals between superiors and subordinates. The procedure is

Figure 3.6 *Management by objectives (MbO)*

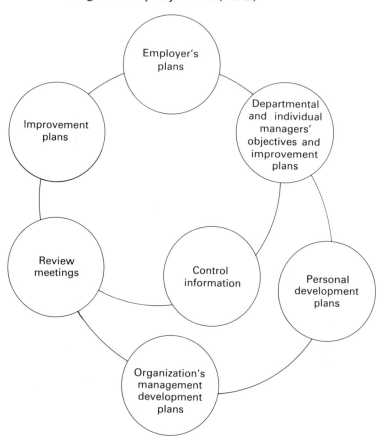

illustrated in Figure 3.6 and an extract from an MbO job description is shown in Figure 3.7.

Where MbO concepts have been used in hotels and catering to set standards, generally speaking it is found that the performance standards of operative staff are 'guest centred', that is, they are concerned with identifying the standards of service to be provided to the guest. The performance standards of heads of departments, on the other hand, are 'profit centred', that is, they identify the cost criteria for producing the services to the guest. Heads of departments are, however, directly responsible for ensuring that the operational performance standards are met by department staff, so their performance standards may incorporate quality management standards as well as the 'profit centred' standards.

Current issues to be faced in job design

With the rapidly changing nature of the workforce and labour market, including the severe skills shortages and the raised expectations of working

Figure 3.7 *Management by objectives: example of performance standards and improvement plans*

Manager, White Hart Restaurant: Objectives for six months ending 30 June

Key result area	Performance standard	Current level of achievement	Control information	Improvement target	Improvement plan
1 Gross profit (a) catering	63%	58%	Monthly stocktake	Achieve budget	Review selling and purchase prices, introduce more high-yield dishes, by 30 April
(b) liquor	60%	58%	Monthly stocktake	Achieve budget	Alter sales mix, introduce premium-priced beer, discontinue sale of cheaper draught beer
2 Sales volume	£60,000 per month	£66,000	Takings sheets	Increase to £84,000	Promote new private function room, spend £2000 on promotion during first quarter
3 Labour	23%	26%	Weekly wages sheet	Reduce to budget, 23%	Increase staff only for booked functions, no more staff to be recruited except to replace those who leave

people, job design now has to consider a wider range of factors than merely designing the task and work content of jobs. Job designers, i.e. most managers, will need to focus more than before on the conditions of work rather than just the job content. Such issues will include more flexible working hours, providing support for women returners, more autonomy, etc. in addition to eliminating menial tasks and tasks requiring scarce skills.

Job design in hotel and catering operations

At one extreme job design can simplify work so that little skill and training is needed. Trends in this direction are very apparent in the hotel and catering industry in several sectors including fast food operations, the use of cook-chill and cook-freeze in many different operations including schools, hospitals, banqueting and 'in-flight' catering. A major reason is the process sometimes referred to as 'de-coupling', whereby the production and service elements are totally separated – pre-prepared meals being produced away from the service point. Such systems are concerned mainly with the 'production elements' of hotel and catering products. However, because of the significant 'customer contact' element, it is difficult to 'simplify out' many of the tasks which customers expect as part of the service and which employees themselves find rewarding, such as social interaction. Consequently while some jobs are being simplified many other jobs in the industry remain rewarding because the very nature of the industry, small units, socio-interaction, autonomy all meet the requirements of what appear to be major contributions to satisfying job design.

Further reading

Armstrong, M., *A Handbook of Human Resource Management*, London: Kogan Page, 188

Handy, C., *Understanding Organisations*, London: Penguin, 1985

Humble, J., *Management by Objectives in Action*, London: McGraw Hill, 1979

Murphy, J., *Quality in Practice*, London: Gill and Macmillan, 1986

Pratt, K. J., and Bennett, S. C., *Elements of Personnel Management*, 3rd ed., Wokingham: GEE, 1989

Robertson, I. T., *Motivation and Job Design, Theory Research and Practice*, London: Institute of Personnel Management, 1985

Sisson K., (ed), *Personnel Management in Britain*, Oxford: Blackwell, 1989

Thomason, G., *Textbook of Human Resource Management*, London: Institute of Personnel Management, 1988

Torrington, D. and Hall, L., *Personnel Management – a New Approach*, London: Prentice Hall, 1987

Ungerson, B., *How to Write a Job Description*, London: Institute of Personnel Management, 1983

Questions

1 Describe the different approaches to job design.
2 Discuss the various influences which need to be taken into account when designing jobs.
3 Discuss what future influences are likely to influence job design.
4 Discuss how job design may differ when applied to management and non-management jobs.
5 Using an employer you know well evaluate their approach to job design.

chapter 4

Recruitment

In the 1990s the hospitality industry, along with most others, is facing considerably increased recruitment and retention problems. By 1995 it is predicted that, in Britain overall, there will be 1.7 million more jobs than in the 1980s whilst there will be only around half a million school leavers available for employment, around 100,000 per year less than ten years before. The National Economic Development Office estimated in 1989 that the tourism and leisure industries alone, apart from other parts of the hospitality industry, were creating around 70,000 new jobs a year (see also Chapter 1). So, not only is the hospitality industry having to compete with many other employers but it will be doing so as the demands for its own products, and hence labour, are growing. The Training Agency, in 1989, reported that staff shortages are the most serious threat to the success of the industry.

At the same time as the demand for labour is growing and some sectors of the labour supply side are declining, the industry also has long standing recruitment and retention problems. Over many years surveys and reports have highlighted problems in the industry which created recruitment problems. These are referred to in Appendix 1 to this book. A very recent report (*Great Expectations*, Mike Hall, Brighton Polytechnic, 1989) identified a number of similar problems which essentially reinforce the persistent nature of some of the industry's employment practices. The main findings of *Great Expectations* were that Brighton's hotel industry did not meet the aspirations of those seeking work and that the industry needed to improve their methods of management in a number of separate but interdependent areas including recruitment, induction, training and welfare, career structures, conditions of employment, industrial relations and management styles, pay, recruitment of women.

Another report, this time concerned with recruitment and retention problems in hotels, restaurants and public houses in London, identified ten clear messages for the industry's employers. These were:

Tackle the industry's image: not that it has a bad one, but that it does not have one
Emphasise the importance of personal qualities
Distinguish between jobs and careers
Publicize the full rewards package, e.g. meals, travel costs, bonuses

Foster job satisfaction

Explore the way jobs are structured and consider other labour markets

Target recruitment well

Explain to unemployed people that work does not always remove rights to benefits

Look for ways to attract young people into the permitted areas of the licensed sector

Use the unusual working hours as an attraction rather than as a barrier.

(Reported in *Tourism Training Initiative Newsletter*, April 1989).

Recruitment advertising in the hotel and catering industry

The quality of recruitment advertising in the hotel and catering industry varies considerably. At one end of the scale, the large companies such as Trusthouse Forte and Bass are able to employ the best of expertise in designing recruitment advertisements. At the other extreme are the small operators who, with no expertise and very limited resources, have to design advertisements which, not surprisingly in many cases, are ineffective. For example, media research has demonstrated that inclusion of earnings in a recruitment advertisement increases the effectiveness of the advertisement and yet the majority of advertisements in the *Caterer and Hotelkeeper* do not include earnings levels.

By itself, good recruitment cannot overcome the problem of high labour turnover. This has to be tackled by keeping all conditions of employment under constant review and by making appropriate improvements to conditions as circumstances dictate. The nature of the hotel and the catering industry, however, is such that most people holding management or supervisory positions are going to be faced frequently with the need to recruit people to fill vacancies.

Labour markets

In order to recruit successfully, however, it is important to have an understanding of labour markets, in the same way as in promoting products and services it is essential to know the nature of the target markets.

There are two principal labour markets and each has very different characteristics, particularly from a recruitment point of view.

Primary labour market

The primary labour market consists of those people who through education, training and experience are committed to an industry, sometime even a sector of an industry. In the hotel and catering industry these would include hotel managers, chefs, hotel receptionists, hall porters and cocktail bar staff.

Figure 4.1 *Welwyn Hatfield Council Equal Opportunities policy statement (reproduced by courtesy of Welwyn Hatfield Council)*

This District Council is committed to the principle of equality of opportunity in employment, training and service delivery. This, because it recognises the substantial disadvantage many people face because of their sex, race, colour, age, marital status, religious belief, sexual orientation, or disability.

In accordance with this principal and alongside its statutory legal obligations such as are contained in the Sex Discrimination Act 1975, Race Relations Act 1976, Disabled Person (Employment) Act 1944 and 1958, Equal Pay Act 1970 and Equal Pay (Amendment) Regulation 1983 this Council will strive to achieve the objectives of equal opportunities in all areas of its work.

Accordingly it is the Council's aim to ensure that no job applicant, employee or service user, will receive less favourable treatment on the grounds of sex, race, colour, age, marital status, religion, sexual orientation or disability.

The District acknowledges that responsibility for the successful implementation of equality of opportunity in employment and service delivery, lies primarily with all employees and Council members. Therefore the Council will act to encourage and promote all appropriate measures which will achieve this aim. Furthermore, it will ensure that the Council's equal opportunity policy statement will be implemented and will require full co-operation and understanding from all employees and Council members, in the actions that need to be taken to secure that Welwyn Hatfield is an equal opportunity district.

As part of this process of striving to achieve equal opportunities the Council will promote enhanced awareness, on the part of all employees and Council members, of discriminatory or potentially discriminatory practice, attitudes and behaviour so that they can be identified and eliminated.

The Council will add to its recruitment material, the fact that it is "striving to be an equal opportunities employer" and will forward to all job applicants a copy of the equal opportunities policy document.

In pursuit of the above objectives, the Council will develop procedures, to ensure that individuals, in the case of employment, are selected, promoted, and treated on the basis of their relevant aptitudes, skills and abilities, commensurate with the post. The aim is that no one should receive unfavourable treatment or be hindered in their career development because of their sex, race, colour, age, marital status, religion, sexual orientation or disability.

Likewise in the area of service delivery, the Council will develop procedures that will attempt to ensure, that no member of the public, will be dealt with less favourably, or inequitably, because of their sex, race, colour, age, marital status, religion, sexual orientation or disability.

As part of the Equal Opportunities Policy, procedures will be developed to ensure that where inequitable treatment is identified steps will be taken to remove it.

The Council will examine all its present application forms, and public documents, to ensure that in line with its statutory duties none is discriminatory, either directly or indirectly, and further are neither sexist, racist, or ageist in content and will amend wherever appropriate.

Apart, from the measures aforementioned the Council will expect arrangements to be made by each division of the Council to promote equal opportunities. The purpose would be to eradicate any attitudes or actions which prevent equal opportunities being implemented.

Such people intend to develop their careers in the industry and in many cases see their opportunities nationally, even internationally. As a consequence they tend to be mobile, both geographically and organizationally.

Secondary labour market

The secondary labour market consists of people, on the other hand, who have skills of use to an employer, but who do not feel committed to a career in a particular industry. They probably attach more importance to a geographical area than to a career. Typically the secondary labour market contains house-wives, students and unskilled working people who choose to work in a particular industry in order to earn a living rather than because of a strong commitment to that industry. The secondary labour market also includes people with skills which may be common to many industries, such as secretaries, maintenance people, book-keepers and accountants.

Discrimination

Whatever the reason for recruitment, plans have to be prepared in the context of employment legislation, which covers issues such as the employ-ment of children and women, sex and race discrimination and the employ-ment of disabled people.

Figure 4.1 is an example of a district council's equal opportunities' statement.

In addition to the statutory obligations of not discriminating on the grounds of sex or race there are employers who decide not to discriminate in other ways also, for example, on the grounds of a person's age. In any event, with the demographic downturn of young people, employers may find that discrimination on grounds of age is no longer a practical proposition, as the older age groups will provide an increasingly important source of labour in the future.

The recruitment process

Recruitment is the process used to attract suitable applicants from whom the most suitable person may be selected for a particular job. It depends upon having the proper information available, including a job description (see Chapter 3), a personnel specification and a knowledge of the labour market. The process starts with the production of a 'personnel' specification, based on a job description or job specification.

Personnel specification

From the job description a 'personnel specification' can be prepared which is a description of the type of person most likely to be able to carry out the job described by the job description. The precise nature of a 'personnel specification' will depend upon the degree of sophistication or otherwise of an organization. Figure 4.2 is an example of one used by THF.

'Personal qualities' are discussed in Chapter 5.

From the job description in Figure 3.3, therefore, a 'personnel specification' could be drawn up and might look something like Figure 4.2. If considered necessary or useful, distinctions could be made between 'essential' or 'desirable' attributes.

From the information in the job description and personnel specification subsequent recruitment steps can be decided upon.

Internal recruitment

The first step always in filling a position is to consider promoting or transferring existing employees. Considerable dissatisfaction can be caused by bringing newcomers in over the heads of present staff, which is often done with the intention of causing as little disturbance as possible to the organization. Unfortunately, because the hopes of some individuals in the organization may be frustrated, they may leave or behave in other unsatisfactory ways and the long-term effect is therefore far more damaging.

It is good management practice, therefore, for all vacancies in a company, and particularly those that may be seen by existing employees to be promotions, to be advertised internally on the staff noticeboard or by circulars. Circulating details to supervisors only is generally not satisfactory as some employees may fear that their supervisors will not put them forward for various reasons.

External recruitment

The next step, if no existing staff are suitable, is to go onto the labour market. This is where most problems arise and where most money and effort can be wasted.

The numerous and varied means of recruitment include:

1   Newspapers: national, local and trade.
2   Agencies, including the Department of Employment and the Youth Employment Offices.
3   Executive selection and management consultants.
4   Posters, e.g. on London Underground, in one's own premises, postcards in local Post Office windows.
5   Colleges.
6   Armed forces.

Figure 4.2 *Example of person specification contents*

Requirements	Essential	Desirable
Physical e.g. Health, Strength, Age, Appearance, Manner, Voice		
Education and experience Secondary Education, Further Education, Work Experience		
Technical knowledge/skills Specific skills and knowledge necessary		
Disposition Personal qualities required, e.g. communicative ability, integrity, motivation, personality		
Circumstances Personal circumstances, e.g. need for accommodation, distance from home to hotel, means of transport, ability to work shifts		

Guidance notes for person completing person specification form

Quality	Brief description
Leadership	Acceptance of responsibility for others. Influence on others.
Maturity	Acceptance of own responsibilities. Realistic ambitions. Settled in life.
Stability	Ability to withstand stress and strain.
Social skills	Development of good relationships with people in work situations.
Sense of purpose	Initiative and persistence in achieving objectives.
Intelligence	Ability to absorb and retain knowledge specific to the job.
Communication	Ability to communicate at all levels.

Notes
1 Approval must be sought from Personnel Department before restricting the specification on grounds of sex or physical capacity.
2 1 = Adequate for normal employment at this staff level
   2 = Above average for this staff level
   3 = High for this staff level.
3 The company has a legal requirement to employ x% of disabled people. Many disabled applicants bring above average qualities of sense of purpose and maturity to the job.

Source: Reproduced by courtesy of Trusthouse Forte Hotels.

Figure 4.3   *Personnel specification for a chef*

Job title	Chef de cuisine
Sex	Male/female
Age range	28–50

ESSENTIAL
Qualifications

(a) educational	No formal requirements
(b) technical	City and Guilds of London 706/1/2 or formal apprenticeship
Experience to include	(a) experience in all corners, but in particular in the larder
	(b) experience of controlling a brigade of not less than five
	(c) recent experience of good quality à la carte service (up to 200 covers a day)
Personal qualities	(a) able to control mixed staff of English, Continental and Asian nationalities
	(b) stable employment record (e.g. no more than three jobs over the last ten years)
	(c) above average intelligence
Personal circumstances	(a) able to work late (11 p.m.) about three nights a week
	(b) will have to live out

DESIRABLE

Qualifications	HCTC on job trainer
Experience	Large-scale banqueting

The choice of media is critical to success and always depends on the type and level of vacancy and whether prospective employees are part of a local, a national or a trade labour market, i.e. a primary or a secondary labour market. Generally speaking the higher level appointments will be advertised nationally; for example, if a company is seeking to appoint an area manager for a group of hotels, the national press such as *The Daily Telegraph* or *The Sunday Times* could be used in conjunction with the trade press. On the other hand, if a waiter or waitress is required, local employment agencies and the local press will probably be adequate.

The likely mobility of applicants is of course vital and in this industry, where accommodation is provided, even less qualified categories of employees are often part of a national labour market and hence are prepared to move large distances. Because of this the trade press can be used effectively. If, for example, a living-in bar cellarperson is required, this can be advertised in a trade paper such as the *Caterer and Hotelkeeper* and the *Morning Advertiser* as well as in the local press, and through agencies. Figure 4.4 illustrates some suitable sources.

Advertising

From Figure 4.4 it is evident that a large part of any recruitment can be expected to rely on advertising and, therefore, apart from the choice of media, the drafting of advertisements is important. To recruit successfully these days, in the face of expert competition from other employers, it is no longer enough just to place an advertisement. It has to be a good advertisement. The rules for creating an effective advertisement are:

1 Be honest.
2 Catch likely candidates' attention with a suitable headline.
3 Hold a person's attention by giving clear, factual information including:

   (a) locality
   (b) job content
   (c) prospects
   (d) qualifications
   (e) experience
   (f) conditions of employment.

4 Describe what action has to be taken in order to apply.
5 Keep the language simple if it is directed at unskilled applicants.
6 Stimulate interest in the employer and promote his image, but remember that the priority is to fill a vacancy, not to advertise the establishment.
7 Avoid box numbers.
8 Avoid meaningless statements such as 'attractive wage' or 'salary according to qualifications'.
9 Test the advertisement on others before finalizing it.
10 Stimulate the reader to act by telling him to call in, write or telephone.

Advertising a vacancy should be the method by which an employer communicates to potential employees that he is seeking to fill a vacancy. If the advertisement is loosely or vaguely worded, it may encourage too many unsuitable applicants or, worse still, it may not attract the most suitable people.

A well-designed advertisement will do more than just communicate basic information, in words; it can, by its graphic design, say a lot about the employer and his style. Bob Payton's advertisement designed by a professional advertising agency illustrates this (Figure 4.5).

There is an often-quoted law of recruitment advertising which states that the ideal advertisement attracts only one applicant and that application will be successful. This is obviously overstating the case but it does illustrate the need to think carefully about the choice and content of advertising. After all, the money wasted on ineffective advertising could well have been spent on new equipment, redecorations or even increases in salaries, and others in the organization will not be slow to point this out.

The Chef's position described in Figure 3.3 could be advertised in the form shown in Figure 4.6. This illustrates an advertisement for a skilled person whereas advertising for unskilled people needs a different approach; for example, if advertising for a barman/barmaid it may well be that the person appointed will need no experience, but some personal qualities instead, such as

Figure 4.4 *Recruitment sources and media (external)*

Staff to be recruited	Sources and/or type of media	Examples
Senior executives, e.g. area managers, regional managers, hotel managers	National press Trade press Consultants Agencies	*Daily Telegraph* *Caterer and Hotelkeeper* Executive selection consultants, 'head hunters' Alfred Marks, Job Centres
Departmental heads, managers of small units, public house managers, etc.	Trade press Specialized sections of national press Agencies Armed services Local radio	*Caterer and Hotelkeeper*, HCIMA Journal – Hospitality *Daily Telegraph*, *Lady* (for Housekeepers, etc.), *Daily Mail* Alfred Marks, Job Centres, Resettlement officers of armed services Capital Radio
Skilled employees, e.g. cooks, waiters	Local press, including London evening papers and Common Market local Press Local colleges Agencies Government Training Centres Rehabilitation Centres BHRCA (foreign employees) Local radio and TV Areas of high unemployment	*Evening Argus, Evening Standard* Alfred Marks, Job Centres
Unskilled employees, e.g. cleaners, porters, kitchen hands, part-timers	Local press Agencies Local colleges Notices and posters Social Services, e.g. probation officers Regional Development Authorities Local radio and TV Salvation Army YMCA YWCA	*Daily Echo* Alfred Marks, Job Centres, Universities, Colleges of Technology (students) Displayed in local Post Office and shop windows or in own premises

Figure 4.5   *Display advertisement*

'good appearance and personality'. For this reason the headline should be directed at young people not barmen or barmaids (see Figure 4.7).

There are three main ways of inserting advertisements in newspapers: display, semi-display and classified. The examples in Figure 4.5, 4.6 and 4.7 are 'display' and because they take up the most space and involve the most work they are the most expensive.

The second method is 'semi-display' which gives the advertiser some prominence in the classified section. Often this is all that is required to attract applicants. An example of semi-display is shown in Figure 4.8.

Classified advertising is the least expensive and usually the least effective. This is because a large number of job advertisements are lumped together and consequently are less likely to catch the reader's eye. This is most likely to be the case when trying to recruit unqualified part-timers, because these are often recruited from normal readers who are not looking for jobs and consequently they will not look up the classified columns. On the other hand, a good display advertisement may well attract their attention and prompt them to apply. Many people, after all, have never thought of themselves working in a bar or restaurant, but the advertisements in Figures 4.5 and 4.7 would probably prompt several to apply. Figure 4.9 shows a typical classified advertisement.

Recruitment agencies

In large organizations where recruitment costs run into thousands of pounds a year, it is often normal to retain a recruitment agency. Usually their services cost relatively little as they receive a commission from the newspaper owners. Smaller firms, on the other hand, will not be able to offer recruitment agencies enough business for them to be interested, but in this case the media themselves will always give advice and guidance.

Word of mouth

One particular method of recruitment has been purposely left until last because of the unique and important part it plays in recruitment. People in this

Figure 4.6   *Display advertisement for a chef de cuisine*

THE SPLENDIDE HOTEL
invites applications for the position of

CHEF DE CUISINE

vacancy larger than hotel name

The Splendide Hotel, part of an independent and progressive group, has an excellent reputation for its cuisine. It is situated on the sea front in Newtown and has two restaurants seating a total of 300 people, plus conference and function rooms able to cater for a further 300.

brief description of employer

The person appointed will be responsible to the Food and Beverage Manager for all kitchen operations including purchasing, gross profit control, menu compilation, and staffing. He or she will have a full-time staff of fifteen including porters.

job description

He or she will be aged 28 – 50 and will have either served a recognized apprenticeship or will have obtained the City and Guilds of London 706/1/2. His/her experience must have been in top class establishments that enjoy a good reputation for their standards of food and service.

person required

The successful candidate will be paid a salary of not less than £12,000 p.a. for a five-day week, including some late evenings. After the first year he or she will receive four weeks' holiday per annnum and will qualify for the Company's pension scheme. Prospects for promotion within the company are excellent. This is a living out appointment.

main conditions of employment

Telephone, or write giving brief details of age, training and experience to

A. Smith, Food and Beverage Manager,

Splendide Hotel
Newtown, Newtownshire
Telephone: Newtown (0021) 12345

how to apply

An example of an advertisement which sets out to create a good impression of the employer. It says a reasonable amount about the job and encourages people to apply in the simplest way.

Figure 4.7 *Display advertisement for a barman or barmaid – local press*

THE SPLENDIDE HOTEL

situated in the centre of Newtown and catering for a busy commercial trade requires

A SMART YOUNG PERSON

to work as a part-time assistant in the cocktail bar. The successful applicant, aged 18–30, will assist the cocktail barman on Tuesday to Saturday evenings each week. Once the person appointed is familiar with the work he or she will stand in for the cocktail barman on Sunday evenings. Hours will be 5.45 p.m. to 10.45 p.m. (The Hotel is on several convenient bus routes which run up to about 11.00 p.m.)

No previous experience in bar work is required as training will be given, but the ability to get on with people will be essential. A meal will be provided during the evening and the rate of pay will be £3.50 per hour.

Splendide Hotel
Newtown, Newtownshire
Telephone Newtown (0021) 12345

If you are interested telephone Mr A. Smith, Food and Beverage Manager.

---

industry know well the value of 'word of mouth' recommendation. Many highly successful hotels, restaurants and public houses do not need to spend a penny on attracting customers. Their reputation is enough. This applies equally to staff and there are many successful managers who never have to spend a penny to recruit new staff. Consciously or unconsciously, their existing employees recruit newcomers for them.

This method of recruitment is particularly good because of the two-way recommendation. An existing employee is recommending someone as a good employer and the applicant is being recommended as a suitable employee. Recognizing the value of this method of recruitment, some firms actually stimulate it by paying bonuses to employees who successfully introduce newcomers to the firm.

However, for large organizations there can be a risk of running foul of Race Relations legislation, because word-of-mouth systems of recruitment have been found to be discriminatory.

Costs

Recruitment, like any other business activity, costs time and money. Most other business activities are measured in some way and standards or ratios are used to indicate the efficiency or otherwise of the activity.

Figure 4.8
Semi-display advertisement

WORKING
HEAD CHEF

required

for busy 60-bedroomed
Hotel.

Large banqueting suite,
100-cover restaurant
and pub food operation.

Ideal candidate will be
required to form five
commis into a cohesive
team, maintain strict
food cost control and
attain percentages.

Candidate will be
totally responsible for
kitchen cleanliness.

Apply in writing to:
Managing Director
Osterley Hotel
764 Great West Road
Isleworth, Middlesex
CVCR25-017

Figure 4.9
Classified advertisement

COOK REQUIRED at Sussex
House Nursing Home for alter-
nate weekends, hours 8 a.m.-1
p.m. If you are a kind, capable
person interested in good home
cooking then you may be the
person we are looking for. Telephone for an informal chat on
Horsham 65356 and speak to
Mrs. Stepney, S.R.N., our
Director of Nursing.   T2 25/26G

This principle should apply equally to recruitment if it is a regular and substantial part of the running costs of the business. Where an agency is retained it will calculate the cost effectiveness of various media, but if an agency is not used this should be calculated internally. Figure 4.10 shows a simple form for the analysis of such costs.

Analyses can be much more complex but something along the lines of the form shown in Figure 4.10 will prove sufficient for the average organization to recognize which means of recruitment is the most effective and which involves the least interviewing, correspondence and other administration.

Recruitment code

Apart from costs, a manager also has wider responsibilities. As a result the Institute of Personnel Management has drawn up the 'IPM Recruitment Code', the main points of which are as follows:

1 Job advertisements will state clearly the form of reply desired (for example *curriculum vitae*, completed application form) and any preference for hand-written applications.
2 An acknowledgement or reply will be made promptly to each applicant. Where consultants are acting mainly as forwarding agents for companies, the parties will agree who will acknowledge applications.
3 Candidates will be informed of the progress of the selection procedure, what this will be, the time likely to be involved and the policy regarding expenses.
4 Detailed personal information (for example religion, medical history, place of birth, family background) will not be called for unless and until it is relevant to the selection process.
5 Recruiters will not take up any reference without the candidate's specific approval.
6 Applications will be treated as confidential.

The full code is contained in Appendix 3.

Figure 4.10   *Recruitment costs analysis*

Media	Daily Globe	Evening Star	Evening Star	Blue Agency	Job Centre
Job	Chef	Receptionist	Waiter	Waiter	Porter
Cost	£240	£80	£80	£140	
Number of applicants	8	20	4	7	16
Number interviewed	5	12	3	6	9
Cost per applicant	£30	£4	£20	£20	
Number of successful applicants	1	4	2	2	2
Cost per successful applicant	£240	£20	£40	£70	

The future of recruiting in the hospitality industry

Traditional forms of recruitment and sources of labour, it appears, are not going to be sufficient to provide the necessary number of people required by the hospitality industry over the next few years. Instead new methods and sources are going to be needed. For example, much more effort will be needed to create a positive awareness of the industry amongst young school children, not just those about to leave school. Another measure that can be developed is to recognize that already, large numbers of young people work in the industry on a casual and part-time basis and more effort needs to be devoted to converting a proportion of these into permanent workers in the industry, by offering real career prospects involving training and personal development. Effort is also needed to attract and retain more women returners and to assist them through the provision of crêche facilities, etc. These could be organized by employers on a cooperative basis. Apart from these sources of labour employers could also consider targeting older people. Age discrimination, according to the Institute of Personnel Management (*IPM Digest*, June 1989), affects not just those over 50; women can start to experience age discrimination from the age of 35 onwards and men from 40 onwards. Other sectors of the population include the one and a half million people who have been unemployed for a long period and maybe ethnic minorities. These are in addition to the many millions of young people in continental Europe who will be keen to work in Britain for a period to improve their English.

Further reading

Armstrong, M., *A Handbook of Human Resource Management*, London: Kogan Page, 1988

Courtis, J., *Cost Effective Recruitment*, London: Institute of Personnel Management, 1984

Herriot, P., *Recruitment in the 90s*, London: Institute of Personnel Management, 1989

Plumbley, P., *Recruitment and Selection*, 4th ed. London: Institute of Personnel Management, 1989

Pratt, K. J., and Bennett, S. C., *Elements of Personnel Management*, 3rd ed., Wokingham: GEE, 1989

Thomason, G., *Textbook of Human Resource Management*, London: Institute of Personnel Management, 1988

Torrington, D. and Hall, L., *Personnel Management – A New Approach*, London: Prentice Hall, 1987

Questions

1 Describe the objectives of recruitment and the various steps you would normally expect to find in a systematic recruitment procedure
2 Discuss which you consider to be the most important steps and why.
3 Discuss what changes are likely to be made in the future to improve recruitment.
4 Using an employer you know well, evaluate their approach to recruitment.

chapter 5

Selection

A key feature of the labour market of the 1990s is going to be its competitiveness, caused by a growth in the number of jobs and a decline in the traditional sources of labour. For the hospitality industry it is likely to be extremely competitive as other service industries expand or emerge and compete for labour. This almost certainly means that organizations will find themselves operating in a 'seller's' market, i.e. prospective employees, selling their labour, will have more power than the 'buyer', the potential employer.

The consequence is that organizations will have to put much more effort into designing attractive jobs and conditions, using effective recruitment methods and developing 'applicant friendly' selection techniques. These techniques will have to serve the dual purpose of ensuring that the proper candidates are selected and also that the employing organization is sold effectively.

The selection process

One of a manager's major responsibilities is to initiate action but to do this he or she has to receive and interpret information in order to arrive at conclusions that will lead to the right action. The further up the hierarchy of management a person moves the more he exercises the skills of judgement and the less he carries out routine and supervisory tasks. In fact, a senior manager's job should normally be devoted almost entirely to making decisions that implement action and to designing systems that enable better decisions to be made. The skill of selecting staff is concerned entirely with this same process. In filling a vacancy a manager obtains information, sorts it, compares it, makes conclusions and implements action. This is illustrated in Figure 5.1.

A manager will use the selection procedure normally for three different occasions:

1 To choose the most suitable person from several applicants to fill one vacancy.
2 To choose the right job from several for an applicant or several applicants.
3 Where there is only one applicant for a vacancy, to decide whether or not to appoint the person and, if so, to know his strengths and weaknesses so that additional supervision or appropriate training can be given, or so that the job can be modified.

In order to do this the manager should go through the procedure (described in Chapters 3 and 4) which requires a comprehensive job description and personnel specification to be prepared. Correct advertising will have attracted candidates and it is then the manager's job to ensure that information is obtained from candidates in a way that enables a comparison to be made with the personnel specification. From this procedure the most suitable applicant will emerge.

To assist in selection there are a variety of tools available to the manager including letters of application, application forms, interviews, group selection procedures, assessment centres and a range of tests sometimes referred to as psychological tests.

Figure 5.1   *The selection procedure simplified*

Selection procedures attempt to predict, as accurately as possible, a person's likely performance in a particular job or, where there are several vacancies, the job in which he or she is most likely to be successful. Most selection methods are of an 'historical' nature, that is they base their predictions on a person's past. However, most people accept that, economic and human considerations apart, the best method would be to employ a person for a period of time and then, if he proved satisfactory, to offer him the job. This is obviously not a practical method, although 'trial periods' are used both consciously and unconsciously in most industries. Selection procedures, instead, need to be designed in order to elicit the most useful and appropriate information in the most economical way.

The personnel specification

In attempting to assess or to measure a person's suitability for a job it is important to know what characteristics are to be measured. The range and descriptions of these characteristics can be vast and in many cases almost meaningless. Some interview assessment forms contain a long list of items including charm, punctuality, honesty, integrity, ability, etc. Many of these are supposed to be assessed (or guessed at) at an interview.

Most characteristics or patterns of behaviour, however, can be grouped under several broad headings and two methods of assessment in particular are of interest. The National Institute of Industrial Psychology (NIIP) system uses seven broad headings and J. Munro Fraser's plan uses five (see Figure 5.2). The five-fold system is a system for measuring to what degree an individual possesses each of five points or groups of characteristics.

The degree to which each of these points is possessed by an individual may be measured by reference to the normal curve of distribution. This can be divided into five grades, A to E, and subdivided into a total of twenty points. Figure 5.3 illustrates this. The average person falls into grade C around the middle of the curve. Those individuals possessing a higher than average degree of a particular point move into a higher grade and, conversely, those with less move down the scale; for example, in the aspect headed 'Qualifications' which includes education, the average person scores around the ten mark because he was in the A or did well in the B stream of a secondary school. On the other hand someone who obtained three 'A' levels would score about sixteen, and someone who could not do better than average in the B stream in a secondary school would probably score no more than seven. The same principle of measurement can apply to all the points.

Figure 5.2 *A summary of two of the most popular approaches to staff selection*

THE SEVEN-POINT PLAN (NIIP). The seven-point plan covers:

1 *Physical make-up* — health, physique, appearance, bearing and speech.
2 *Attainments* — education, qualifications, experience.
3 *General intelligence* — fundamental intellectual capacity.
4 *Special aptitudes* — mechanical, manual dexterity, facility in the use of words or figures.
5 *Interests* — intellectual, practical: constructional, physically active, social, artistic.
6 *Disposition* — acceptability, influence over others, steadiness, dependability, self-reliance.
7 *Circumstances* — domestic circumstances, occupations of family.

THE FIVE-FOLD GRADING SYSTEM (MUNRO FRASER). The five-fold grading system covers:

1 *Impact on others* — physical make-up, appearance, speech and manner.
2 *Acquired qualifications* — education, vocational training, work experience.
3 *Innate abilities* — natural quickness of comprehension and aptitude for learning.
4 *Motivation* — the kinds of goals set by the individual, his consistency and determination in following them up, his success in achieving them.
5 *Adjustment* — emotional stability, ability to stand up to stress and ability to get on with people.

Figure 5.3   *The normal curve of distribution*

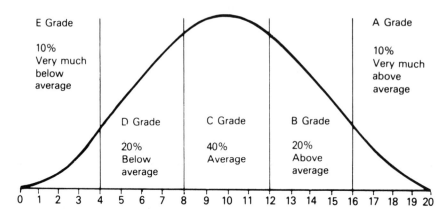

In producing a personnel specification, therefore, inclusion of these aspects with indications of desirable grades or precise requirements would considerably improve the 'pen picture' of the person required. Then during the subsequent selection procedure, candidates should be assessed or measured in the same way, making it a simple task to identify the person with the assessment nearest to the personnel specification. He or she should be the most suitable of the candidates.

Letter of application

Generally speaking it is not possible to use letters of application as a selection method any more than the telephone without the support of an interview or other method. However, well-designed advertisements can ask applicants to give sufficient information from which some candidates can be invited for interview. A typical sentence at the end of an advertisement would read:

> 'Kindly write giving full details, include age, education, training, experience, and earnings to . . .'

The main occasion when selection will depend only upon an application letter is when applicants live at some distance, usually overseas. In such cases the cost of travel excludes the possibility of interviewing.

To attempt to make an appointment purely on the strength of information contained in a letter is very risky, but if done, references and a full curriculum vitae should certainly be taken up first.

Application forms

The application form is used primarily to gather together relevant details so that the selector has this information at his or her finger-tips and can make fair comparisons with the personnel specification and with other candidates' applications.

When designing an application form it is important to remember that it may have to serve several purposes, such as:

1   Deciding whom to invite for an interview.
2   Being used as an interview assessment form.
3   Documenting employees and obtaining referees' names and addresses.
4   Providing a reserve list of potential employees.
5   Measuring the effectiveness of various recruitment media.
6   Analysing the labour market.
7   Obtaining agreement for medical examination, reference enquiries, etc.

The information required on an application form will, therefore, include some or all of the following:

(a)   Position applied for.
(b)   Personal data: name, address, telephone number, age, sex, marital status, children, nationality.
(c)   Education: schools, subjects studied, exams passed, and further education.
(d)   Professional qualifications.
(e)   Experience: jobs, duties, responsibilities, employers, earnings, reasons for leaving.
(f)   Skills: e.g. word processing, PBX, languages.
(g)   Military experience: branch of the service, rank attained, experience.
(h)   Personal circumstances: when available, prepared to travel or to move, current holiday plans.
(i)   Medical history.
(j)   Interests, hobbies, sports, other activities.
(k)   Record of offences. (Note: This is subject to the Rehabilitation of Offenders Act.)

The exact nature and extent of the information asked for will depend on the type of job and the employer's administrative requirements, but it should be confined to information necessary for sound assessments to be made.* It is not appropriate, therefore, for one 'blanket' type form to be used for all job categories. The type of form used for senior executives which asks about professional qualifications and total employment history would not be suitable for an unskilled worker, such as a room-maid, where the last five years' work history may be quite sufficient.

When designing an application form legal aspects also have to be considered, particularly, discrimination legislation. Questions about marital status and number of children for example, may be permitted so long as everyone, regardless of sex, is asked such questions, and decisions are not based on this information to the exclusion of other information.

*See the recruitment code in Appendix 3.

The interview

The next step after candidates have completed and submitted their application forms, or discussed their qualifications on the telephone is to invite selected candidates in for interviews. The interview is the most commonly used method of selection. It is also considered by many to be one of the least effective, largely because it bears no resemblance to what a person is likely to be employed to do and also because few managers are properly trained in interview techniques. In one survey of graduate recruits 52% reported that their selection interviews had left them with a poor impression of the company, due to lack of skill on the part of the interviewer (*Personnel Management*, October 1989). Consequently many bad appointments are made because the candidates have not had the opportunity to show their paces, or because the interviewer could not interpret rightly the available information. It is not possible in this book to discuss interviewing in depth, but excellent books have already been written on the subject (see the list of Further reading at the end of this chapter). In conducting an interview, however, it is important to keep to a plan, see Figure 5.6 for an example, and the simplest method is to follow chronological order – starting at childhood and working up to the present day. Questions normally become more searching as one approaches current or more recent experiences, and must therefore be designed to test fully a person's claimed level of competence and likely level of achievement.

Main types of interview

The most common method is the individual interview, i.e. one interviewer interviews one candidate at a time. Whilst this method usually enables the candidate to relax more quickly, there is the risk of bias or preference – particularly if the interviewer's decision is made independently of other colleagues.

The second method is a panel interview or selection board – very common in the public sector. This will usually consist at least of the line manager concerned and a personnel specialist. This approach reduces the risk of bias, particularly as the panel increases in size. The approach can be varied by candidates being seen individually in turn by each member of a selection panel.

There is one type of interview sometimes referred to as a 'stress' interview. The intention is to create a stress situation to see how an applicant reacts. It is only valid if a person is likely to encounter stress situations, e.g. difficult customers, regularly and such interviews should only be administered by trained interview specialists. Even so there are serious doubts about the ethics of conducting such an interview without giving the candidate prior notice – in which case much of the effect of the stress interview will be lost.

If necessary make notes during an interview, but do explain to the candidate that this is necessary so that nothing of importance can be forgotten. The following *dos* and *don't*s on page 83 will be useful.

Figure 5.4 *Application form for non-management positions*
(This is an example of contents – but not of spaces provided)

Application form

Surname

First names

Address

Dependants

Splendide Hotel
Newtown, Newtownshire
Telephone Newtown (0021) 12345

Telephone no.   Nationality

Are you a Registered Disabled Person? If yes please give your registration number

Have you ever been convicted of any criminal offence? If so please give details:

Education *Only complete this section if your full-time education ended less than 5 years ago*

School *last attended*   Exams passed

Details of Further education   Course and exams passed
Other training courses including HCTB courses

Have you been previously employed by this Company? YES/NO. If yes please give dates and position held

Date available   How did you learn of this vacancy?

Details of previous employment – last three positions. If this covers a period of less than five years give details of other positions held

Name and address of employer	Date		Position	Wage	Reason for leaving
	From	19..			
	To	19..			
	From	19..			
	To	19..			
	From	19..			
	To	19..			
	From	19..			
	To	19..			

I agree to being examined by the company's doctor should a medical examination be required

I understand this incorrect or misleading information may render me liable to instant dismissal and that any appointment is subject to satisfactory references.

Applicant's signature   Date

Figure 5.5 *A typical extended application form*

Trusthouse Forte (U.K.) Limited

Application For Employment

PLEASE COMPLETE EACH SECTION IN CAPITALS USING BLACK INK
AND RETURN THIS FORM TO THE HOTEL FROM WHICH YOU OBTAINED IT.

The information which you give on this form will be treated as **Strictly Confidential**

GENERAL INFORMATION

What position are you applying for?   Date available to start:

How did you hear of this vacancy?   Uniform Size: Wages Expected:

PERSONAL AND SOCIAL DETAILS

SURNAME: Mr/Mrs/Miss/Ms   FIRST NAMES

Address   Maiden Name (if applicable)

Telephone   HOME
                        WORK
Nat. Ins. No:

Birth Date   Marital Status: Single □   Married □
                        Divorced □   Widowed □   Separated □

Birth Place   No. of Children & Ages

Nationality

Are you a member of any professional organisation or association?

Hobbies and other interests

Do you hold a current Driving Licence?   Do you own a car?   Yes □   No □
                        Yes □ No □
Have you ever been convicted of a
Criminal Offence?   Yes □   No □   If 'yes', explain

OFFICE USE ONLY

Interviewers Notes: **2.** Qualifications & Experience
1. Personal Qualities
    Appearance, Personality, etc.

---

3. Circumstances (Domestic)   **4. Action to be Taken**
    Health   **Offer to be made:** Authorised By:
    Availability   Job:
                        Wage:
                        Start Date:
                        Applicant informed:

OTHER INFORMATION

Are there any other qualifications you have gained or courses you have attended you think we should know about?
Yes or No   If 'yes' explain

Typing   words p.m.   Shorthand   words p.m.
What machines can you operate?
What languages do you speak?

HEALTH DETAILS

Name and address of your Doctor

Have you, within the past three years, had any illness or accident
which caused you to be off work for two weeks or more?   YES/NO
If yes, what was the illness or accident?

Have you, within the past three years, attended an out-patients clinic or had a course of
treatment (tablets, injections or physiotherapy) lasting one month or more?   YES/NO
Are you now receiving any such treatment?   YES/NO
Do you smoke?   YES/NO
Have you any permanent disability?   YES/NO
Are you a Registered Disabled?   YES/NO
If yes,   what is your number?
    what is the expiry date?
    what is the disablement?
Are you suffering from or have you ever suffered from
    fits, epilepsy or black-outs?   YES/NO
    diabetes?   YES/NO
    depressive illness or nervous trouble?   YES/NO
    such diseases as typhoid, cholera, hepatitis, recurring diarrhoea?   YES/NO
    skin disease or dermatitis?   YES/NO
    allergy (to any drugs or to handling any substance)?   YES/NO
    earache or ear infection?   YES/NO
Have you ever been refused employment or dismissed on medical grounds?   YES/NO
If 'yes' explain

The answers supplied to the above questions are true to the best of my knowledge.
Furthermore, I undertake to report immediately to my Manager if I or a member of my
household should be suffering from vomiting, diarrhoea, skin rash, septic skin lesions or
discharges from ear, eye, nose or any other site,
    1. After returning to, but before re-starting work, after any of the above illnesses, and
    2. After returning from a holiday abroad, having suffered from vomiting and
diarrhoea for more than two days.

EDUCATION   (Secondary and above)

From   To   Name and Address of School, College, etc.   Qualifications

EMPLOYMENT (Show last employment first, include training and military service.) We need your employment record covering the last five years. For any period of unemployment please put dates and address of Department of Employment, where registered.

From   To   Name and Address of Employer   Job Title   Reason for Leaving

FOR NON-BRITISH & NON-EEC NATIONALS

Date of Entry into U.K.?   How long are you intending to stay in UK?

Do you have a Work Permit?   Yes ☐   No ☐ If yes, what type and number?

EMERGENCY INFORMATION

In case of emergency who do we contact?

Address
Tel. No.   Home   Work   Relationship

REFERENCES
DELETE INFORMATION WHICH IS NOT APPLICABLE

(no information will be sought from your present employer without your consent)
NAME
ADDRESS
             Telephone
Type of reference – School/College/Employer/Character

NAME
ADDRESS
             Telephone
Type of reference – School/College/Employer/Character

NAME
ADDRESS
             Telephone
Type of reference – School/College/Employer/Character

DECLARATION

I understand that the completion of the Form does not guarantee employment. I certify that all the information given on this Form is true and accept that any mis-statement or suppression of material may mean the cancellation of any appointment which is also made subject to the receipt of satisfactory references.

DATE   SIGNATURE OF APPLICANT

Please return this form to the hotel from which you obtained it.

Do
1 Have a clear job description, personnel specification, details of conditions, and an interview plan that contains prepared technical questions.
2 Use a quiet, comfortable room.
3 Suspend all phone calls and other interruptions.
4 Introduce yourself, be natural and put the candidate at ease.
5 Explain clearly the job, conditions of employment and prospects.
6 Ask questions that begin with When, Where, Why, Who, What and How. This avoids receiving 'Yes' and 'No' as an answer and encourages the candidate to talk.
7 Avoid asking unnecessary questions already answered on the application form.
8 Listen and let the candidate talk freely, but at the same time guide and control the interview.
9 Encourage the candidate to ask questions.
10 Close the interview firmly and explain the next step in the procedure.
11 Treat all candidates as though they are potential employees and customers.
12 Write up your assessment immediately after each interview (see Figure 5.7 for an example).

Don't
1 Keep the candidate waiting.
2 Oversell the job.
3 Conceal unpleasant facts about the job.
4 Interrupt or rush the interview.
5 Preach to the candidate.
6 Read out to the candidate what is on the application form: he or she filled it in and knows it already.
7 Ask questions that indicate the answer.
8 Ask questions that only get 'Yes' or 'No' for an answer.
9 Allow the first impression to influence the whole interview.
10 Ask unnecessary personal questions.
11 Raise hopes unnecessarily.
12 Leave candidates with a bad opinion of your organization; they may be potential customers in other contexts.
13 Wait until the end of the day or even till the following day to write up your assessments.

The three 'C's – Contact, Content, Control

Some interviewers evaluate the quality of interviewing by referring to the three 'C's – Contact, Content, Control.

Contact refers to the ability to 'make contact' with the candidate, to develop a rapport. This is achieved by setting out to enable the candidate to relax so that the 'real' person comes through. This is a difficult situation to achieve because for many candidates the interview can be very nerve-racking. However, a number of techniques, usually combined, can help, such as those listed on page 86.

Figure 5.6   *An example of what can be included in an interview plan*

Interview plan

Part 1	
Introduction	Introduce oneself, describe position held and responsibilities, give brief description of unit, company, job, conditions, prospects, reasons for vacancy, hours of work, rate of pay.
Part 2	
Facts	What made applicant decide to come into the industry? Any connections with the industry, e.g. brought up in hotels?
Life	Where did applicant go to school, college, university? What qualifications did he or she attain? Special interests at school, college, both academic and non-academic. What was the first job after leaving school?
All jobs	Reasons for joining. Reason for leaving. Responsibility when first appointed and upon termination. Earnings when appointed and upon termination. What did applicant think of employer, manager? What was the most important lesson learnt there? What changes could be made? Main problems there. Main achievement there.
General	What is applicant's most important achievement? Hobbies and interests. What is ambition in life — next year, five years, ten years?
Technical expertise	A series of questions to test an applicant's technical knowledge should be asked.
Attitudes	Towards e.g. college training/informal training. Recent legal changes. Unions, customers, work, management.
Family	Any domestic responsibilities at home? When available to start? What hours/days prepared to work? Mobility.
At present	Working? Type of job, duties, progress made in that job. Prospects, wages, benefits, reason for leaving, reason for coming to this position. Health, personal and of family. Criminal convictions.
Part 3	
Close	Answer applicant's questions. Explain next step in selection procedure. Check on travelling expenses.

Figure 5.7 *Selection interview appraisal report (for a senior appointment)*

NAME .... AGE .... APPRAISED FOR ....

INTERVIEWED BY .... DATE ....

1 PRESENT CIRCUMSTANCES:

Firm .... business .... size ....

Position held .... location ....

Salary .... benefits .... pension .... holidays ....

Availability .... preferred location ....

Notice given/received .... other appointments pending ....

Salary expectation ....

Responsible to: ....

Responsible for: ....

a) no. and type of staff ....
b) duties ....

Prospects: ....
....

Reasons for leaving: ....
....

Reasons for wanting this appointment: ....
....

2 PERSONALITY AND APPEARANCE:

Appearance: ....

Dress: ....

Self-expression, accent, voice: ....

Manner: ....

Acceptability: ....

3 FAMILY BACKGROUND:

Origins .... married/single .... children ....

Views of candidate and his/her spouse on conditions of employment, including travel:
....
....

4 EDUCATION:

Type of education .... achievements ....

5 PROFESSIONAL QUALIFICATIONS:

Type .... place ....

Method of achievement; number of attempts:
....
....

Interview in an informal setting, but where there are no risks of disturbances or of being overheard

Avoid having a desk between the interviewee and yourself – a desk creates a psychological barrier

Offer a cup of tea or coffee

Invite a candidate to smoke if he or she wishes

Discuss common ground, e.g. a hotel or a manager known to both of you

Use body language, e.g. move towards the candidate to emphasize that you are interested in what is being said

Use encouraging statements such as, 'That's interesting', or 'Tell me more about that'.

Figure 5.7   *cont.*

6   EXPERIENCE:

....

....

....

....

....

7   APPRAISAL

Intelligence and ability

....

....

Knowledge and experience:
(breadth and depth) ....

....

Career development — salary progression:

....

....

Motivation, personal relationships, adjustment, stability:

....

....

Health, outside interests, etc.:

....

....

8   RECOMMENDATION:

....

....

....

....

....

Source: Croner's Personnel Records 1/86, with kind permission of Croner Publications.

Content refers to the need to ensure that the interview covers all the important ground, including a person's technical competence, ability to get on with others and maybe the ability to take on increased responsibilities. It is particularly difficult to judge a person's future potential but one useful piece of information can be provided by a person's perspective of what is challenging. The question, 'What is the biggest work-related responsibility you have ever had?', can be very informative. One person may answer, 'To have catered for 5,000 at an agricultural show', whereas another candidate may answer, 'To have prepared a cold buffet for 200'. Such answers enable the interviewer, having checked the facts, to determine which of the applicants is more likely to fit in with the employer's scale of expectations.

Figure 5.8 *Comparative career progression charts*

Another important piece of information useful in predicting a candidate's growth potential is his career progression chart. From this one can look for growth in responsibility, such as size of establishment, number of subordinates, increase in standards (e.g. star rating) and earnings over a period of time. Figure 5.8 shows three career paths.

Manager A (aged 33) has had an erratic career, manager B (aged 33) appears to be on a growth path whilst manager C (aged 40) has 'plateaued out'. If all three were applying for a position with, say, around 150–200 subordinates, everything being equal, then manager B appears to be most likely to be suited. Obviously many other factors have to be considered such as the number of job changes or promotions in each person's career and the reasons for the changes.

Another important aspect of 'Content' is to ensure that the interviewer communicates all the necessary information to the candidate, pleasant and unpleasant (e.g. unsocial hours). The interview is, after all, a two-way process.

Control refers to the interviewer's ability to ensure that the interview plan is completed in the time allocated. This will require the skill to guide the candidate through the career and technical questions and to bring the candidate back if he or she begins to wander from the subject without changing the 'Contact' or rapport being built up.

One final rule and a useful one by which an interviewer's skill can be measured is to estimate the amount of time devoted by the interviewer to listening and to talking. Generally speaking the less the interviewer talks, the better he or she is at formulating questions, listening and making the right assessment.

Group selection procedures and assessment centres

The main weakness of the interview is that it relies on one technique only. This weakness can be compensated for to some extent by training and by involving a number of people in the process. One way of improving the reliability of a selection method, however, is to introduce more techniques so that the combination of techniques exposes more of a candidate's skills, personality traits, etc. to scrutiny. This is increasingly done through *assessment centres* or *group selection procedures* which trace their roots back to methods used to select officers for the armed services.

These are specialized techniques and should always be conducted by people trained in their design, operation and interpretation. The purpose of a group selection procedure is to observe candidates' behaviour in a situation or in a variety of situations similar to those they would have to face in the organization. A group selection procedure could include:

1   The analysis of problems with reports and presentations
2   Group discussions and debates
3   Business games, 'in-tray' exercises
4   Individual interviews
5   Tests; aptitude, personality, interest
6   'Informal' drinks and dinner.

Group selection procedures and assessment centres are normally used to identify personality traits, skills etc. and to predict behaviour that is difficult to assess in an interview or from personal history. These traits may include leadership ability, persuasiveness, self-confidence, ability to stand up to pressure, mental flexibility. They are used both for recruiting new employees (usually senior) and for assessing promotion potential of existing employees.

Psychological tests

The testing of individuals in education, at work and in other aspects of our lives has been going on in various forms for many years. Its main industrial purpose is to help to predict future performance in particular fields by understanding individual and group behaviour. As with other selection procedures testing assists in identifying the most suitable person for a job, and in identifying the most suitable jobs for individuals. As the HCITB's magazine *Service* stated: 'Much of the disappointment arising from failures and drop-outs in training could be eliminated by the use of simple tests of the ability and potential of applicants.'

Most tests can normally only be administered under the supervision of a trained person registered with the National Foundation for Educational Research.

The five main groups of tests are:

1 *Intelligence (IQ) tests* These measure the stage of development of intelligence in children and the intelligence of adults relative to the general population. The mean score is 100. Such tests are commonly used to determine if a person will be able to cope with certain intellectual tasks.

2 *Attainment tests* These measure the degree to which a person has acquired knowledge or skill. A craft test such as the City and Guilds of London Professional Cookery examination is typical. Applicants for jobs such as cashiers, book-keepers or other clerical staff could be given simple attainment tests which could easily be devised by supervisors along with a personnel or training specialist. But it is important, in designing such tests, to recognize that failure to do the test may not indicate total unsuitability, but only a need for training. Many more skill or attainment tests, including those shown in Figure 5.9, could be used in this industry.

Figure 5.9 *Attainment tests — examples of uses*

Example of category of employee	Nature of test
Chefs and cooks	Demonstrate knowledge of recipes and practical skill in making up certain dishes
Waiters and waitresses	Demonstrate knowledge of recipes, the accompaniments for certain dishes, and the service of some complex dishes
Barmen and barmaids	Demonstrate knowledge of and ability to prepare certain of the more popular drinks Demonstrate the ability to compute the cost of rounds of drinks
Cashiers and receptionists	Demonstrate knowledge of some common reception routines, the ability to operate appropriate office machines and to compute typical cash transactions

3 *Aptitude tests* This group of tests identifies an individual's innate suitability for particular types of work and can indicate whether a person would be more suited to one type of work rather than another.

4 *Interest tests* These tests indicate broadly which type of work an individual would prefer, such as: indoor, outdoor, computational, gregarious, individual, routine, creative.

It is important to stress that an interest in, or preference for, particular work need not indicate an aptitude for that work. However, where an aptitude for a certain type of work is supported by an interest in the same type of work the chances of that individual succeeding are much higher.

5 *Personality tests* These tests determine an individual's reactions to different situations from which general conclusions can be drawn

regarding likely future behaviour. They are concerned mainly with measuring non-intellectual characteristics. In particular most attempt to measure how a person relates to the world around him and they do this by measuring the degree to which a person possesses certain personality traits, such as drive, stability, persuasiveness, self-confidence, introversion, extroversion. Some personality tests, such as Cattell's 16PF,* are claimed to be extremely comprehensive, covering all possible aspects of personality encountered in normal individuals.

Test batteries

It will be clear that each of the groups of tests mentioned above, with one or two possible exceptions, attempts to measure limited aspects of an individual. These are intelligence, attainment, aptitude, interests and personality. Each individual employed, however, needs levels or aspects of each of these characteristics and one type of test only may not do justice. As a result some selection specialists use a battery or variety of tests that measure several of those aspects of a person that may be considered of importance. Additionally, a test battery may be only part of an overall procedure incorporated, for example, into a group selection procedure or assessment centre.

References

It is important to remember that references are only as reliable as the judgement of the person giving them, and because of the fear some employers have of putting a bad or indifferent reference in writing, many written references are worthless. The best procedure for obtaining references, therefore, is to telephone referees and to discuss a candidate's application on the telephone. This discussion should be written up afterwards so that it can be put into a person's file.* Alternatively, a standard letter or questionnaire asking previous employers to confirm certain details can be used, see Figure 5.10.

References must only be sought after a person has been offered an appointment subject to references, as he may not have informed his current employer of his plans to move; unless, of course, he has given specific permission for references to be applied for before being offered an appointment (which is common in the public sector).

Successful selection, that is, placing suitable people into the right jobs, is vital to the prosperity of an organization. But selection can only be successful if it is carried out methodically, and this requires a clear job description and personnel specification, plus a system which ensures that the most suitable candidates are attracted and identified. This will require well-designed advertisements and application forms that elicit appropriate information.

---

*Raymond Cattell, *Sixteen Personality Factor Questionnaire* (16PF).
*Remember that under the Data Protection Act the subject may have the right to see this if the data is on computer.

Figure 5.10 *A reference inquiry letter*

Splendide Hotel
Newtown, Newtownshire
Telephone Newtown (0021) 12345

Dear Sir,

We have received an application for employment from Mr   who says that he was employed by you. It would be very helpful to us if you could answer the questions at the bottom of this letter and return it to us in the enclosed pre-paid envelope. The information will of course be treated in the strictest confidence.

If at any time we can be of similar assistance please do not hesitate to contact us. We hope that this enquiry does not cause you too much inconvenience.

Yours faithfully,

Please delete one

Full name

Position held   Correct/Incorrect

Dates employed: from   to   Correct/Incorrect

Reason for leaving   Correct/Incorrect

Would you re-employ him if you had a suitable vacancy?   Yes/No

Would you prefer us to telephone you?   Yes/No

Would you care to add any comments regarding suitability for the job applied for?

Interviews and other selection techniques, as outlined above, will then have to be conducted enabling the assessor to predict, as accurately as possible, a candidate's performance if he or she were to be appointed. This will involve knowing which characteristics are desirable and it will also involve using techniques that identify or measure those same characteristics.

Future trends

For the industry's smaller employers the need to adopt more effective selection techniques, or at least to apply commonly used ones more effectively, is vital. For the larger organizations there is a need to examine both the techniques they use but also where the emphasis is placed. Currently, for example, most applicants are eliminated before interview, on the basis of their application form – amongst the least reliable of the selection tools. The most systematic methods are used on the smallest number, those who remain after the first screening. Maybe more effort needs to be devoted to ensuring that the good candidates who are lost through the initial screening are not lost by using more systematic methods in the earlier stages of the process. This would require considerably more thought in designing recruitment literature, so that self-selection plays a bigger part in bringing forward a smaller number of candidates but who are better candidates, followed maybe by self-administered tests.

Careful selection is an investment in team building and while it is more time-consuming than haphazard recruitment, the reduction in labour turnover which normally results, together with the consequent improvement in efficiency and customer satisfaction, make it worthwhile.

Further reading

Armstrong, M., *A Handbook of Human Resource Management*, London: Kogan Page, 1988

Gratus, J., *Successful Interviewing, How to Find and Keep the Best People*, London: Penguin, 1988

Lockwood, A. and Jones, P., *People and the Hotel and Catering Industry*, Eastbourne: Holt, Rinehart and Winston, 1984

Pratt, K. J., and Bennett, S. C., *Elements of Personnel Management*, 3rd ed., Wokingham: GEE, 1989

Pugh, D. S., and Hickson, D. J., *Writers on Organisations*, 4th ed. London: Penguin, 1989

Rae, L., *The Skills of Interviewing, a Guide for Managers and Trainers*, London: Gower, 1988

Sisson K., (ed.), *Personnel Management in Britain*, Oxford: Blackwell, 1989

Thomason, G., *Textbook of Human Resource Management* London: Institute of Personnel Management, 1988

Torrington, D. and Hall, L., *Personnel Management – A New Approach*, London: Prentice Hall, 1987

Questions

1 Describe the objectives of selection, the alternative methods and the various steps you would normally expect to find in a systematic selection procedure.

2 Discuss which you consider to be the most effective selection methods and why.

3 Compare and contrast interviews, psychological tests and 'group assessment' procedures.

4 Discuss what changes are likely to be made in the future to improve selection procedures.

5 Using an employer you know well evaluate their approach to selection.

chapter 6

Appointment and induction

First impressions are often the most lasting impressions, and the first impressions formed by many employees upon starting employment with a new organization are unfortunately not often good. While they may be false, the employee is not to know this. Impressions have been shaped by the advertisement, the interview and interview arrangements, treatment of travel expenses, etc., and new employees arriving to start work are in many cases thrust straight into the job without even minimal introduction to the employer's methods and rules, let alone introductions to colleagues and management. The first hours and days are critical and if properly dealt with can create the right relationship that contributes to employees' staying with an employer. Figure 6.1 shows information from the National Economic Development Committee's research into the industry's manpower and shows the low level of formal induction. This shows that less than 10% of hotel and restaurant managers in the industry actually carried out a formal induction of new employees.

Induction has been defined in the Department of Employment, Glossary of Training Terms as, 'Arrangements made by or on behalf of the management to

Figure 6.1 *Induction in the hotel and restaurant industry*

Method	Per cent
None	24
Introduce and show around	13
Introduce, show around, explain rules	30
Introduce, show around, explain rules, give supervised job trial	14
Brief chat	2
Take through booklet describing job	3
Supervised job instruction	3
Special induction course/procedure	8
No response	3
	100

Source: EDC manpower survey — interviews with managers

familiarize the new employee with the working organisation, welfare and safety matters, general conditions of employment and the work of the departments in which he is to be employed. It is a continuous process starting from the first contact with the employer.'

As this definition shows, the process of correctly inducting an employee starts even before the formal offer of employment. When the employer has made a decision, the successful applicant should be told immediately that the employer wishes to make an offer. This should be done, if possible, at an interview (not at the selection interview) or by telephone so that agreement can be reached about details such as starting date, outstanding holiday arrangements, etc.

Letter of appointment

A formal letter should then be sent off incorporating all conditions of employment and also the job description. An example of a typical letter of offer is shown in Figure 6.2.

This letter satisfies several requirements.

1 It gives the new employee full details concerning the job and conditions.
2 It fulfils the requirements of Employment Legislation by giving the employee details of certain conditions of employment and obviates the need to do this within thirteen weeks of his or her joining.
3 It demonstrates an efficient, businesslike and, by its tone, sympathetic approach that should make the person feel he or she is joining a worthwhile organization.
4 It obtains written acceptance of the offer and also written permission to write off for references.
5 It states exactly when and where the person is to come, and what to bring on the first day.

Documentation

The next step is to arrange that when the employee arrives all documentation proceeds smoothly. This includes obtaining the P45 and, where the employee is to be paid through a bank, the bank's address. A personal file or dossier will have to be opened which will contain all relevant correspondence and documents including the application form and acceptance of offer, and in time a variety of other documents. In larger companies an engagement form should be completed to ensure that no documentation procedures are missed out. This could look like the one illustrated in Figure 17.5 (page 206) and would be produced with sufficient copies for each interested department, including the wages department.

Figure 6.2 *Example of a letter offering employment*

Mr J. L. Cook   **Splendide Hotel**
3 Seaside Gardens   Newtown, Newtownshire
Newtown   Telephone: Newtown (0021) 12345
Newtonshire

Dear Mr Cook   27 September 1990

Appointment as chef de cuisine

This letter is to confirm the conversation that we had yesterday in which I was very pleased to tell you that your application for the position of chef de cuisine has been successful.

I should like to confirm that you will be commencing employment on Monday 8 October next and that the following are details of the conditions of employment that we agreed.

Your pay is at the rate of £1,500 per month, paid monthly in arrears. All meals will be provided whilst on duty. The company undertakes to ensure that any future changes in the agreed terms will be communicated to you in writing within one month of the change.

Your normal hours of work are forty-five over a five day week. The actual hours will be agreed on a weekly basis with the food and beverage manager. As this is a management appointment there is no entitlement to overtime payments.

Your entitlement to holidays (excluding public holidays) and holiday pay (including accrued holiday pay on termination of employment) is four weeks per annum. Your holiday will fall within the period 1 May–30 September each year, the actual period to be fixed in accordance with the rota drawn up by the hotel manager.

You are covered by the company's sick pay and pension schemes, details of which are set out in the accompanying handbook.

You are entitled to receive one week's notice of termination during the first four weeks of employment, then four weeks for up to four year's service, and thereafter an additional week for each year of service up to a maximum of twelve weeks. You are required to give the company similar notice.

You are subject to the company's disciplinary procedure – details of which are set out in the accompanying handbook. If you have any grievance regarding your employment, you should raise it with your departmental manager, either orally or in writing. If the matter is not settled at this level, you may pursue it through the company's grievance procedure, details of which are set out in the accompanying handbook.

This offer is subject to satisfactory references and satisfactory medical report from the company's doctor.

A copy of this letter is attached for you to sign and return to me. I shall treat it both as an acceptance of the offer and permission to write to your referees.

You will find attached a copy of the job description which we discussed at the interview, and if you have any queries do not hesitate to contact me.

In the meantime I should like to wish you every success and happiness with the company and look forward to seeing you in my office at 9.30 a.m. on 8 October. Would you kindly bring your P45 with you.

Yours sincerely

J. E. Jones
General Manager

Enclosures: Job description, details of company schemes covering sickness, pensions, discipline, grievances, health and safety.

Introduction to work-place, colleagues, rules, etc.

The second part of inducting new employees is concerned with ensuring that they know and understand what is required of them in order to do their jobs satisfactorily. This includes telling them or preferably showing them the layout of the place of work, introducing them to colleagues and explaining to them the function of other relevant departments. It will also be necessary for them to know about house rules such as 'no drinking' and relevant laws such as licensing hours and 'no smoking' in food areas.

Training needs

The third aspect is concerned with determining the employee's ability to do the job itself effectively and this will depend upon a person's training and experience. No training may be needed, or merely working under close guidance and supervision for a few days may be adequate. On the other hand, detailed training may be required and this is often the case in larger organizations that are prepared to employ untrained people and have standard methods common to many branches.

Induction checklist

Whatever the level of competence, however, it is advisable to use a checklist to ensure that an induction procedure deals adequately with all necessary aspects of induction. In this context it is important to remember that what may not appear important to the employer may be very important to employees. Figure 6.3 shows the checklist used by a hotel. An induction checklist is also shown on page 320.

Where it is discovered that some items mentioned on the list are not provided for in an induction programme, the latter may need to be amended. At the same time this example of a checklist is not claimed to be complete and further items could be added to it.

Induction – each employee is an individual

Introducing staff into an organization inevitably involves some of the mechanistic processes just described, but it has to be remembered that each member of staff is an individual. Precisely how one introduces or inducts each new individual to an organization depends upon many factors, such as the newcomer's experience and knowledge and the type and level of job he or she is to undertake. It is vital, however, if induction is to be successful, to try to put oneself in the new employee's place. As Rafael Steinberg writes, 'He arrives unknown. His face is not recognized. His interests and idiosyncrasies are ignored by people he meets. He has suddenly become a number, an anonymous replaceable cog. Quite naturally, without thinking about it, he resists this depersonalization and strives to introduce a measure of humanity to his strange new world.'*

Probably the simplest and most common method of induction is a short discussion in a supervisor's office followed by informal chats. This may be quite practical where a person's superior is readily available. However, where this is not the case, unless a checklist is used, many points may remain unclear for a considerable time.

Another method is the 'sponsor' or 'mentor' method in which a newcomer, after an initial talk with his own supervisor, is introduced to an established employee who will 'show him the ropes'. This should not be confused with 'sitting next to Nellie' which is concerned primarily with training and not induction. If this 'sponsor' technique is used, however, the sponsor should be carefully selected to ensure that he or she knows what the duties are and has the necessary knowledge to carry them out. These would include many of the items listed on the induction checklist. In addition, however, a well-chosen sponsor will introduce the new employee to 'the inner face' of the organization, i.e. informal systems, unwritten rules, etc. A copy of this list should be given to the sponsor who would return it to the newcomer's supervisor once everything had been completed. This might take as little as a few minutes, or could be spread over several days.

Finally some induction programmes make use of formal training techniques in classroom situations. This is normally only used by larger employers that can afford the facilities and these programmes, apart from the initial documentation, may include talks, discussions and films on the company's history, organization, rules and regulations. In addition, a large part of the programme may be devoted to job training.

The advantage of formal systems such as the 'sponsor' and the classroom methods is that because one person is clearly responsible for the induction of newcomers it is more likely to be organized and conducted properly.

Induction can be considerably simplified by the preparation of clear 'handouts' or manuals elaborating aspects of employment that may need some explanation. Pension schemes and grievance procedures, for example, are ideally explained in written form owing to the amount of detail involved. Many other subjects, too, can be included in manuals such as trade union or staff association agreements, suggestion schemes, holiday arrangements, sick leave and fringe benefits.

What a 'job' consists of

Induction is not something that takes place on the first morning of a new job; it can be a relatively long process, with some people taking many weeks to settle in. This is because every job has two parts to it. First there is the work itself and second there are all the peripherals to the job including conditions and social contacts.

*Rafael Steinberg, *Man and the Organization* (Time-Life International, 1977).

Figure 6.3   *Orientation checklist for new employees, Newport Marriott Hotel (USA)*

NEWPORT
Marriott

Name of Employee	Department	Hire Date

Manager, please check each item as it is covered with the employee and return to personnel by_____

1. **INTRODUCTION**
   Department Head/Supervisor/
   Co-workers

2. **EXPLAIN WORK SCHEDULE**
   Work schedule (posted as soon as
   business for following week can be
   forecasted)
   Changes must be approved by
   manager

3. **EXPLAIN ATTENDANCE
   REQUIREMENTS**
   Attendance (Mandatory on scheduled
   days)
   Punctuality (Must be on time)
   Reporting absences (Phone
   supervisor/manager at least 2 hours in
   advance of scheduled time and if
   unable to reach, leave a message with
   Security)
   Punch own time card
   Punch in in uniform at shift starting
   time.
   All work must be on the time clock & a
   mgr. must approve any overtime
   before it is worked.

4. **EXPLAIN GENERAL RULES**
   Employee entrance/exit (by Security)
   There is no employee parking
   No return after work policy
   Red sticker policy (items subject to
   inspection by Security or
   Management)
   No personal phone calls & employee
   pay phone
   Hotel telephone number and
   department extension
   Groom standards (dress code &
   hygiene)

Professional conduct/behavior
required
Smoking policy
No gum chewing
Uniforms (includes name tag)
Employee restrooms (uniformed
employees use locker rooms)
Employee cafeteria (time card
stamped/wear name tag)
NOTE: Proper behavior is required in
the Cafeteria; including cleaning up
after eating—emptying trash and
ashtray. No food/beverage is to be
taken out of the Cafeteria.
Use service elevators
No eating in areas outside cafeteria
without management approval
Notify supervisor before leaving at the
end of your shift
No wandering out of work area
without management approval
Phone answering procedures (give
name, do not screen calls)
Employee lockers (unauthorized
substances or materials)

5. **EXPLAIN TRAINING PROGRAM**
   Who will train
   90-day probation period
   Encourage asking questions

6. **MEAL**
   30 minute meal period (punch in and
   out for meal)

7. **EXPLAIN RELATION OF WORK TO
   OTHERS**
   Chain of command
   Guarantee of Fair Treatment
   Relation of job to other jobs
   Relation of department to other

departments and to hotel
Individual responsibility to guests
(Agressive Hospitality/Customer
Concern)

8. **EXPLAIN IMPORTANCE OF JOB**
Employee's contribution to job
Rewards of enthusiasm, job
satisfaction, advancement
(Promotions based on qualifications)

9. **QUALITY/QUANTITY OF WORK**
Importance of accuracy/speed when
experienced
Importance of courtesy and smile

10. **SAFETY**
Fire/emergency procedures
Nearest fire extinguisher (location)
Report ALL accidents IMMEDIATELY
(no matter how minor) to your
supervisor/manager
Clean as you go policy
Job safety analysis

11. **EXPLAIN PAY POLICIES**
Starting pay rate/performance
reviews/increases (PAF)
Pay periods (Sat.–Fri.) payday/time
Thursday
Accurately report all tips on tip sheet
each week and sign name

12. **EXPLAIN BENEFITS**
NOTE: Full time is 30 hours or more
per week

Vacation policy (eligible if full-time
after 1 yr., part-time after 2 yrs.)
Sick leave (for full-time employees,
after 6 months)
Holidays (full/part-time)
Medical Insurance (full-time; if not
enrolled within 1st 30 days there is a
90 day waiting period before
insurance is effective! May also have
to take a physical exam)
Group Term Life Insurance (additional
life insurance; same enrollment
requirements as Medical Plan)
Dental Plan (full-time/after 6 mos. in
Medical Plan sign up at hire or at
change from PT-FT)
Credit Union (full-part-time
employees)
30% Gift Shop discount

13. **DISCIPLINARY PROCEDURES**
Verbal Warning
Coaching and Counseling
Written Warning
NOTE: Policies on this list with an (*)
are important. When not followed an
automatic written warning may result.
Suspension pending termination

14. **REVIEW POSITION DESCRIPTION**

Initial

I have received the Newport Marriott Hotel Handbook and understand that it is my
responsibility to study and use the handbook as a reference to the benefits and rules of
the company. If I have any questions I will ask my manager or the Human Resources
staff.

I understand that the Human Resource Director is my Equal Employment Opportunity
representative, and that he/she will insure my rights under the Marriott Guarantee of
Fair Treatment.

Regarding medical, dental, group term-life, and disability insurance coverages; I
understand that I must see the human resources representative and complete the
enrollment forms within 21 days of hire, or eligibility, to assure full coverage without
an additional waiting period.

FOR EMPLOYEES WHO HAVE BEEN ISSUED UNIFORMS AND/OR EQUIPMENT: The
uniforms and/or equipment issued to you are to be used only while performing services
for Marriott Corporation. In the event you leave the Corporation, you must return the
uniforms and/or equipment in good condition minus normal wear and tear. Also,
uniforms and/or equipment damaged due to normal wear and tear shall be returned for
replacement and, if lost, you will be personally responsible to accept the expense of the
uniforms and/or equipment. Marriott Corporation will be authorized to deduct (by your
signature below) from any of your earnings, present or future, the value of said
uniforms/equipment.

I have read, or have had read to me, the items listed above. The items on the other side
have been explained to me and I understand and agree to abide by these and all other
rules of this hotel.

Employee's Signature_____   Date:_____

Explained by (Mgr/Supervisor):_____   Translator:_____

Figure 6.4 *The main elements of a job*

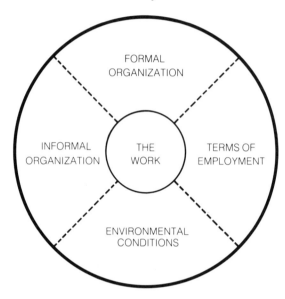

People will not be able to cope with the *work* part of their job unless they understand and are reasonably happy with the surrounding elements. These include:

Location and physical layout
Colleagues and informal relationships
Management, supervision and formal relationships
Customers
Conditions of employment and contracts
Company and house rules.

The induction process is concerned with introducing an employee to all these elements as quickly as possible so that he or she need not worry about them any more. This enables him or her to concentrate on the work which is the main purpose of the job rather than having to learn and worry about all the elements surrounding the work.

Benefits of induction

The employer benefits from effective induction by:

1 Reducing staff turnover.
2 Improving staff efficiency and work standards.
3 Improving staff morale.

The employees benefit by:

1 Fitting in and feeling part of the team.
2 Being accepted as part of the team.
3 Becoming competent and hence confident in the shortest possible time.

Measuring the effectiveness of induction programmes

The purpose of induction procedures is to introduce new employees into the workforce and, with most employers, to reduce the likelihood of the new employee leaving. The effectiveness of induction can be measured by measuring labour turnover in three specific ways. These are:

1 The survival curve which measures an employer's ability to retain its entrants. It shows employee wastage as a curve which can be divided into the induction crisis, differential transit and settled connection.
2 The labour turnover rate, which measures leavers as a proportion of the labour force.
3 The length of service distribution which shows the employer's ability to build a stable team.

These are discussed in detail in Chapter 14.

In meeting the individual's needs it is important to recognize features of the employer's organization and the industry. The hotel and catering industry has a number of features which distinguish it from many other employers and these should be borne in mind when induction programmes are being prepared. These include:

1 The industry employs a large number of people from the 'secondary' labour market, i.e. people such as housewives who have not trained specifically for employment in the industry and who may not want a career.
2 The industry has its own traditions and jargon, much of it either based on a highly specialist use of normal words or, in the case of kitchen work, based on French.
3 Immediate customer contact, frequently with little, if any, supervision.
4 Complex interdependent operations, which can be seriously interrupted by one person not performing his or her role properly.

In the obviously difficult field of managing people, comparing human beings with machines should be avoided, but in the use of induction a very useful parallel can be drawn. Time spent in carefully installing and running-in a new piece of machinery usually results in that machinery giving long reliable service. It is as well to remember that in this context most human beings behave in very much the same way as machines.

Further Reading

Armstrong, M., *A Handbook of Human Resource Management*, London: Kogan Page, 1988

Fowler, A., *Getting off to a Good Start, Successful Employee Induction*, London: Institute of Personnel Management, 1983

Hornsey, T. and Dann, D., *Manpower Management in the Hotel and Catering Industry*, London: Batsford, 1984

Lockwood, A. and Jones P., *People and the Hotel and Catering Industry*, Eastbourne: Holt, Rinehart and Winston, 1984

Pratt, K. J., and Bennett, S. C., *Elements of Personnel Management*, 3rd ed., Wokingham: GEE, 1989

Pugh, D. S., and Hickson, D. J., *Writers on Organisations*, 4th ed. London: Penguin, 1989

Sisson, K., (ed.), *Personnel Management in Britain*, Oxford: Blackwell, 1989

Thomason, G., *Textbook of Human Resource Management*, London: Institute of Personnel Management, 1988

Torrington, D. and Hall, L., *Personnel Management – A New Approach*, London: Prentice Hall, 1987

NOTE: The Hotel and Catering Training Company publishes a large list of useful publications, including *Staff Induction*.

Questions

1 Describe the objectives of induction and the various steps which you would normally expect to find in a systematic induction procedure.

2 Discuss which you consider to be the most important steps and why.

3 Describe also who should be involved in the procedure and what they should be responsible for.

4 Discuss what changes are likely to be made in the future to improve induction procedures.

5 Using an employer you know well evaluate their approach to induction.

chapter 7

Performance appraisal

Each time a supervisor praises or reprimands a subordinate some form of performance appraisal has almost certainly taken place. In fact, appraisal is occurring constantly at work. From time to time, however, it may become necessary for a supervisor to get away from the hurly-burly of the work place and to examine objectively the performance of his or her subordinates. The supervisor needs to do this because the employer should know the strengths and weaknesses of the employees and because employees need to know how they stand. The supervisor should examine each employee's performance against expectations and at the same time consider the person's potential as well. He or she should then decide what steps should be taken in both the employer's and the individual's best interests. This process has several titles but is commonly called 'performance appraisal' and should be an essential part of any worthwhile human resource policy of all but the smallest employers.

A survey carried out for the Institute of Personnel Management (Phil Long, 1986) identified a number of different reasons why employers review the performance of their employees. These are shown in Figure 7.1. From this it is apparent that performance appraisal is aimed at improving performance both of the individual and of the employing organization. This is achieved by:

1   Identifying both individuals' and group weaknesses and strengths so that weakness can be corrected and strengths developed and built upon.
2   Identifying each individual's hopes and aspirations so that, where these do not conflict with the organization's objectives, they can be satisfied. This is

Figure 7.1   *Reasons for reviewing performance*

To assess training and development needs	97%
To help improve current performance	97%
To review past performance	98%
To assess future potential/promotability	71%
To assist career planning decisions	75%
To set performance objectives	81%
To assess increases or new levels in salary	40%
Others – e.g. updating personnel records	4%

necessary because when most individuals' hopes and aspirations are frustrated for too long they will begin consciously or unconsciously to work against the employer's interest.

From a properly conducted appraisal programme an employer should obtain the following:

1 An analysis of training needs which enables individual and group training programmes to be produced.
2 A succession plan and management development programme that earmarks individuals for promotion and identifies their particular development needs.
3 A reasonably objective basis for salary review.
4 Improved communications.

The individual also benefits by knowing:

(a) How he or she stands and what help is to be given to improve performance.
(b) What his or her career prospects are.

There are three main steps in conducting appraisals correctly:

 (i) Having an up-to-date and objective job description, and performance targets.
 (ii) Comparing the person's performance with the job description and targets.
(iii) Communicating and discussing the supervisor's and the person's views regarding his or her performance, and the recording of both the supervisor's and the subordinate's views.

Job descriptions have already been discussed in Chapter 3 and it now becomes apparent why they should contain as many objective, measurable items as possible; for example, if the word 'satisfactory' is used, superior and subordinate may interpret the word differently. On the other hand, if an objective term such as '60 per cent gross profit' is used, neither person can dispute the interpretation of this figure so long as each is clear about what is included in the calculation. In comparing a person's performance with his or her job description, therefore, it is necessary to bring together as much relevant information as possible such as budgets, forecasts and other records.

The approach to appraisal

There are many different approaches to appraisal but it is possible to divide schemes into those concerned mainly with:

Outputs, i.e. results oriented.
Inputs, i.e. job behaviour or personality traits.
A combination of the two above.

The IPM survey referred to above identified a number of different approaches:

Results-oriented	63%
Job behaviour-oriented	52%
Personality trait rating	29%
Alphabetical/numerical rating	28%
Narrative – free essay	2%
controlled writing	44%
Forced distribution global rating	10%

The appraisal form

The type of form used to record the appraisal should be incidental to the interview itself although a well-designed form can help in preparing for and conducting an interview. In cases where the form itself is of more importance than the interview the approach to the management of people is likely to be mechanistic. It enables the employer to achieve some of his objectives without fully considering the individual's own needs and aspirations.

The contents of the form therefore should be dependent upon the purpose of the appraisal scheme and the nature of the approach. One concerned with 'inputs' would concern itself with the following type of information:

1 Personal details, e.g. name, length of service, job
2 Performance report covering:
  Knowledge
  Skill
  Application
  Initiative
  Expression, written and spoken
  Ability to plan and to organize
  Ability to work with others
  Ability to direct others
  Specific job targets or objectives and the measure of achievements
3 Training needs in present job
4 Potential
5 Training or development needs if promotable
6 General salary recommendation
7 Employee's comments.

One concerned with 'outputs', on the other hand, would be more likely to look like Figure 3.7, a typical Management by Objectives format.

Types of appraisal scheme

Some schemes require the manager making the assessment to place ticks in graded boxes, or to award letters, grades or points, as judged appropriate. They are relatively easy to operate, but just how reliable or fair they are is very debatable. They are particularly difficult for use for the assessment of non-quantifiable factors such as personality traits.

The British Psychological Society was reported (IPM Fact Sheet 3 1988) to have found that such schemes are less popular now because of the difficulties associated with them.

In 'written assessment' schemes much greater importance is attached to a freely written report. These types of schemes have the advantage of encouraging the manager making the assessment to think broadly rather than having to use pre-selected 'labels'.

There are systems that compromise between these two extreme types and which ask the manager to fill in boxes and to write a broad statement as well. One such scheme is shown in Figure 7.2.

Pratt and Bennett (1985) describe three commonly used techniques for rating performance. The first is the 'linear rule' which requires the appraiser to place a tick along a numerical scale or in a box which represents a rating for the characteristics. They point out the distinction which needs to be made between measuring *results*, such as quantity of work, and *traits*, such as reliability. The second technique is known as BARS (Behaviourally Anchored Rating Scale). In this technique people familiar with a job select appropriate aspects of a job and describe examples of behaviour ranging from ineffective to effective along a scale for each aspect. An appraiser can then identify individual performance on the scale. Third, Pratt and Bennett describe management by objectives (MbO) which is described in Chapter 3 of this book.

Ideally a system of assessment should reduce the non-quantifiable (usually inputs) to a minimum and should concentrate the assessment on objective criteria (usually outputs), so that facts rather than opinions are used as a basis for the interview and report.

There appear to be several critical issues which contribute to successful appraisal schemes. These include:

1   Appraisers and appraisees need sufficient time to prepare for the appraisal interview.
2   Adequate publicity including objectives, methodology and access to further information about the scheme.
3   Top management support.
4   Training of the appraisers and the appraisees.

Who should be appraised?

These days where appraisal schemes are operated most managers and supervisors are included. The IPM survey showed the following participation:

Directors (board level)	52%
Senior management	90%
Middle management	96%
Junior management	92%
First line supervisor	78%

Clerical/secretarial	66%
Skilled/semi-skilled	24%
Knowledge workers, e.g. those who provide professional, scientific and advisory services	55%
Others, e.g. graduate trainees	7%

The appraisal interview

The crucial aspect of appraisal is the conduct of the interview itself. Some managers find that asking their subordinates to examine and complete an appraisal report themselves makes the situation easier. This is sometimes known as 'self-appraisal' and enables a supervisor to study beforehand a person's views concerning his or her own performance. This obviously means that the supervisor is better equipped to get the best results from the interview as he or she knows where the person is likely to be most sensitive. At the same time, if the person has identified known weaknesses, the supervisor can concentrate on means of improvement and on the future without dwelling on shortcomings and the past.

Some schemes are now going even further and allow the appraisee to actually design the basis of the performance review – selecting what he or she thinks is relevant to a review.

Many managers, however, find this approach too liberal and prefer to maintain a more 'normal' superior–subordinate relationship. Unfortunately this can involve the manager in playing two roles – judge and counsellor. This and the associated problems were referred to in Charles Margerison's article 'A constructive approach to appraisal', in *Personnel Management* (July 1976) when he wrote:

Of course, they (managers) recognize that appraising a subordinate's performance and helping him improve it in the future is important. However, for many managers the appraisal interview is embarrassing. They are put in a position of having to make an evaluation of their subordinates and this act in itself hardly leads to a genuine discussion of performance. Once an evaluation has been made, the subordinate is left either agreeing or disagreeing with it. If he agrees, there is little to be said. If he disagrees, there are serious implications.

If I as a subordinate disagree with your evaluation, then I am in danger of becoming a mutineer – I am rebelling against your assessment and in the process putting myself on the side of the revolutionaries. Is it possible for me to contradict my superior when I know that he has the power to influence my future rewards and career?

This conflict in the conduct of appraisal interviews is very difficult for many to overcome, as McGregor (1957) wrote, 'Managers are uncomfortable when they are put in the position of playing God' (Harvard Business Review, 1957), but if the manager can concentrate on the *counselling* and *problem-solving* rather than making judgements and examining shortcomings, this problem can be over-come to some extent.

Experts in performance appraisal have various ideas on the different types of approach to performance appraisal interviews.

Figure 7.2 *Example of an appraisal form*

Performance review: Part 1   Confidential
Name of employee   Job   Branch
Completed by   Name   Position

Overall assessment *Put tick in*   Whichever grade you award please
  appropriate boxes   elaborate here on this person's
                                           performance:

Excellent   □   Satisfactory □
Good   □   Poor   □

Detailed assessment

		Excellent	Good	Satisfactory	Poor	Remarks
For all staff	Technical competence					
	Application					
	Initiative					
	Relations with: Supervisor					
	Colleagues					
	Customers					
For supervisory staff	Ability to direct others					
	Planning and organizing ability					
	Expression: Written					
	Oral					

Performance review: part 2   Confidential

1 Is this person promotable, and if so, what type of job would most suit his/her
   abilities and aspirations?
2 List what training can be given, or other action taken, to assist in improving performance or preparing for promotion
3 What salary increase would you recommend? Give reasons

High   □   Low   □
Standard   □   None   □

4 Have you discussed this appraisal with your subordinate? Yes/No
   If no, why not?
   If yes, what were his/her comments?

Appraisal styles

Pryor and Mayo (1985) suggest that there are six styles on a continuum consisting of dominating, telling, advising, joint, self-assessment and abdicating. These relate to the interaction between the appraiser and the appraised and can be seen on their Appraisal interaction model in Figure 7.3.

Figure 7.3 *Appraisal styles*

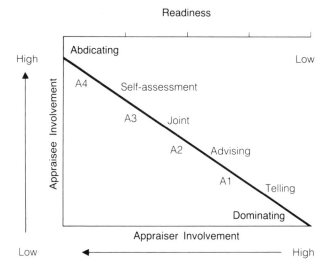

Source: Personnel Management, June 1985

As with selection interviewing, appraisal interviewing is a skilled technique and those responsible for conducting these interviews need training and practice, along with the ability to examine and criticize their own performance. Here are some useful rules to follow:

Do

1 Plan the interview by obtaining all necessary information and by giving the person to be interviewed prior notice of the interview and its purpose.
2 Remember that interviews are a means of two-way communication and that the best interviewers do little talking themselves.
3 Suspend phone calls and other interruptions and allow plenty of time for the interview.
4 Put the interviewee at ease and try to make the occasion an informal one. (For example, avoid having the desk between yourself and the interviewee.)
5 Make the interviewee feel that the main purpose of the interview is to benefit him or her.
6 Start by praising strong points. Remember a person's 'ego' and that any subsequent criticism will be rejected as unfair or even untrue unless the balance is maintained by acknowledging good points.
7 Ask for interviewee's reasons for any shortcomings and ask for suggestions for improvement.
8 Finish the interview firmly on a positive note reiterating what performance is expected and what assistance the employee can expect in the form of training or other help.
9 Remember always that giving a person a poor appraisal can be a reflection on the manager's own ability.

Don't

1 Rush the interview. It is one of the most important occasions in a person's working year.
2 Prejudge the outcome of the interview and therefore don't finalize the form until afterwards.
3 Read out the printed form. Your appraisal should come over in your own words.
4 Preach or be pompous. This is an occasion to discuss how a person's performance can be improved with your help.

Small organizations

In the smallest organizations with no more than a few employees a formal approach will be unnecessary and could even disrupt some healthy superior–subordinate relationships. Even so, those employees with potential and prospects should be told of this so that they are less likely, as a result, to go to another employer for advancement.

Appraisal is one of the most personal and potentially unsettling situations that occurs in a working person's life. It can be, after all, an examination and judgement of the main role in life and consequently it can be very damaging to the ego. It must therefore be positive, constructive and helpful. It should not be an occasion for apportioning blame or responsibility for past shortcomings or failures. If these are discussed, they should be used as examples to illustrate points from which both sides can learn in order to take steps to build for the future. Appraisal must be creative and must result in new objectives and in agreement on the means by which these objectives can be achieved.

Further reading

Armstrong, M., *A Handbook of Human Resource Management*, London: Kogan Page, 1988

Fletcher, C., *Performance Appraisal and Career Development*, London: Hutchinson, 1985

Jones, P., and Lockwood, A., *The Management of Hotel Operations*, London: Cassell, 1989

Lawson, I., *Appraisal and Appraisal Interviewing*, 3rd ed. London: Industrial Society, 1989

Lockwood, A. and Jones P., *People and the Hotel and Catering Industry*, Eastbourne: Holt, Rinehart and Winston, 1984

Pratt, K. J., and Bennett, S. C., *Elements of Personnel Management*, 3rd ed., Wokingham: GEE, 1989

Randell, G., *et al*, *Staff Appraisal*, 3rd ed., London: Institute of Personnel Management, 1984

Sisson K., (ed.), *Personnel Management in Britain*, Oxford: Blackwell, 1989

Thomason, G., *Textbook of Human Resource Management*, London, Institute of Personnel Management, 1988

Torrington, D. and Hall, L., *Personnel Management – A New Approach*, London: Prentice Hall, 1987

Questions

1 Describe the objectives of a performance appraisal scheme and the various steps or phases which you would normally expect to find.

2 Discuss which you consider to be the most important steps and why.

3 Discuss what changes are likely to be made in the future to improve performance appraisal procedures.

4 Discuss the relationship between performance appraisal and approaches to management, such as Management by Objectives (see Chapter 3).

5 Using an employer you know well evaluate their approach to performance appraisal.

chapter 8

Training

One of the features of working life today is that whatever training is obtained at the start, it will almost certainly become redundant or obsolete during the same working lifetime. The need to train, to acquire new knowledge and new skills has become an everyday aspect of each individual's working life. In some cases this may merely be an updating process, but in others it will require a complete change from one occupation to another.

Some jobs and whole industries will disappear and others will emerge. Fortunately for the hospitality industry there is no likelihood of the main services it provides becoming redundant in the immediate future. Jobs within the industry may change, but the industry itself is predicted to continue to flourish.

The responsibility for ensuring that working people are equipped to cope with these changes is threefold. The State carries a part of the responsibility, particularly in providing education and training for school-leavers and for those who need retraining owing to the decline of their own industries, nationally or regionally.

From the hotel and catering industry's point of view the government was instrumental in a number of important initiatives aimed at improving the industry's standards. The most important probably was the establishment in 1966 of the Hotel and Catering Industry Training Board (HCITB), now known as the Hotel and Catering Training Company (HCTC). While many industrial training boards were disbanded in the 1980s, the government decided for a number of reasons to retain the HCTC. These reasons included the obvious growing, even vital, importance to the economy of tourism, and also the tremendously fragmented and still predominantly untrained workforce in hotels and catering generally. The Education and Training Advisory Committee for the hotel and catering industry demonstrated that less than 40 per cent of the workforce, including management, had any appropriate training and that the output of all the college courses would not keep pace with replacement needs, let alone needs generated by the growth of the industry.

Apart from the traditional training work of the HCITB, the government also set up a national scheme for the development of open access and distance learning programmes designed for anyone wishing to acquire technical expertise without having to have prior qualifications and without having to attend conventional college courses. A number of courses have now been developed for the industry, principally by the HCTC and the British Institute of Inn-keeping. These open learning programmes aimed mainly at managers and supervisors without prior qualifications include:

Computing studies
Supervisory skills
Food and beverage management
Licensed house management.

Employers, too, have their share of responsibilities and they discharge these by providing training intended to suit their individual needs, or by participating, as do some employers in the hotel and catering industry, in group schemes, which generally provide a good standard of training quite economically. Some employers provide excellent training, whereas others are quite content to recruit trained individuals from the labour market without putting any trained people into the market themselves. The Industrial Training Act of 1964 recognized this and attempted to stimulate industrial training and to spread the burden over most employers.

Within some sectors of the hospitality industry staff training is steadily becoming more effective. However, the generally high labour turnover still reduces the effectiveness of the training effort, although companies such as McDonald's cope well with the problem. They do this by using extremely well thought out and well supervised training programmes. In addition, like many of the best of the large retailers, they budget for and plan training time into all recruits' work. Their 'crew members' only progress to more responsible roles when they have completed satisfactorily the preceding training.

In contrast many of the industry's traditional employers, particularly the smaller, privately owned businesses, do not implement proper training for a number of reasons:

1   Many proprietors and managers have had no formal training themselves and, therefore, are unaware of the standards that can be achieved and of the benefits of training.
2   Many employers are concerned constantly with immediate operational problems and do not plan ahead.
3   Many are undercapitalized and cannot afford the investment.
4   Many believe that it is the responsibility of others, such as colleges, to provide them with trained staff.

At the same time, however, there is a constant up-grading in the industry and a move towards both 'High Tech' (modern technology) and 'High Touch' (high customer contact) each demanding more training, with the leading employers now putting more resources into training.

The third part of the responsibility rests with individuals. No amount of training will be effective unless an individual wishes to make the most of what is available. The State and employers may provide facilities, but it remains ultimately for the individual to make the most effective use of these facilities for the benefit of himself, his employer and the community. In this respect a recent government report (Training in Britain, HMSO 1989) found that nearly half the working population could not 'imagine themselves undertaking training ever. Another 38 per cent could imagine themselves training – but had done little about it.' Obviously there is a need for both government and employers to do something about such an attitude.

Industrial training is concerned primarily with bridging the gap between individuals' and groups' actual performance and the performance required to achieve an undertaking's objectives. These objectives may include such things as expansion, increasing sales, increasing profitability and improving standards. On other occasions training may be needed merely to maintain the employer's position in the market. However, there are some useful signs, or symptoms, that may indicate a need for training and these include:

1 Failure to attain targets such as gross profit on food or liquor, turnover, net profit
2 Dissatisfied customers
3 Slow service
4 High labour turnover, low morale
5 Friction between departments such as restaurant and kitchen, or housekeeping and reception
6 High accident, breakage, wastage rates
7 Staff unable or unprepared to adapt to changes.

It is not suggested that training alone can solve all these problems. If a hotel or restaurant is badly planned or wrongly situated, no amount of training (apart from training the executive responsible) can rectify this. However, training can often provide the solution or part of the solution.

Training should also consciously try to help individuals to reach the limits of their capabilities and realistic aspirations – so long as these do not conflict with organizational goals.

The main components of training

There are three main components that an individual requires in order to do a job effectively. These components are knowledge, skills and attitudes. Each of these can be developed or improved upon (from the organization's point of view) by effective training. Each component, however, needs a different training approach. Knowledge, for example, can be imparted by talks, lectures and films, but these techniques would prove almost valueless in imparting the second component, skill, such as handling a knife. In this case, practice is necessary. The third component, a person's set of attitudes, is the most difficult to impart or to change, even with soundly based training, and it requires deep understanding of human behaviour by those responsible for training. Training techniques in this field may include discussions, case studies and role playing. It is agreed, however, by many behavioural experts that because attitudes are extremely difficult to modify it is better to select people with the right attitudes rather than attempt to train people who have attitudes which conflict with those of the employer.

In order to design effective training programmes the following principles should be known and understood:

1 Training can only be successful if it is recognized that learning is a voluntary process, that individuals must be keen to learn and consequently they must be properly motivated; for example, if trainee waiters are losing earnings in the form of tips in order to attend a course, they may well begrudge the time and therefore may be unwilling to participate actively.
2 People learn at different rates and, particularly in the case of adults, often start from different levels of knowledge and skill and with different motives and attitudes.
3 Learning is hindered by feelings of nervousness, fear, inferiority, and by lack of confidence.
4 Instruction must be given in short frequent sessions rather than a few long stints; for example, if a trainee is being instructed in the use of kitchen equipment, ten lessons lasting forty-five minutes are obviously far better than one lesson lasting seven and a half hours.
5 Trainees must play active roles – they must participate; for example, lecturing puts the trainees into a passive role, whereas discussions or practical work give them active roles.
6 Training must make full use of appropriate and varied techniques and of all the senses, not just one, such as the sense of hearing.
7 Trainees need clear targets and progress must be checked frequently.
8 Confidence has to be built up by praise, not broken down by reprimand. Learning has to be rewarding.
9 Skills and knowledge are acquired in stages marked by periods of progress, 'standstill' and even a degeneration of the skill or knowledge so far acquired. Instructors must know of this phenomenon ('the learning curve'), as it can be a cause of disappointment and frustration for many trainees.

These principles of learning illustrate and emphasize that it is both difficult and wasteful to treat individuals as groups. So far as possible training needs to be tailored to suit individual needs. The techniques to be used depend on a variety of factors, including whether it is knowledge, skills or attitudes that are to be imparted and whether individuals or groups are to be trained. The two main approaches are 'on the job' and 'off the job' training.

On the job training

In the hospitality industry much of the staff's work is performed in direct contact with customers. For this reason much of the training of new staff has to be performed 'on the job' so that experience of dealing with customers can be obtained. 'On the job' training, therefore, plays a vital part in the industry's approach to training. In one large survey conducted in the United States 'experiential learning' was ranked as the most effective form of training. If handled correctly, it can be very effective for the teaching of manual and social skills, but it requires that training objectives are clearly defined and that those responsible for instruction are proficient in training techniques. Unfortunately, newcomers are often attached to experienced workers who are not in any way equipped to train others. This is often referred to as 'sitting next to Nellie'. Apart from not having a suitable personality, the trainer may not even have been told what to instruct and what not to instruct. Instead, if experienced workers are to be entrusted with the training of newcomers, they should be chosen because of their ability to deal sympathetically with trainees, because of their knowledge of the job itself. They should then be given appropriate instructor training before being asked to train newcomers. The progress of trainees should be checked from time to time by the person responsible for training. Responsibility for training should not be abdicated to the instructor. An example of an 'on the job' training programme for a cocktail barman is shown in Figure 8.1.

Note that the programme in Figure 8.1 is in progressive stages. It requires each phase to be completely covered before the next is started. In addition, this particular programme is only a checklist and therefore presupposes that the instructor already has the detailed knowledge. Because of this, in many cases it will be necessary to expand this type of list by specifying in a document such as a training manual exactly what has to be instructed under each new heading. Appendix 7 is an abridged version of a short book on training 'on job' or staff trainers.

Off the job training

'Off the job' training takes place away from the working situation. A variety of methods and techniques may be used but the particular choice will depend on what is to be imparted. The main methods are listed below:

1 *Talks* are best used for imparting knowledge such as company history and policies, legal matters, regulations, recipes, and an outline of methods and procedures. In giving a talk, progress must be checked frequently by use of questions and answers.
2 *Discussions* are best used to elaborate on and to consolidate what has been imparted by other techniques.
3 *Lectures* often mean little more than talking at trainees and are therefore to be avoided as there is usually little trainee participation.
4 *Case studies, projects, business games* are best used to illustrate and to consolidate principles of management such as planning, analytical techniques, etc.
5 *Role-playing* is best used to develop social skills such as receiving guests, handling customer complaints, selling, interviewing or instructional techniques. Ideally this should be supported by tape recordings and closed circuit television recordings, if possible.
6 *Films, charts, and other visual aids* should not normally be used as instructional techniques by themselves, but should support talks, discussions, case studies and role playing. Films on a variety of hotel and catering subjects are obtainable from several training organizations.

Figure 8.1 *Example of an 'on the job' training programme for a cocktail barman. (This is basically a list of duties and tasks)*

First stage

1 Bar preparation and cleanliness
(a) Washing down of bar counter, bottle shelves
(b) Polishing of mirrors, glass shelves
(c) 'Bottling up'
(d) Use of counter towels, drip mats and trays
(e) Preparation of accompaniments including lemon, olives, cherries
(f) Use of beer dispense equipment

2 'Cash'
(a) Price lists
(b) Use of cash register
(c) Cheques and credit cards
(d) Charging to customer accounts
(e) Computation of costs of rounds and 'change giving'

3 Main points of law
(a) Licensing hours and drinking up time
(b) Hotel residents and guests
(c) Adulteration
(d) Weights and Measures Act

4 Service of simple orders
(a) Beers, wines by the glass
(b) Spirits and vermouth with mixers
(c) Use of accompaniments such as ice, lemon, cherries
(d) Cigarettes, cigars

Second stage

1 Bar preparation and cleanliness
(a) Requisitioning of stock
(b) Cleaning of beer dispense equipment
(c) Preparing weekly liquor and provisions order

2 'Cash'
(a) Checking float
(b) Changing till roll
(c) 'Off sales'

3 Further law
(a) Betting and gaming
(b) Young persons
(c) Credit sales of intoxicating liquor

4 Service of simple mixed drinks
(a) Shandies
(b) Gin and Italian, gin and French

Third stage

1 Bar preparation and cleanliness
(a) Rectification of faults such as 'fobbing beer', jammed bottle disposal unit
(b) Preparation for stock taking

2 'Cash'   Cashing up

3 Service of all drinks contained in house list
(a) Knowledge of recipes
(b) Use of shaker and mixing glass

7   *Programmed texts and teaching machines* satisfy many of the principles of learning (mentioned on page 115). In addition, they can be used by individuals at any convenient time – not requiring the presence of an instructor. They cannot, of course, be used to teach some things such as manual skills and they can be very expensive to design.

An example of a fairly typical 'off the job' programme for cooks is shown in Figure 8.2.

Figure 8.2   *Example of first day of an 'off the job' training programme for cooks employed by a firm with many establishments offering standardized service*

Time	Subject matter	Method of instruction
9.00/9.45	Company history Present organization and objectives Personnel policies	Talk, discussion and film
9.45/10.30	Kitchen equipment; cleanliness, safety, uses	Demonstration and discussion
10.30/11.00	Hygiene	Film and discussion
11.00/11.15	Coffee	
11.15/12.00	Principles of cookery; grilling	Demonstration and discussion
12.00/1.00	Portioning, preparation and presentation	Demonstration and practical work
1.00/2.00	Lunch	
2.00/4.00	Practical cookery	Practical preparation of simple dishes
4.00/4.15	Tea	
4.15/5.00	Costing and portion control	Talk and discussion
5.00/6.00	Clearing up	

Training needs analysis

Having looked at what training attempts to do, at the main principles of learning and at the main techniques available, the next step is to consider the design of training programmes. This starts with an identification of training needs, sometimes referred to as a 'training needs analysis', which is conducted by the person responsible for training in consultation with line managements. It should attempt to identify those *problems and opportunities* that line management could solve and exploit with the assistance of appropriate training. It should be produced by studying the training needs of individuals as identified in 'appraisal reports', and by detailed discussions with the line managers. The individual's job description, actual performance and potential should be the basis for these discussions together with organizational plans for the future.

From the consolidation of individual training needs will emerge organization or corporate training needs. Some will be 'essential' and some 'desirable'. These priorities should be laid down by senior management and will consequently fit in with the undertaking's business objectives.

In the case of an industrial catering contractor or a group of restaurants, for example, there may be plans to expand the number of units and in order to do this a variety of key staff for the new units will be needed over a given period of time. It will be important, therefore, to identify those people who can be transferred or promoted and the training that will be needed in order to prepare them. This may range from preparing some assistant managers for full management to preparing junior kitchen hands to take over some more skilled responsibilities such as cooking.

The question of having sufficient trained personnel to fit into expansion plans is a critical one to the successful growth of an organization and it is one area where the training function together with effective recruitment can prove to be of considerable value to a company.

All training needs obviously do not emerge from the annual training needs analysis. They also arise from unexpected changes in trading conditions or business emphasis; for example, many restaurant operators do not pay sufficient attention to the profits that can be generated by liquor sales. In this case, if a company decides that sales of drinks are to be promoted, effective training of waiters and waitresses in product knowledge, service and selling techniques can play a big part in boosting sales and profits. Likewise, a brewery may change its emphasis from running tenanted houses to running managed houses. In this case it will have to recruit and train managers to run the public houses; it will also have to train district managers in the supervision of managed houses.

The identification of training needs process may identify training needs in three broad areas. The first is the organization's needs; for example, improved customer relations. Such a need may affect all employees. The second need is a group need; for example a particular group of employees such as head receptionists may need training in maximizing room occupancy. The third is that of individuals; for example the proposal to computerize the payroll could result in the need for the payroll clerk to be trained in appropriate computer skills.

Effectiveness of the different forms of training.

A survey conducted by Syracuse University in the United States on the effectiveness of different forms of training in the hospitality industry found that the most effective forms of training for both management and non-supervisory staff was 'personalized experiential learning'. The next most effective in the case of management grades was self-directed learning and in the case of non-supervisory staff it was textual material, e.g. books. The fuller findings are shown below in Figure 8.4.

Figure 8.3   *Identifying training needs*

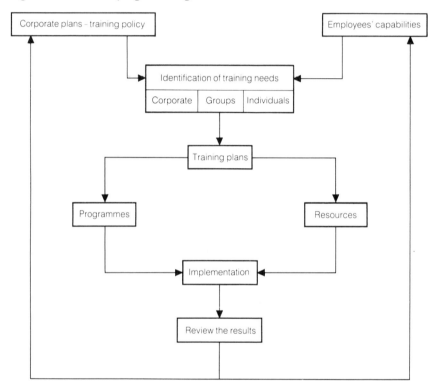

Figure 8.4   *Rank order of training effectiveness for non-supervisory groups*

1   Personalized experiential learning; e.g. on job training, 'mentor' supervision
2   Textual material; e.g. text books, manuals
3   Self-directed learning resources; e.g. resource area, programmed learning
4   Observational learning; e.g. exhibits, working models
5   Interactive simulations; e.g. games, role play
6   Visual lecture aids; e.g. flip charts, OHPs
7   Expert formal presentations; e.g. lectures, panel presentations
8   Impersonal passive electronic media; instructional TV and radio

Source: CHRIE conference paper 1988, Dr R. Foucar/Szocki, Syracuse University, USA.

Line management support

It is vital that line management is seen to support training by participating in it as far as possible, because if all instruction is left to the training staff an undesirable gap can develop between line management and the 'trainers'. The best way to overcome this is to ask line management, such as unit and departmental managers, and the most skilled operators, such as chefs and wine-waiters, to be trained to take some training sessions. This ensures that the instruction given is in line with working requirements and conditions, but, of more importance, it persuades line management that training personnel are working with and for line management.

The subject of training can be very extensive and because of this in some cases it becomes an 'end' in itself rather than a means to an end. It is therefore vital for it to be seen in perspective.

Training is one of the tools of management that should be used to increase an employer's efficiency. It enables the undertaking's goals to be achieved by properly equipping its personnel with the knowledge, skills and attitudes necessary to achieve those goals. But at the same time training should also enable individuals to achieve whatever realistic aspirations they have in their work by enabling them, through increased competence and confidence, to earn more and to gain promotion.

Further reading

Armstrong, M., *A Handbook of Human Resource Management*, London: Kogan Page, 1988

Boella, M. J., *Effective Staff Training*, Brighton: Brighton Polytechnic, 1986

Donnelly, E., Kenny J., and Reid, M., *Training and Development*, London: Institute of Personnel Management, 1986

Gode, W., *Training your Staff*, 2nd ed. London: Industrial Society, 1989

Pratt, K. J., and Bennett, S. C., *Elements of Personnel Management*, 3rd ed., Wokingham: GEE, 1989

Sisson K., (ed.), *Personnel Management in Britain*, Oxford: Blackwell, 1989

Thomason, G., *Textbook of Human Resource Management*, London: Institute of Personnel Management, 1988

Torrington, D. and Hall, L., *Personnel Management – A New Approach*, London: Prentice Hall, 1987

Note: The HCTC publishes a large number of useful publications, including:

1   *Planning Your Training*
2   *Implementing Your Training*
3   *Reviewing Your Training*
4   *Staff Induction*
5   *Health and Safety*
6   *On-the-Job Training*
7   *A Guide to Systematic Training*
8   *Training Your Staff*

Questions

1 Describe the objectives of systematic training and the various steps or phases which you would normally expect to find in its operation.

2 Discuss which you consider to be the most important elements and why.

3 Discuss what changes are likely to be made in the future to improve training and what areas employers are most likely to concentrate on.

4 Discuss the relationship between training and approaches to management, such as Management by Objective (see Chapter 3).

5 Using an employer you know well, evaluate their approach to training.

chapter 9

Management development

The well-being of any undertaking depends upon its staff and, in particular, on its management. Senior managers have a vital responsibility to ensure that suitable people are available and are being developed to succeed to management posts as they arise.

In the 1990s this task promises to be more challenging and difficult than ever before, for a number of reasons. These include:

1 Shortage of younger people, more older people
2 Expectations of those available to join or rejoin the labour market, e.g. the married woman returner, ethnic minorities, retired people
3 Increased competition between employers
4 Internationalization of markets and operators
5 Increased development needs and expectations of management.

In particular, this last issue has to be confronted by employers. The United Kingdom's management is still one of the least qualified when compared with our major competitors including the USA, France, and Germany, all of whom are competitors in the tourism market. In the USA and Japan 85% of managers have degrees, in France and Germany the figure is 65% whilst in Britain the figure is only 24% (*The Making of British Managers*, CBI, 1987).

Management development may be defined as those activities designed to provide the organization with a competent management team which is able to meet its short-, medium- and long-term objectives. These activities may include:

The improvement of managers' techniques in planning and controlling the organization's structure and resources.
The acquisition of new information on the environment.
Helping managers adapt their attitudes or mental modes.
(After Dr Graham Milborrow, *Management News*, June 1985.)

As part of this exercise an organization needs to plan for natural replacement caused by retirements, resignations, deaths, etc., and it needs to ensure that sufficient competent management is available for expansion plans. However, in a healthy organization these plans must also extend to satisfying an individual's reasonable aspirations; for example, if an employer stands in the way of an employee's trying to obtain a recognized qualification by not allowing adequate time off, the employee will almost certainly place his qualification before his job and will seek an employer who will assist him. Plans that only accommodate the employer's needs will result in dissatisfaction, frustration, low morale and high labour turnover.

The senior management of an organization must therefore ensure that adequate plans and resources exist to recruit, motivate, train, develop, and retain its existing and future management. This is all part of the management development role, but in this chapter only the planning of management succession and the development of individual management skills will be discussed. Other aspects of the full management development function such as recruitment, induction and appraisal have been dealt with in other chapters.

Figure 9.1   *A management succession or replacement form*

Position	Present job holder	Most suitable replacement Put present job in brackets	Second recommendation Put present job in brackets
Hotel Manager (Splendide)	J. Jones	A. Smith (Food and Beverage Manager, Splendide)	R. Barker (Front Office Manager, Grand)
Promotion potential		Ready for promotion	Promotable with training
Training and/or development needed		None	Food and beverage experience needed
Signed by	J. Jones	Date	20/1/86
Approved by	J. Walker	(Area Manager)	

Succession plans

In larger organizations management development and succession plans will be interdependent. The approach to succession planning itself will vary according to an organization's own needs. In an organization which operates within one large homogeneous market (McDonald's for example) it may be possible to develop all an organization's management along similar lines. In another organization, operating in very different markets with very different products

(Bass for example), it may be necessary to develop managers specifically for particular market segments – the managers of their international hotels may need languages whereas the managers of their public houses may not.

Succession planning has two main elements. Firstly, there have to be decisions regarding the sources of future management. These may be all 'home grown', or they may be imported from other organizations or there may be a mixture of both sources. Secondly, there is the process needed to identify management needs and the management to fill these needs. In small organizations this will be a simple informal system because senior management is likely to know everyone with potential. In large organizations complex, formal systems may be needed because of the large number of job opportunities, managers and potential managers involved. There will also be the need to manage the entire process so that an appropriate management team results.

A succession plan is produced by comparing future management requirements with currently available management. In order to do this, organization charts should be drawn up which show the structure of the undertaking at the present time and at various future dates, for example, three months, one year, three years, five years. Each job shown may have two boxes immediately next to it or under it in which the names of suitable successors can be inserted. A replacement form is shown in Figure 9.1, and a succession chart in Figure 9.2.

The names shown in Figures 9.1 and 9.2 would result from discussions between the most appropriate levels of management, using appraisal reports as a basis. This emphasizes the need for a section on promotion potential to be included in the appraisal report. Increasingly, promotion potential is being assessed through the use of assessment centres (see Chapter 5).

So long as the basis for discussion is that replacement will be due to normal retirement, accident or the voluntary departure of the incumbent, the most appropriate levels of management to be involved in discussions will be:

1   The present holder of the job for which a replacement is being discussed
2   The present job holder's superior
3   The superiors of those proposed as replacements
4   A member of senior management fully aware of future plans
5   A personnel specialist (if one is employed).

In some cases one person will fulfil more than one of these roles. The final plan, particularly for the more senior levels, must carry the approval of senior management.

In order to identify likely successors in the first place it is usual to ask each member of management to nominate those he or she considers to be most suitable as successors. However, where this is done it must be recognized that there may be the danger of rigid departmental career paths, whereas in some cases, interdepartmental transfers and promotions will be more desirable in order to broaden experience.

In the largest organizations which are broken down into regional or functional operating companies, the danger of 'sitting on' talent, consciously or unconsciously, has to be avoided. This can be achieved by all management

Figure 9.2 *A succession chart*

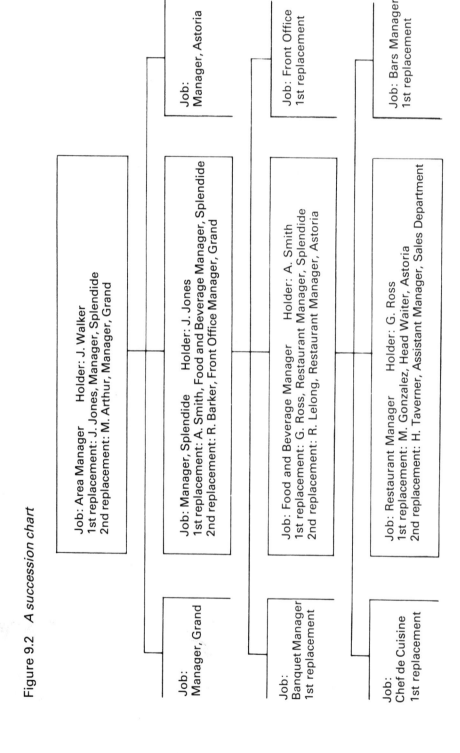

Job: Area Manager   Holder: J. Walker
1st replacement: J. Jones, Manager, Splendide
2nd replacement: M. Arthur, Manager, Grand

Job: Manager, Splendide   Holder: J. Jones
1st replacement: A. Smith, Food and Beverage Manager, Splendide
2nd replacement: R. Barker, Front Office Manager, Grand

Job: Food and Beverage Manager   Holder: A. Smith
1st replacement: G. Ross, Restaurant Manager, Splendide
2nd replacement: R. Lelong, Restaurant Manager, Astoria

Job: Restaurant Manager   Holder: G. Ross
1st replacement: M. Gonzalez, Head Waiter, Astoria
2nd replacement: H. Taverner, Assistant Manager, Sales Department

Job:
Manager, Astoria

Job: Front Office
1st replacement

Job: Bars Manager
1st replacement

Job:
Manager, Grand

Job:
Banquet Manager
1st replacement

Job:
Chef de Cuisine
1st replacement

above a certain level of seniority being dealt with as a 'group resource', in which case appraisals and other management development processes will be monitored by a central department.

What do managers do?

Before designing detailed management development plans it is important to consider what managers do so that the development plans meet the needs of the organization and of the individual. The Council for Management Education and Development suggested that there are a number of management competences which fall into three main levels. These are concerned with different issues dependent upon the seniority of the managers concerned. An example is shown in Figure 9.3.

Figure 9.3   *Competences needed by middle management*

Management level	*Management competences*				
Supervisory/ operational/ junior					
Middle/tactical	Managing systems	Managing people	Finance management	Changing systems	Political sensitivity
Senior/strategic management					

This can be expressed in other ways. Essentially, as a person moves up the organizational hierarchy, tasks will change from being mainly of a routine nature, concerned with supervising operations through to non-routine interpretation of management information and organization of change.

Development of managers

Following the succession plan, individual training and development programmes have to be designed. It is here that an understanding of how a manager acquires his knowledge, skills and attitudes is vital. People do not become managers in a classroom, although they can acquire much of the necessary knowledge and basic skills there. Most of their expertise is obtained in the hard practice of managing people in the work place (see Figure 9.5). A management development programme must therefore contain a balance of formal training and planned experience. It is not something that operates for one period only of a manager's life. It should be updated constantly to continue throughout a manager's working life. Over a period of years, therefore, a programme may include spells in line management and in various specialist departments; for example, a young executive's first ten years with a company could be shown as in Figure 9.4.

Figure 9.4   *Example of a career path for a young executive*

Year	Approximate age	Position
1	21	Trainee management programme, various departments and establishments
2	22	Junior supervisory position, e.g. assistant manager/
3	23	manageress of a hotel or restaurant
4	24	Specialized function, e.g. new projects department, sales office, training department
5	25	Line management, e.g. unit management, food and beverage management
6	27	Specialist function, e.g. sales management, training officer
7	28	Assistant to area manager
8	30	Line management, e.g. manager of medium to large unit, area manager

During this period the executive may also attend a dozen 'off the job' courses on such subjects as:

Supervisory skills
Budgetary control and forecasting
Techniques of instruction
Interviewing and selection techniques
Project planning
Finance for non-financial executives.

Whether these are internal or external courses depends on the needs of the organization and the individual. Generally speaking, internal courses are more precisely designed to satisfy the needs of the organization, whereas external courses have to be broadly based to appeal to a wider market.

The value of external courses lies to a great extent in the opportunity to exchange views with managers from other organizations, but this only has value if those attending can bring about organizational changes. This prerogative normally lies only with more senior managers and therefore the value of external courses probably increases with the seniority of those attending (so long as they are geared to their needs).

The more junior people will be mainly concerned with acquiring knowledge and skills appropriate to their employer's needs and, so long as the numbers justify it, these courses should be run internally to ensure that only relevant matter is covered.

The British Institute of Management in 1985 reported that, 'there is a growing body of opinion which favours in-company courses – they argue that the "grape-shot" approach to cover a multitude of interests is not effective.'

Recent research from the United States showed that the most effective management training, not surprisingly, was 'On-job' training. Figure 9.5 shows the rank order of the different forms of training.

Figure 9.5 *Rank order for effectiveness of training of management grades*

1 Personalized experiential learning
2 Self-directed learning resources
3 Interactive simulations
4 Visual lecture aids
5 Textual material
6 Observational learning
7 Expert formal presentation
8 Impersonal passive electronic media

Source: 'A Model of Excellence of Training Managers and Non-supervisory Employees in the Food Service Industry', CHRIE Conference Paper 1988. Dr Reg Foucar-Scocki, Syracuse University, USA.

Trainee management courses

As the first step in a young manager's career, the design of trainee managers' courses is critical. It is in the first months that the basis of knowledge and skills and, in particular, an understanding of the employer's attitudes and values will be formed. During this period, however, unless worthwhile targets are set and some experience of supervision is obtained, most trainees will feel frustrated. For this reason there are many critics and opponents of the traditional 'Cook's tour' involving spells of training in the most important departments. In some cases this criticism is well deserved because no objectives are laid down and the trainees are merely used as cheap labour, or not used at all.

However, in order to be a successful manager, knowledge and experience of certain departments are vital and the well-designed 'Cook's tour' serves this purpose; at the same time objectives must be agreed with departmental supervisors and trainees must be given their training objectives in written form. They should not move from one department to the next until departmental training objectives have been attained. Trainees should maintain training logs or diaries and, in addition, they should be given projects. Regular progress interviews should be held to ensure that the trainees' objectives are being achieved.

In considering an individual's development programme, which is updated and modified year by year, it is vital to examine both 'strengths' and 'weaknesses', remembering that they may well be strengths and weaknesses only so far as the employer is concerned. In another type of organization the same characteristics may be seen in a completely different light. Ideally the weaknesses should be corrected and the strengths built upon. However, this will not always be possible because some 'weaknesses' may not be merely lack of knowledge or skill but of a 'personality' or attitude nature and these are often very difficult to correct even if it were in the individual's interest to do so. For example, a highly creative person may prefer to work as an individual. He or she may not enjoy or wish to work with others, nor to control them. The 'weakness', so far as the employer is concerned, is that he or she cannot direct or lead others, so the employer decides to give the individual 'a spell managing others' to make him or her into an 'all-rounder'. In some cases this may work out, but in others it could have disastrous results, with the person concerned eventually leaving. Equally damaging, the individual could unsettle subordinates, whom, it must be remembered, he or she may not have wanted to control in the first place.

It is vital, therefore, in designing management development programmes to recognize those 'weaknesses' that can be corrected and those that cannot. It is far better to build on strengths and to provide opportunities for these to be developed and exploited to the utmost, rather than to try to compensate for 'weaknesses' that may only be weaknesses in the employer's mind in any case. Re-design of a job may therefore be one outcome of the management development process.

The future of management development

Until recently management development in Britain was a largely unco-ordinated set of dispersed activities which depended upon initiatives coming from individuals, or employers or education and training institutions. The Management Charter Initiative and other related activities is an attempt to bring some order into the present situation. This is based upon some key principles:

1 Open access, enabling many more to benefit from management education.
2 Flexible and innovative forms of education, including 'distance learning', in-house projects.
3 Corporate and individual development plans.
4 A shift towards work-based assessments rather than end of course exams.
5 Credit accumulation which may also recognize learning acquired through experience.

The most likely outcome of the current developments will be a range of management courses starting with a Certificate in Management, followed by a Diploma and culminating with the Master in Business Administration (MBA).

Within the hospitality industry, in most cases, management development will remain the personal responsibility of individual managers. A small number of employers, particularly the larger ones, are now offering a compre-hensive range of management development options ranging right up to the MBA. The industry however consists in the main, of small privately owned enterprises and their perceptions and financial resources are likely to limit the extent to which they fund the development of their management, irrespective of the need to do so.

Further reading

Armstrong, M., *A Handbook of Human Resource Management*, London: Kogan Page, 1988

Jones, P., and Lockwood A., *The Management of Hotel Operations*, London: Cassell, 1989
Jones, P., and Lockwood A., *The Management of Hotel Operations*, London: Cassell, 1989
Pratt, K. J., and Bennett, S. C., *Elements of Personnel Management*, 3rd ed., Wokingham: GEE, 1989
Sisson K., (ed.), *Personnel Management in Britain*, Oxford: Blackwell, 1989
Thomason, G., *Textbook of Human Resource Management*, London: Institute of Personnel Management, 1988
Torrington, D. and Hall, L., *Personnel Management – a New Approach*, London: Prentice Hall, 1987

Questions

1 Describe the objectives of management development and the various steps or phases which you would normally expect to find in the operation of an effective management development programme.

2 Discuss which you consider to be the most important steps and why.

3 Discuss what changes are likely to be made in the future to improve management development procedures.

4 Discuss the relationship between management development and approaches to management, such as Management by Objective (see Chapter 3).

5 Using an employer you know well, evaluate their approach to management development.

chapter 10

Job evaluation

A methodical, fair approach to the award of wages and salaries is vital to a harmonious relationship between employers and employees. In organizations of any reasonable size, this can probably only be achieved if the relative value of each job is recognized and to do this a system of ranking jobs in order of importance needs to be used. It is important that a person, such as a chef, who has completed a relatively long and formal training and has acquired knowledge and skill should be paid more highly than a person whose job needs little knowledge or skill. It is simple to distinguish between jobs with skill and those without, but the problem arises when comparing jobs which are less easily differentiated; for example, when comparing those of a cook and a waiter. Both demand particular skills and knowledge but management has to decide whether to award more, and how much, to one rather than the other. A system of comparison that embraces all jobs within an enterprise needs to be adopted to ensure that wages are distributed fairly. Such a system, usually called 'job evaluation', provides a sound basis for comparisons to be made. Some systems attempt to be objective and analytical, whereas others are somewhat subjective, but if managed properly they can be equally successful. Job evaluation may, therefore, be defined as the process which establishes the relative value of jobs in a jobs hierarchy.

Employers introduce and use job evaluation for a number of different reasons. A recent survey conducted jointly by the Institute of Personnel Management and the Wyatt Company found the following reasons for using job evaluation:

Figure 10.1 *Reasons for using job evaluation*

	Existing schemes	New schemes
Fair pay	54%	49%
Company pay	16%	11%
Performance pay	9%	16%
Pressure	7%	—
Management information	6%	16%
Explain job	5%	6%
Relatives		
Other	3%	2%

Source: Personnel Management, January 1990

Figure 10.2a *Job evaluation: non-analytical methods*

Title	Broad description	Advantages	Disadvantages
Ranking	A simple method whereby the relative importance of the total job is assessed. Jobs are put in order of importance and may then be divided into groups	Very simple to use	Assessors need to know all jobs in some depth
Grading or classification	A simple method in which a grading structure indicating relative job values is designed. Each job is then placed within the most appropriate grade	Very simple to use	Assessors need to know all jobs in some depth. Marginal jobs may be placed in higher or lower grade because system may not be sufficiently discriminating.

Figure 10.2b *Job evaluation: analytical methods*

Title	Broad description	Advantages	Disadvantages
Points assessment	A commonly used and very acceptable method. Factors common to most jobs in the organization are identified such as knowledge and responsibility. Maximum points are allocated to each factor weighted according to importance. Each job examined is broken into the various factors. Each factor is then awarded points between zero and the maximum. The total of points awarded will give the score for the job and thereby its standing relative to other jobs. Bench-mark jobs will be used to assist in allocating points	Simple to under-stand and operate	Takes longer to implement than ranking or grading. It can lead to considerable discussion on weighting of factors

Figure 10.2b *Job evaluation: analytical methods – cont*

Title	Broad description	Advantages	Disadvantages
Factor comparison	Similar in some respects to points assessment but in some cases monetary values are used instead of points. Fewer factors, also, will normally be used than in points assessment. Bench-mark jobs will normally be used	Simple to operate once it has been designed	Difficult to arrive at monetary values
Direct consensus method or paired comparisons	A complex technique where evaluators representing all interested parties are asked to indicate which job of a pair or which factors within pairs of jobs they consider more important. The evaluators will probably deal with several or even many jobs. The paired comparisons of all evaluators may then be fed into a computer which will produce the ranking of all jobs considered.	Reduces individual subjectivity to a minimum	Complex, usually needs a computer
Time span of discretion	This technique measures one factor only: the length of time in which an individual's work or decisions remain unchecked, e.g. a typist four hours, a managing director four years	Simple, once the concept has been fully understood	Sometimes difficult to determine true discretion span

Symptoms that can indicate a need for methodical job evaluation can include:

(a) Employees leaving because wages are not awarded fairly and, in particular, because some newcomers earn more than long-serving employees.
(b) No formal periodic review of wages or salaries.
(c) Difficulties, due to wage levels, in transferring and promoting employees.
(d) A need to pay 'extras' or bonuses to get people to do what is, or should be, part of their normal job.
(e) Some employees working excessive overtime.

In order to carry out effective job evaluation precise job descriptions and even job specifications are required because without these the comparison of jobs becomes difficult, if not meaningless. Also, because comparisons of jobs are to be made, the preparation of job descriptions, must be standardized throughout the undertaking, and the actual evaluation should be conducted by one specialist or the smallest possible number of people to ensure a consistent result.

As Figure 10.2 shows there are many different job evaluation techniques. The first type – the non-analytical – considers the total job when jobs are being compared. In the case of *ranking*, jobs are placed in order of importance. They may then be placed in clusters of closely ranked jobs.

In the case of *grading* or *classification*, a number of grades will have been decided upon. A typical job illustrating the grade will be chosen which is known as a 'bench-mark' job. All other jobs are then placed into the most appropriate grades using the 'bench-mark' job for guidance (see Figure 10.3).

Figure 10.3 shows a typical approach, which is the system devised by the Institute of Administrative Management, and demonstrates its application to jobs in the hotel and catering industry.

Points assessment This method allocates points for each factor of a job. The points for all factors are added up and the total of points indicates the job's relative position in the job hierarchy.

The type of factors evaluated in each job may include:

1 *Knowledge* This may be simple knowledge acquired in a few days or, at the other extreme, may be acquired by several years of study and application.
2 *Skill* This refers mainly to manual skills. These may be acquired within a very short period, such as the skills needed to operate a limited range of equipment, or they may take many weeks, even months of practice such as typewriting, or the varied skills needed by a competent cook.
3 *Responsibility* This may be of the type where a person makes important decisions that are not checked for a long period; alternatively they may be simple decisions that are checked immediately. This factor may include responsibility for people, equipment, cash.
4 *Physical demands* Some jobs, such as cooking, are physically demanding, or they may make little physical demand such as book-keeping or typing.

Figure 10.3   *A job grading or classification system (using the Institute of Administrative Management method)*

Level definition	Example of jobs
1 Very simple tasks of largely physical nature	Porter* Cleaner
2 Simple tasks carried out in accordance with a small number of clearly defined rules, and which can be carried out after a short period of training of up to 2–3 weeks. The work is checked and closely supervised	Room attendant* Lift attendant Counter assistant Barperson Hall porter
3 Straightforward tasks, but involving more complicated routines and requiring a degree of individual knowledge and alertness, as the work is subject to occasional check	Commis waiter* Clerk
4 Tasks calling for the independent arrangement of work and the exercise of some initiative, where little supervision is needed. Detailed familiarity with one or more branches of established procedure required	Receptionist* Waiter Cashier Store keeper Florist
5 Routine work, but involving an individual degree of responsibility for answering non-routine queries and/or exercising some measure of control over a small group of staff	Head waiter* Senior receptionist Assistant housekeeper
6 Non-routine work, involving co-ordination of several lower grade functions, possibly some measure of control over small group of staff. Also non-routine work involving recognized individual knowledge and some responsibility without follow-up	Head housekeeper* Banqueting manager Restaurant manager
7 Work necessitating responsibility for sections involved on routine tasks and/or where there are also individual tasks to be undertaken, calling for specialist knowledge	Chef de cuisine* Front office manager *Bench-mark jobs

5   *Mental demands*   All jobs, to a greater or lesser extent, make demands on a person's mental abilities including the ability to concentrate and to apply oneself; for example, a senior receptionist's job will be much more demanding mentally than a porter's.

6   *Social skills*   Some jobs require more social skill than others. A restaurant manager, for example, will require a high degree of tact and patience, whereas a chef may require little or no social skill.

7   *Working conditions*   This includes physical and social inconveniences such as heat, long hours, and whether sitting or standing. This may also take into account hazards such as risk of burns, cuts or even physical violence.

These seven examples give a broad indication of the types of factors considered. Others may be used and, in addition, a breakdown into 'sub-factors' may also be desirable. The main methods of evaluation or how these factors may be measured are shown in Figure 10.2 (a and b).

The normal method of awarding points for each factor is to have a scale with 'bench-mark' jobs on it. When evaluating a particular factor of a job it will be placed at or between what appear to be the most appropriate 'bench-mark' job or jobs; for example, in evaluating one factor, such as knowledge, the list of bench-mark jobs is examined and the job being evaluated is then placed in the most appropriate position on the scale (See Figure 10.4).

Figure 10.4   *Example of bench-mark jobs (for one factor only)*

Points   *Bench-mark jobs for knowledge – maximum points: 30; minimum points: 0*

Points	Bench-mark jobs
30	Hotel manager
24	Front office manager
18	Restaurant manager
12	Station waiter
6	Hall porter

In evaluating the knowedge required of a head waiter, for example, it would fall between the station waiter and the restaurant manager in Figure 10.4, consequently being awarded somewhere around 15 points. The same procedure would then be adopted for all other factors to be evaluated. The bench-mark jobs will not necessarily be the same for each factor. After this has been done for all factors the points are totalled and the job grade should be determined by reference to a grade table such as shown in Figure 10.5.

Figure 10.6 shows the technique applied to two jobs; a restaurant manager's and a commis waiter's. In this example the factors outlined on page 136 are used but in designing a scheme other factors entirely may be considered.

After totalling the points a look at a grade table will indicate the grades of the two jobs – refer back to Figure 10.5. The commis waiter's job, therefore, is a grade 3 and the restaurant manager's a grade 6.

This is a very simplified example of a points assessment system. Some systems may be much more complex than this, but no matter which technique is used, the principles of job evaluation are:

1   Job descriptions must be precise and up-to-date.
2   Because wages and salaries depend on the results, evaluation must be scrupulously fair and consistent.
3   It is the job, not the job holder, which is being evaluated.

People at work measure their value to their employer, to a large extent, by reference to the amount that they and their fellow workers are paid. If, therefore, there appears to be unfairness or injustice in the methods or level of payment, employees will lose faith and confidence in their employer and will react accordingly. Arriving at a fair distribution of wages is not easy and only

Figure 10.5   *Example of a grade table*

Grade	Points (Total of all factors)	Example of job
7	121–140	Chef de cuisine
6	101–120	Restaurant manager
5	81–100	Senior receptionist
4	61–80	Waiter
3	41–60	Clerk
2	21–40	Hall porter
1	0–20	Kitchen porter

Figure 10.6   *Example of a points assessment system showing the evaluation of two jobs*

Factor	Maximum points	Example evaluation of two jobs Commis waiter	Restaurant manager
Knowledge	30	5	18
Skill	20	10	20
Responsibility	30	3	24
Physical demands	10	5	4
Mental demands	20	8	15
Social skills	20	12	18
Working conditions	10	5	3
Total	140	48	102

too often in the hotel and catering industry it is the result of expediency rather than methodical planning and application. It is vital, however, to recognize the relative importance of each job and, if they exist, to remove any causes that can lead to dissatisfaction. In order to do this it is vital, therefore, to adopt a methodical system of evaluating jobs so that wages and salaries appear to all to be fairly distributed.

Having said this, the recent IPM/Wyatt survey found less than full satisfaction with job evaluation amongst those employers using the process. They found:

1 The process is time consuming and inefficient; it is demanding of resources.
2 It is difficult to ensure high quality results.
3 The centralized process runs counter to the current trend in employee relations, i.e. it tends to be unitarist rather than pluralist in approach.

For these reasons some employers have dropped job evaluation in favour of market pricing or competency awards.

Job evaluation in the hospitality industry

Job evaluation is commonplace in the public sectors of the hospitality industry. Many jobs are evaluated using one or other of the job evaluation methods. It is also used by a number of larger operations, such as Bass, who use the Hay-MSL to determine pay rates for their managers. Otherwise job evaluation is not very common, due largely to the large number of small employers. Instead wage levels are frequently determined by expediency rather than by a methodical approach. Newcomers are frequently recruited and paid more than existing staff doing the same jobs. Also staff often leave because their employers refuse to grant increases even though the employer knows it will be necessary to pay replacements more than the outgoing staff are asking for.

Further reading

Armstrong, M., *A Handbook of Human Resource Management*, London: Kogan Page, 1988

Pratt, K. J., and Bennett, S. C., *Elements of Personnel Management*, 3rd ed., Wokingham: GEE, 1989

Sisson K., (ed.), *Personnel Management in Britain*, Oxford: Blackwell, 1989

Thomason, G., *Textbook of Human Resource Management*, London: Institute of Personnel Management, 1988

Thomason, G., *Job Evaluation: A Practical Guide for Managers*, London: Institute of Personnel Management, 1980

Torrington, D. and Hall, L., *Personnel Management – a New Approach*, London: Prentice Hall, 1987

Questions

1 Describe the objectives of job evaluation and the alternative approaches.

2 Discuss what you consider to be the most important elements and why.

3 Discuss in which sectors of the hotel and catering industry job evaluation is most likely to be found and why.

4 Using an employer you know well, evaluate their approach to job evaluation.

chapter 11

The administration of wages and salaries

An employer pays wages and salaries, one of the elements of the total remuneration package, in order to attract, retain and motivate the work force he or she requires. In order to be effective the remuneration package needs to be aimed at supporting the employer's overall human resource policy. For example, if an employer's policy is to encourage long service and career development amongst most of its employees the employer may offer an incremental payment system which rewards long service in itself. If the employer chooses to recruit from a volatile, young and relatively cheap labour market it will probably offer low rates of pay with little room for significant increases. Some employers will mix their policies, encouraging managers to make careers with them whilst not encouraging long serving operative staff. Obviously wage payment is a highly charged subject and in the hotel and catering industry it is a very contentious one owing to a variety of complications. Apart from lack of method in setting basic rates, in some sectors other factors such as tipping, service charges and the provision of meals and living accommodation, all have to be taken into consideration. Within a single establishment it is quite possible to find a complete permutation of all the various benefits received by employees. Some live in and earn tips, some live out and do not earn tips, some are provided with meals and some are not. In addition, in the largest organizations, some subsidiaries encourage tipping, whereas others do everything to eliminate it and also levy service charges. This may be even further complicated by some executives being provided with company cars and other benefits. On closer examination, however, it may well be found that these same executives are worse off (in cash and kind) than their own residential managers.

Mars and Mitchell claim the payment system in hotels has particular problems because it consists of:

1 basic pay and subsidized lodging and subsidized food;
2 tips and service charges (where applicable) and 'fiddles' and 'knock-offs' (Mars and Mitchell 1976).

Although Mars and Mitchell were writing in 1976 regular surveys amongst returning industrial release students indicate that little has changed in this respect. Mars and Mitchell attach particular importance to the 'fiddles' element because of the power it provides to management. They suggest that management lays down parameters within which 'fiddles' are acceptable, but at the same time if someone displeases them for other reasons, they can dismiss the person for fiddling. Undoubtedly, whether fiddling is institutionalized or not, it is a major source of income to employees, and causes headaches to the industry's employers.

Types of employees

Within the hotel and catering industry, there are four main types of employee. From a payment or earnings point of view these are:

Salaried employees; usually paid monthly by cheque or credit transfer and usually consisting of managers and senior supervisors.
Full-time operatives; usually working around a 30–45 hour week and who know from week to week that they have guaranteed work; paid usually weekly in cash.
Part-timers; usually working fewer hours than a full timer and who generally know from week to week that they have guaranteed work; usually paid by the hour in cash. With some employers part-timers qualify, pro-rata, for the same fringe benefits, such as holidays, as the full-time members of staff.
Casuals; normally working on a 'session' by 'session' basis (e.g. one evening) with no guarantees about future work; usually paid by the session in cash.

Formal wages administration

A major responsibility of managers is to decide how to distribute fairly among all employees the money set aside for payment of staff. This may range from as little as 10 per cent of revenue in some efficient public houses to over 40 per cent in top-class hotels. This money may derive from normal revenue or may also come from retained service charges. Managers may decide by looking at what competitors are paying, what the wages council rate is, what has been historically the employer's practice and, in many cases, what is necessary to overcome the current crisis. The result is that considerable anomalies exist in many hotels, catering establishments and, indeed, in whole firms. As mentioned in the last chapter, newcomers may be paid more than similar staff with long service and more senior staff may earn less than some juniors. Such anomalies are not necessarily confined to the smaller employers.

The exact policy to be adopted by an employer with regard to his wage and salary systems will depend to a great extent upon his business objectives, his personnel policies and his style of management; for example, in organizations where labour turnover is not considered to be important, there may be little method or formality in setting rates of pay. In other organizations, however, where it is recognized that a stable labour force is a valuable asset, much more method will be applied to wage and salary matters. This is typically so in the public sector.

Where there are many employees with differing levels of skills, fair salary administration may depend upon job evaluation which measures the relative importance to the organization of different jobs. But after jobs have been evaluated, rates will have to be set for each grade to ensure that there are realistic differentials between grades so that more senior jobs and promotions are rewarded by worthwhile differences in earnings; promotion then becomes something to aim for. This is illustrated in Figure 11.1.

Figure 11.1   *Example of a grade and wage table*

Grade	Basic wage
1	£100 p.w.
2	£110 p.w.
3	£121 p.w.
4	£133 p.w.

Determining the rate for each job or for key jobs depends on many factors including the make-up of the workforce, statutory requirements, competitors' rates of pay, other industries' rates of pay, cost of living, and the location of the employer. Because of this, in order to establish or to maintain competitive rates of pay, it will be necessary to study advertisements in the press, to keep in touch with staff agencies and the local office of the Department of Employment, and with the local associations of hoteliers and caterers. In making decisions, as a result of this research, it is vital to ensure that all factors affecting rates of pay are taken into account, such as tips and service charges, actual hours worked, the provision or otherwise of meals and accommodation. Some employers with units in different regions may, in addition, require different rates or even entirely different structures for each branch or region.

Increments

In some situations, in order to encourage good performance and long service, it may be appropriate to provide merit and service increments and where this is done there will normally be overlaps between grades, enabling someone in a low grade, but with long service or high merit, to earn more than someone in a high grade with short service. This recognizes that a person's competence and value to an organization may increase with service, and because of this the increment is granted both as an increased share of his overall contribution and to encourage the employee to stay. Figure 11.2 shows a scale for such a scheme.

In the example shown in Figure 11.2 an employee could anticipate, with satisfactory service, to move from the minimum to the maximum in a period of about four years giving an average annual increase of about 6 to 7 per cent. The exact rate could be determined by performance appraisals and by the employer's financial policy. The advantage of this system, if publicized, is that an employee knows what he can expect to earn by gaining promotion or by staying with an employer. In addition, some employers have age-related scales or rates of pay, usually for employees up to about 21 years of age. Increases in these cases would normally be granted on each employee's birthday.

Figure 11.2 *Example of an incremental wage scale*

Starting wages or salaries offered to newcomers may not normally be more than 20 per cent above the minimum and this should only be permitted where appropriate experience in the type of job justifies it. Some trade unionists are opposed to incremental scales, saying that every job should have a set rate and that age and service are irrelevant if the job is performed satisfactorily. Furthermore, they claim that such systems can have an adverse effect on staff turnover because management, in order to keep payroll costs down, will encourage labour turnover, thus retaining a high proportion of employees at the lower end of the scales.

Reviews should take place regularly and should fit into the employer's budgetary and financial cycle. In seasonal establishments reviews may take place towards the end of the season in order to retain those employees management wants to keep.

Communicating details of any increases should be done as soon as possible after the decisions have been taken, but, as mentioned in the chapter on appraisals, they should not be part of any performance review or appraisal. Where a person is promoted, the increase should take place upon promotion and not be subject to trial periods as this can indicate doubts about the person's ability to hold down the new job at the very time he or she needs the employer's fullest confidence. Nor should the individual concerned have to wait for the annual review, because a person should be paid the rate for the job being done.

Apart from increases for merit, service and promotion, some systems also allow for cost of living increases to be made from time to time. These will probably be related to some government data such as the retail price index, but where these are granted it is important to bear in mind that they have little positive motivational effect – unlike a promotion or merit award. That is because they are usually granted to all employees without discriminating between the good and the not so good. On the other hand it is important to keep in mind that the absence of 'cost of living' increases may have a negative effect – that is the employee's relative level of earnings may fall and force them to seek employment elsewhere. It can be said that although 'cost of living' awards have little positive, motivational effect, their absence may have a negative effect such as a higher labour turnover.

As with all systems, there is no need to adhere inflexibly to the systems described – systems should be servants not masters – but experience shows that once a systematized salary structure is operational the whole question of pay becomes less contentious and, in particular, where there are disputes or dissatisfactions over differentials management has a basis for dealing with these rationally.

Where systematic salary administration does not exist, on the other hand, there will almost certainly be anomalies, unfairness and, consequently, dissatisfaction. Staff turnover will be high not just because of dissatisfaction with levels of pay, but because of some imagined or genuine grievance, such as learning that a newcomer is being paid more.

Further reading

Armstrong, M., *A Handbook of Human Resource Management*, London: Kogan Page, 1988

Genders, P., *Wages and Salaries*, London: Institute of Personnel Management, 1981

Mars, G., Mitchell, P., and Bryant D., *Manpower Problems in the Hotel and Catering Industry*, Farnborough: Saxon House, 1976

Sisson K., (ed.), *Personnel Management in Britain*, Oxford: Blackwell, 1989

Pratt, K. J., and Bennett, S. C., *Elements of Personnel Management*, 3rd ed., Wokingham: GEE, 1989

Thomason, G., *Textbook of Human Resource Management*, London: Institute of Personnel Management, 1988

Torrington, D. and Hall, L., *Personnel Management – A New Approach*, London: Prentice Hall, 1987

Questions

1 Describe the objectives of a systematic wage and salary administration system.

2 Discuss in which sectors of the hotel and catering industry systematic wage and salary administration is least likely and most likely to be found and why.

3 Discuss what you consider to be the most likely consequences of the lack of systematic wage and salary administration and why.

4 Discuss what changes are likely to be made in the future to improve wage and salary administration procedures.

5 Discuss the relationship between salary administration and performance appraisal (see Chapter 7).

6 Using an employer you know well evaluate their approach to wage and salary administration.

chapter 12

Incentives

The competition amongst employers to attract effective employees, and the nature of the taxation system, have obliged employers over the years to seek ways and means of making the total remuneration package more attractive to employees. In some cases benefits, such as free meals, are offered, merely because other employers do so. In other cases, various incentives are offered in order to focus the employee's attention on the business objectives of the employer, e.g. to increase hotel room occupancy or to increase the number of contracts run by a contract caterer.

What motivates?

In Chapter 2 the contributions of a number of different theorists were considered. Most of these are crucially concerned with what motivates people to work. In spite of the vast body of knowledge coming from people like Taylor, Mayo, McGregor, Maslow and Herzberg there is still no consensus. Many managers still hold to the belief that money, because of what it can buy (including security and status), is a major motivator. Others tend to the more complex views of Maslow and Herzberg, arguing that people work for a composite package, including money, security, self-esteem, esteem of others, job satisfaction, etc. At a practical level this discussion obviously concerns the merits or otherwise of incentive schemes. Some people argue that employees should be given an adequate wage or salary and, so long as other prospects are adequate such as the regular review of earnings and the likelihood of promotion, people will give what they consider to be a 'fair day's work'. The prospect of incentives will not spur them to continued greater efforts. It is also argued that incentive payments are most effective when people are dependent upon them, that is, the nearer the basic pay is to subsistence levels, the more effective an incentive scheme. The effect of such an attitude on employer/employee relationships, however, is hardly likely to be positive.

In work of a highly creative nature the prospect of incentive payments is considered unlikely to stimulate greater creativity. There are others, however, who argue that incentives will certainly influence productivity saying, for example, that in a selling situation the prospects of earning commission will definitely stimulate greater 'selling' effort. It is also argued that because of the growing interdependence of working people they can no longer increase their own earnings without the involvement of their colleagues. In many cases nowadays this is true, but in this industry there are still many opportunities for individuals to increase considerably their earnings – particularly in the 'selling' areas, such as waiting, bar work, hotel reception and function catering. Within the scope of this book it is not possible to consider further the arguments for and against incentive schemes. There are unfortunately innumerable examples supporting both viewpoints. It is intended here to look at the main forms of incentives operated in the hotel and catering industry including tips, the 'tronc', service charges, bonuses and commissions.

In other industries other forms of incentive payments are also used. These include methods such as piece rates or measured day work, which are usually based on work measurement techniques, whereas those commonly used in the hospitality industry are more normally related to financial targets such as gross profits, turnover, and variable costs (e.g. gas, electricity). In some cases they may be entirely discretionary.

Although *tipping* and the *tronc* were mentioned along with other forms of financial incentive, it is probably better to think of them as part of normal earnings. Financial incentives are normally intended to stimulate and promote *extra* productivity, whereas tips, the tronc and service charges are considered by many employees as a matter of right and something without which they could not have a reasonable living standard.

Tipping is a form of payment that originated when many workers in the old inns were not employed by the innkeeper but were retained by guests to do particular jobs such as carrying bags, cleaning garments, etc. Many consider it an anachronism in this day and age and a view that has been expressed by many people for many years is that it needs to be eliminated as rapidly as possible. Professor Nailon of Surrey University, however, writes* that it is not necessarily a bad practice but that it may have profound effects on interdepartmental relationships. Also it removes from management an important area of personal control.

Service charges many argue, on the other hand, are quite acceptable methods for an undertaking to employ to raise revenue, so long as the sum allowed for distribution to the workforce is distributed on a fair basis. In many tourist countries it is common to find that tariffs are inclusive of taxes and service charges, and tipping is being eliminated.

Where the service charges are part of an employee's remuneration a minimum level should be specified so that a person can know how to regulate his or her affairs; for example, if an employer knows that his waitresses normally earn £20 a week from the service charge and £90 per week in wages, he could, without much risk to himself, offer a minimum guaranteed income of £110 per week. This guaranteed income could be paid weekly and the excess periodically, such as quarterly or half-yearly, thus spreading payment over good and bad spells of trade. Where a service charge is included in the bill, tipping may be discouraged and notices on bills, menus, brochures and in guest rooms discourage guests from giving tips in addition to paying the service charge.

*HCIMA Review, vol. 2, no. 4.

Principles of incentive schemes

In designing an incentive scheme, whether for this industry or any other, there are several principles that should be adhered to for it to be effective in the long term. These are:

1 The undertaking's major business objectives should be promoted and their achievement assisted by incentive payments. These payments should enable individuals to identify with the success of the undertaking; for example, if food gross profit is vital, the chef and maybe his staff as well should be rewarded for achieving gross profit targets. But only elements over which a person exerts control should be included. A chef, for example, has no control over the rent and the rates, therefore there is no point in including these in a scheme for the chef.

2 When an incentive scheme is to be introduced *all* workers should be considered because of the effect the scheme may have on existing earnings differentials and the possibility of creating friction between staff.

3 Payments should be related to results by comparing actual performance with forecasts, targets, standards, or budgets. This may be done individually or on a group basis.

4 Targets should be realistic, that is achievable with reasonable effort and agreed with the person or groups concerned.

5 Targets should be reviewed regularly, and at least annually, so that payments are something to be earned with effort rather than something which becomes a matter of right. They should also be reviewed if circumstances change considerably; for example, if a vast new office block opens next door to a snack bar, trade will probably increase greatly, through no effort of the manager. The turnover and other targets should, therefore, be reviewed at the same time bearing in mind that extra work will be created and that wages and salaries may have to be increased.

6 An incentive scheme should be simple and clearly understood by those within the scheme.

7 Payment of the incentive should be made as near as possible to the period in which it was earned. Long delays in payment cause irritation and reduce the incentive element.

8 All elements of a scheme and any rules should be objective. Management should not incorporate 'discretionary' rules such as 'management reserves the right to withhold payment without giving a reason'. Incentives, if earned, should be a matter of right, not for management to dispense on a discretionary basis, and the terms of the incentive scheme should become part of the 'Contract of Employment'.

Incentives are normally used to stimulate performance and particularly to increase sales and control costs. Figures 12.1, 12.2 and 12.3 are included as examples.

Having looked at these examples, which are intended to illustrate principles only and which demonstrate that incentive schemes can be designed for many departments in an organization, it is vital to bear in mind that their introduction may have undesirable consequences which could exclude their being used; for example, the chef may well place commission above customer

Figure 12.1   *Example of an individual incentive scheme (chef)*

1 *Job*	Chef
2 *Commission*	1 per cent of all 'gross profit' (for this purpose revenue less purchases and labour costs) in excess of £2000 per week, after achieving the following targets
3 *Targets*	1 Purchases not to exceed 45 per cent of revenue 2 Kitchen labour not to exceed 15 per cent of revenue

4 *Example of calculation*
Period 7

Food cost	£6000	(37.5%)	Revenue	£16000
Labour cost	£2200	(13.75%)		
	£8200			
'Gross profit'	£7800	(48.75%)		

Gross profit £7800 − £2000 = £5800 × $\frac{1}{100}$ = £58.00
Commission to be £58.00

Figure 12.2   *Example of a group incentive scheme*

1 *Department*	Front Office
2 *Commission*	£60 for every 1 per cent in excess of occupancy targets, distributed to all front office staff pro rata to salaries
3 *Target*	85 per cent occupancy

4 *Examples of calculation*
Period 7
Actual occupancy 90.0% therefore 5.0 × £60 = £300 to be distributed

Salaries: Head receptionist	£7000
2 Senior receptionists @	£6500
2 Cashier/receptionists @	£5000
Total salaries	£30,000

$\frac{£300 \text{ commission}}{£30,000 \text{ salaries}}$ = £0.01 per £ salary

Therefore the following commissions will be paid
Head receptionist   £7000 × £0.01 = £70
Senior receptionists   £6500 × £0.01 = £65
Cashier/receptionists   £5000 × £0.01 = £50

satisfaction and buy cheap materials or keep labour costs too low for efficient service. In the case of the receptionists they may overbook (more than is desirable) and consequently lose customers for the future. On the other hand, in looking at the restaurant manager's scheme, it can be seen that because the commission is related to net profit, the manager has an interest in successfully controlling all aspects of the business, including turnover, purchases, wages, variables, and, of course, customer satisfaction. In designing an incentive scheme, therefore, one has to ensure that the benefits to the individual do not stimulate him or her to take measures that may not be in the employer's own

Figure 12.3 *Example of an individual incentive scheme (manager)*

1 *Job*	Restaurant manager
2 *Commission*	˙5 per cent of net profit up to budget
	10 per cent of net profit between 101 per cent and
	130 per cent of target budget
	20 per cent of net profit in excess of 130 per cent of
	target budget
3 *Target budget*	£40,000 net profit

4 *Example of calculation*

Year ended 31 December 1990   Actual net profit = £56,000

Commission rate	Qualifying net profit	Commission
5%	£40,000	£2000
10%	£12,000	£1200
20%	£ 4000	£ 800
TOTAL	£56,000	£4000

NOTE: In this example it is interesting to note that although the top rate of commission is 20 per cent and consequently well worth striving for, the actual rate of total commission is only just over 7 per cent.

interests. Incentives can cover such things as sales, profits, occupancy, suggestion schemes, new staff introduction bonuses, and new business introduction bonuses.

Financial incentives can reward individual employees or groups of employees through increased payment for their increased contribution to the enterprise. However, they can achieve little on their own. They must be part of a comprehensive, well-balanced human resource policy that is based upon offering every employee adequate wages and other conditions before incentives are offered.

Further reading

Armstrong, M., *A Handbook of Human Resource Management*, London: Kogan Page, 1988

Pratt, K. J., and Bennett, S. C., *Elements of Personnel Management*, 3rd ed., Wokingham: GEE, 1989

Roots, P., *Financial Incentives for Employees*, London: BSP Professional Books, 1989

Sisson, K., (ed.), *Personnel Management in Britain*, Oxford: Blackwell, 1989

Thomason, G., *Textbook of Human Resource Management*, London: Institute of Personnel Management, 1988

Torrington, D. and Hall, L., *Personnel Management – A New Approach*, London: Prentice Hall, 1987

Questions

1 Describe the objectives of incentive schemes and the various alternatives in regular use.

2 Discuss which you consider to be the most important principles if incentive schemes are to be effective. What do you understand by 'effective'?

3 Discuss what external factors influence the nature of incentive schemes.

4 Discuss the relationship between incentive schemes and alternative methods of wage and salary administration.

5 Discuss the role played by wages, and salaries and incentives in achieving an employer's human resource policy.

6 Using an employer you know well, evaluate their approach to incentive schemes.

chapter 13

Fringe benefits

The importance of fringe benefits in employment policies has grown in recent years partly because of relatively high levels of personal tax and partly because of pressure from other sources such as the rapidly increasing competition for employees. Fringe benefits are intended primarily to motivate employees to give better performance and to encourage them to stay with the employer. They include benefits that attract little or no tax such as meals, holidays, and deferred earnings such as pensions. The total list of benefits offered today is considerable and is continually growing as employers look for new ways to woo employees. They can be divided into three main types: financial, part-financial and non-financial.

Financial benefits include: commissions, bonuses, profit sharing, share options.
Part-financial benefits include: pensions, meals, cars, subscriptions.
Non-financial benefits include: holidays, sick pay, medical insurances.

In considering fringe benefits it is vital to recognize that what may be considered an 'incentive' or 'motivator' today may lose its motivating effect with time. This may be because what is offered by only one or two employers to start with will be offered by many employers as they follow suit. Alternatively, what may have been offered as a reward for exceptional services one year becomes expected and a 'matter of right' within the next two or three years.

Having made this point, it is necessary to bear in mind also that although the presence of many fringe benefits in a 'compensation package' may not be a positive incentive to work harder or to perform better, the absence of fringe benefits, on the other hand, may be a disincentive and will leave an employer at a disadvantage in recruiting or retaining staff.

In some cases offering high salaries, commissions or bonuses may compensate for lack of fringe benefits, but owing to the fact that non-cash benefits are taxed lightly or not at all, these have been playing a bigger part in employee compensation in recent years. They can add another 25 per cent to the total payroll costs but a similar increase to salaries, due to personal tax, would almost certainly not enable employees to purchase the same type of benefits, or to enjoy the same standard of living.

Fringe benefit programmes should be designed to further the employer's objectives and should, in particular, be designed to assist in human resource planning. Where, for example, it is desirable to have a stable, mature management team providing plenty of continuity, such as is required by many brewery companies, a very generous pension and life assurance scheme, along with loan facilities (for house purchasing among other things), will assist in retaining the management team. On the other hand a dynamic young organization may want a fairly steady flow of 'whizz kids', the majority of whom will not want to stay for long because there will not be room for all of them. In this case high salaries and good incentives payments will be preferable, as this type of person will not be so interested in benefits such as pensions.

The differing needs of employers, along with pressures exerted by competing organizations and by statutory requirements, will all help to dictate what type of fringe benefits programme needs to be offered. There are many different components and the permutations can be numerous. The major ones, however, as listed in a survey published in *Catering Times*, are shown in Figure 13.1.

Figure 13.1   *Some fringe benefits offered in the industry*

Staff restaurant, free meals
Luncheon vouchers

Living in accommodation, staff hostel
Assistance with finding accommodation

Free uniform, laundry services

Holidays
Pension scheme, sickness leave

Maternity leave, paternity leave

Medical services, private medical insurance

Social and sports clubs, cinema and theatre passes

Company newspaper, staff newspaper

Discount buying, discounted holidays/meals in company hotels or restaurants

Savings schemes, loans, house purchase assistance, re-location grants

Long service awards

Christmas bonus, birthday gift/cards

Suggestion bonus, language proficiency, employee introduction bonus

Jury service pay

Share option scheme

Volunteer reserve paid time off

Source: Company induction material

Financial benefits

Commissions and bonuses   These were covered in more detail on pages 145–50 but, as was said there, they should be directly related, as far as possible, to performance. Discretionary 'handouts' have little positive motivational value.

Profit sharing   Although many profit sharing schemes may not be justified directly on motivational grounds, because individuals do not receive a commission or bonus related to their own efforts, and because these awards may be expected as a matter of right, profit sharing may well be justified for indirect reasons. There is a growing view that employees have a proprietorial interest in the undertaking which employs them and that consequently, they should have a share of any increased profits. Awarding a bonus of this kind may not assist directly in increasing profits but withholding an award may have an adverse effect on employees' morale. Whether this share of increased profits should be in the form of a bonus or salary increase depends on current performance of the employer's business; for example, if there is a strong upward trend in profits an increase in salaries could be awarded, whereas if a year's performance was exceptional and not certain to be maintained, a bonus may be preferable from the employer's point of view, because it is a 'once only' payment and because it does not have a gearing up effect on future wage increases, pensions, etc.

Share option schemes   These enable executives to buy options on company shares with loans provided by the employer. The better the company performs, the more the value of the executives' shares increases. These schemes are strictly controlled by law; for example, they do not allow an executive to sell his shares until a certain number of years has elapsed. All of the above schemes are now offered in the hotel and catering industry.

Part-financial benefits

There are many benefits which may be awarded that can be described as partly financial. These are benefits that the employee cannot normally dispose of in cash or kind, but which enable him or her either to save spending personal resources on these benefits or to enjoy a higher standard of living. These benefits include such things as pensions and life assurance schemes, company cars, expense accounts. The major 'part-financial' benefits are as follows:

Pensions   Most schemes grant a fraction of final earnings for each year of service. The better schemes grant one-sixtieth of final salary (sometimes the average of the last few years) for each year's service, thereby enabling a person with forty or more years' service to retire on forty-sixtieths (or two-thirds of final salary), the maximum pension currently permissible. Provision is also normally made for a person's dependants whether he or she dies in service or in retirement.

One of the benefits to employers of comprehensive pension schemes is that they enable employers to retire their older employees, particularly for health reasons, replacing them by younger people, knowing that the older ones will be well provided for in retirement.

Life insurance   In itself this is hardly a benefit that will persuade a person to join one employer rather than another. From the employer's point of view, however, the major value is that it provides for the dependants of employees who die in service. Without this provision the employer may feel that there is a moral, if not a legal responsibility to look after an employee's dependants, particularly if that person dies in the course of work. If no insurance is provided, some other provision may have to be made on a discretionary basis and, where large numbers of people are employed, cases may be treated inconsistently. Also, the burden may fall more heavily in one year rather than another and, worst of all, if the employer goes out of business the dependants of ex-employees may be completely unprovided for.

Company cars   Generally speaking these are provided for one of two reasons. First, it is because an employee needs a car in order to do the job. This would include a variety of people such as regional or area managers and stock takers. Second, cars are provided to improve a person's standard of living without incurring the full tax liability that paying an equivalent cash amount would impose.

The provision of company cars is a highly contentious benefit, however, for reasons such as these:

1 Cars are very nearly 'cash equivalent' and therefore if a car is provided to one employee in a particular job grade because it is needed, another employee of similar grade but who does not need or receive a car may well expect a cash equivalent. To complicate this further, if a cash equivalent were paid this would be taxed fully, whereas only part of the estimated value of the car to the other employee would rank for tax.
2 Cars are status symbols both within the organization and within the community at large and wherever status is concerned people are very sensitive and often irrational.

House purchasing   Purchasing a house is usually the biggest investment that a person ever makes and often moving house is one of the biggest obstacles to employee mobility. (The fact that labour mobility in the hotel and catering industry is high while home ownership by the industry's employees is low are probably not unrelated.) By helping employees to buy a house employers can increase the stability of their labour force. At the top of the scale this assistance can take the form of cheap loans, but, more practically, it can be confined to the employer acting as guarantor.

Removal or relocation expenses   These payments are intended to indemnify an employee for the cost incurred in moving home when being appointed, transferred or promoted by the employer. The amount allowed should be such that the employee is no worse off financially as a direct result of moving house. The expenses included in this, however, can be extensive, including estate agents costs, legal fees, furniture removal, new school uniforms, temporary accommodation, etc.

The employer's responsibility should be confined purely to indemnifying the employee for the actual costs incurred in the employee's transfer from one home to another. Considerations of capital appreciation should be excluded.

Today because of the considerable differences between property values in the South and the North of England some employers, including major hotel companies, are now experiencing difficulties in transferring employees. Assistance in house purchase and mobility grants may need to be developed by employers so that transfer from the North to the South does not result in big changes in employees' standard of housing.

These are the major part-financial fringe benefits offered by many employers. There are many others as well which enable employees to enjoy a better standard of living and these include advantageous purchasing of food, insurance, furniture, etc. These can all be arranged through the employer's own suppliers or agents.

Non-financial benefits

Although the main benefits in this category can cost the employer considerable sums of money, they do not normally provide employees with any direct financial advantages. Instead they afford employees other benefits such as a degree of security or more time for leisure.

Fringe benefits are often provided where it is recognized that financial incentives may have little effect due to taxation. The main benefits in this category are:

Holidays These can be used as a stimulus to labour stability; for example, extra days over the minimum can be granted after a certain number of years' service. Extra holidays must be reasonably obtainable, however, because working for fifteen years, for example, for extra holiday entitlement will contribute nothing to retaining staff. It is much better to grant two to four extra days after two to four years' service, leading up to an extra week after five years. The table in Figure 13.2 illustrates one example.

Sick pay schemes As with several other conditions of employment details of paying during sickness have to be entered in the statement of conditions of employment. This is required by the Employment Protection (Consolidation) Act 1978 and, in the absence of such details, an employer may have to pay a

Figure 13.2 *Example of a service-related holiday entitlement scheme*

Years of service	Holiday entitlement per annum
During 1st year	4 weeks (pro rata to actual service)
2nd year	4 weeks and 2 days
3rd and 4th year	4 weeks and 3 days
5th and 6th year	4 weeks and 4 days
7th year onwards	5 weeks

sick employee the full wage or salary until dismissal of the employee having given full notice of termination.

It is for this reason as well as for normal human considerations that employers should formulate a sick pay policy that is consistent with their human resource management practices and which is affordable.

It is important to recognize that in some employment situations sickness leave, with pay, can increase considerably the incidence of absence. This appears to be particularly so in the public sector where sick leave may be seen as another form of holiday entitlement.

Private medical treatment   Private medical treatment is one particular fringe benefit that is being granted to many more employees these days. The direct advantage to the company is that employees can be treated at a time convenient to the company and not when it is convenient to the National Health Service. This is particularly appropriate to key members of the staff. Sometimes the cover provided by the company includes the employee's family as well.

Some employers may feel it is too expensive or even inappropriate to pay for this service, but even so employers can arrange 'group rates'* and monthly deductions of premiums from salaries enabling their employees to benefit from preferential rates at no cost to the employer. A combination of these two methods can be adopted where senior employees are paid for by the company and the remainder of the employees have the option of participating in the group scheme.

This chapter has dealt with the major benefits that can be offered to employees. All employees will not qualify for all these benefits automatically. Some benefits should be incentives to stay with the organization and to seek promotion; therefore they should be granted only for service and seniority. On the other hand some may be offered to all employees upon joining, for example, discounted purchasing facilities.

Fringe benefits play a vital part in an employer's personnel policy as the nature of all the benefits offered influences considerably the type of employees who will be attracted to the employer and who will stay. And since the cost of fringe benefits can add another 25 per cent to the payroll cost, it is essential that the range of benefits offered and their likely effects are fully considered.

Further reading

Armstrong, M., *A Handbook of Human Resource Management*, London: Kogan Page, 1988

Pratt, K. J., and Bennett, S. C., *Elements of Personnel Management*, 3rd ed., Wokingham: GEE, 1989

Sisson K., (ed.), *Personnel Management in Britain*, Oxford: Blackwell, 1989

*The HCIMA has negotiated a group rate with BUPA for its members who may not have the benefit of a company scheme.

Thomason, G., *Textbook of Human Resource Management*, London: Institute of Personnel Management, 1988

Torrington, D. and Hall, L., *Personnel Management – A New Approach*, London: Prentice Hall, 1987

Questions

1 Describe the objectives of fringe benefits schemes and the various alternatives in regular use.

2 Discuss which you consider to be the most important principles if fringe benefits are to be effective. What do you understand by 'effective'?

3 Discuss what external factors influence the nature of fringe benefits.

4 Discuss the relationship between fringe benefits, incentive schemes and alternative methods of wage and salary administration.

5 Discuss the role played by fringe benefits, wages and/or salaries and incentives in achieving an employer's human resource policy.

6 Using an employer you know well, evaluate their approach to fringe benefits.

chapter 14

Labour turnover and termination of employment

One of the problems in considering the industry's labour turnover is that 'the industry' consists of many sectors and there are also many differences within sectors. Consequently we find tremendous differences both between and within sectors. For example, in many public sector organizations such as the school meals service, labour turnover can be in single figures. On the other hand in the private sector – fast-food, for example – labour turnover can easily be well over 100% per annum. Turnover figures of several hundred per cent per annum are not unusual.

There are of course many factors influencing labour turnover. These include:

1 The nature of the industry itself: e.g. seasonal; limited career structures; fragmented; large number of small units; high proportion of 'secondary' labour force.
2 The nature of individual units: e.g. location; size; staff/work ratios.
3 The nature of individual managers: e.g. lacking formal management training; acceptance of high labour turnover.

These and many other factors are discussed in more detail by Mars *et al.* (1979), Johnson (1980) and Hornsey and Dann (1984).

For the industry as a whole the HCITB estimated labour turnover to be 95 per cent per annum (HCITB 1984). If one adds the vacancies arising from growth, in the region of 1.4 million vacancies arise each year. The pattern is shown in Figure 14.1.

In order to understand and control labour turnover properly at a unit level, not only is it important to analyse it by department as illustrated in Figure 14.2, but it is necessary to look at the 'survival curve'. This is a means of identifying when labour turnover is most critical; is it occurring during the early induction period, the subsequent 'settling-in' period or after employees have become settled? Such an analysis (see Figure 14.3) can indicate causes such as poor induction or a change of supervisor or manager. With such information the employer may be able to take appropriate measures.

Whilst labour turnover is analysed by department and by length of service, the actual reasons for employees leaving need to be determined also. Some employers do little or nothing about such an analysis while others obtain very

Figure 14.1   *Annual number of recruits and sources*

Recruited from:			
	Outside the industry	Other sectors within the industry	The same sector (including promotions)	Total
Managers	19,000	22,000	12,000	53,000
Supervisors	17,000	15,000	30,000	62,000
Craftspeople	41,000	54,000	76,000	171,000
Operatives and others	718,000	180,000	193,000	1,091,000
TOTAL	**795,000**	**271,000**	**311,000**	**1,377,000**

Figure 14.2   *Labour turnover in three hotels*

Sampled departments	Two large London hotels A	B	Medium-sized county town hotel
Kitchens	140%	80% ⎫	47%
Wash-up, porters	550%	135% ⎬	
Coffee shop	125%	100%	17%
Hall porters	68%	105%	0%
Housekeeping	150%	146%	28%
Weighted average *all* departments	110%	105%	40%

detailed information. Figure 14.4 shows how one of the fast food companies analyses employees' reasons for leaving.

With such information management may then be in a position to consider changes and improvements to their personnel practices in order to reduce labour turnover. Causes of turnover may include:

1   Wage and salary rates falling behind the rates offered by competitors.
2   Better conditions generally (such as reduction in split shifts) being offered by competitors.
3   The decline in quality of supervision and departmental managers.
4   Recruitment, selection, induction and training practices needing improvement.
5   Unfair or uneven work distribution.

The analysis of labour turnover is discussed further in Chapter 17. Both the staff turnover report itself and the information deduced from such reports are of a statistical nature, that is, they are mainly concerned with groups and numbers of people. The actual termination procedures adopted, however, are concerned with individuals and these are divided into two main types: voluntary, where the employees leave of their own free will, and involuntary, where the employer decides that employment should terminate.

Figure 14.3   *A survival curve*

Figure 14.4   *A list of reasons for leaving an employer*

Codes:

1	Another job	11	Retirement
2	Returned to college or school	*12	Failure to return after leave of absence
3	Medical reasons	*13	Conclusion of temporary employment
4	Marriage	*14	Reduction in labour force
5	Relocation	*15	Unsatisfactory performance
6	Dissatisfaction with wages	*16	Misconduct
7	Undisclosed personal reasons	*17	Gross misconduct
8	Resigned without notice	*18	Absenteeism
9	Dissatisfaction with work	*19	Permanent disability
10	Dissatisfaction with conditions	*20	Death

*Involuntary leavers

Voluntary termination

Almost invariably this arises where an employee has the opportunity to take other employment that offers more attractive conditions, but, because employees leaving voluntarily have not been dismissed by the employer, they are probably the employees that an employer would most like to retain. It is for this reason that these employees should be interviewed to determine their reasons for leaving. The *exit* interview may reveal specific information regarding conditions of employment, competitors' conditions, the quality or otherwise of supervision, training and selection procedures. Finally, a well-conducted exit interview can ensure that employees leave on good terms. Ex-employees are, after all, to some extent an employer's ambassadors, broadcasting his reputation among other potential employees. In some cases it may be advisable to supplement an exit interview by talking to a departing employee's past supervisor in order to check the reasons given by the employee.

Involuntary terminations

In this industry, along with some others, dismissal is often used as the first remedy for a variety of ills, rather than being used as the last. In fact, in some sectors of the industry dismissals are quite indiscriminate; for example, it is common practice for complete bar staffs to be dismissed because of bad liquor stock results. The innocent suffer the same fate (dismissal) as the guilty.

One recognizes that pilferage in this industry is a serious problem, but other measures such as more methodical selection, checking of references, better conditions of employment, and better career prospects, along with stricter and more accurate means of control, are better solutions than indiscriminate sackings. Where pilferers are caught, however, they should be prosecuted rather than being allowed to get away with their crime, often because the employer wants no trouble or publicity.

The dismissal of an employee is a very serious measure, particularly now that the law provides employees with protection against unfair dismissal. The law on dismissals is dealt with in more detail in Chapter 16.

The vast majority of terminations, however, are not a consequence of pilferage, and in most cases are as unwanted by the employer as by the employee. The most common reasons are:

1 Lack of ability.
2 Continual late arrival, absenteeism, or disobedience.
3 Personality.

In all these cases when contemplating dismissal other remedies should be considered first; for example, lack of ability may well be the fault of the employer because he did not select or place the employee carefully enough, or because he did not provide appropriate training. In the second case tighter discipline could possibly overcome the problem and a discussion with the employee to discover the underlying causes would possibly be helpful. In the third case, if it is a 'clash of personalities', and if the organization is big enough, a transfer may be the solution. On the other hand, once a decision is made to terminate employment it must always be borne in mind that the employer may have to prove in an industrial tribunal that the dismissal was 'fair' as laid down by the Employment Protection (Consolidation) Act 1978. Documentary evidence, therefore, of unsatisfactory work or behaviour, and of warnings given may be vital in proving the case. It is important, therefore, to operate a formal system of warnings that can be used as a last resort by the employer should he be called to an industrial tribunal. Typical warnings could look like those shown in Figure 14.5.

Redundancy

The other main form of involuntary termination is of course redundancy. This is where a job is eliminated owing to such things as changes in methods, or mergers. In this case the law lays down certain minimal payments to be made to the employee. In addition to this payment some employers, recognizing the

Figure 14.5　*Examples of written warnings*

The following examples are all reproduced courtesy of Trusthouse Forte Hotels.

RECORD OF VERBAL WARNING Disciplinary Procedure (THF)

Employee's name: ....

Hotel: ....

Department: ....

Position: ....
I have had reason to issue a verbal warning to the above employee in respect of:
....

Signed: ....
　　　　　　　　　　Supervisor/Head of Department/Manager

Date: ....
To be retained on the employee's personal record file, and removed at the end of six months if there is no further offence.

FIRST WRITTEN WARNING – CONDUCT Disciplinary Procedure (THF)

Employee's name: ....

Hotel: ....

Department: ....

Position: ....
Further to your interview on .... (date), regarding the following offence, I have cause to issue you a first written warning as to your future conduct.
Details and date of offence ....

In the event of a recurrence or continuance of the above, or any other breach of discipline within twelve months, you will be issued with a final warning and thereafter will be liable, should there be no improvement in your record, to disciplinary action, which could include dismissal.

Signed: ....
　　　　　　　　　　　　　　　　　　　　　　　　Manager
Date: ....
A copy of this warning will be retained in your personal file, but will be removed at the end of twelve months if your conduct has been satisfactory during that period.

I confirm that I have received a copy of this written warning.

Signed: ....

Date: ....

FIRST WRITTEN WARNING – PERFORMANCE Disciplinary Procedure (THF)

Employee's name: ....

Hotel: ....

Department: ....

Position: ....
I regret I have to warn you that considerable improvement must occur in your performance as set out below. Assistance and guidance will be given to you to achieve the required standard, but unless this is reached within the period specified, you will be issued with a final warning, and thereafter will be liable, should there be no improvement in your performance, to dismissal.

Area of sub-standard performance   Details of improvement required
....
Signed: ....
                                                                                   Manager
Date: ....

Date by which performance will be reviewed: ....

A copy of this warning will be retained in your personal file, but will be removed at the end of twelve months if your conduct has been satisfactory during that period.

I confirm that I have received a copy of this written warning.

Signed: ....

Date: ....

FINAL WARNING – PERFORMANCE Disciplinary Procedure (THF)

Employee's name: ....

Hotel: ....

Department: ....

Position: ....
I regret to have to tell you that following the written warning regarding your performance given to you on .... there has been no improvement in your performance. This is therefore a final warning and if there is no improvement by .... you will be liable to dismissal.

Signed: ....
                                                                                   Manager
Date: ....

A copy of this warning will be retained on your personal file but will be removed at the end of twelve months if your conduct has been satisfactory during that period.

I confirm that I have received a copy of this written warning.

Signed: ....

Date: ....

FINAL WARNING – CONDUCT Disciplinary Procedure (THF)

Employee's name: ....

Hotel: ....

Department: ....

Position: ....

Further to your interview on .... (date), I have cause to issue a second and final warning as to your future conduct.

Details and date of offence ....

Any recurrence or continuance of the above, or any other breach of discipline within twelve months, will lead to disciplinary action, which could include dismissal.

Signed: ....
                                                              Manager
Date: ....

A copy of this warning will be retained in your personal file, but will be removed at the end of twelve months if your conduct has been satisfactory during that period.

I confirm that I have received a copy of this written warning.

Signed: ....

Date: ....

STATEMENT OF DISCIPLINARY ACTION Disciplinary Procedure (THF)

Employee's name: ....

Hotel: ....

Department: ....

Position: ....

Further to your interview on .... (date), it has been decided that the following disciplinary action will be taken (delete as appropriate).

1. Dismissal with .... weeks notice
2. Summary dismissal for gross misconduct

Details and date of offence ....

If you wish to appeal against this disciplinary action you have a right to do so in accordance with the Disciplinary Procedure. The Personnel Officer is available to advise you how to do this.

Signed: ....

Position: ....

Date: ....

TO BE SIGNED BY THE EMPLOYEE
Right of Appeal
I acknowledge that I have received a copy of this statement. I understand that I have the right of appeal against this disciplinary action which *I do/do not wish to take up. Any appeal must be made within 5 working days of the date of dismissal.

Signed: ....   Date: ....

*Delete as appropriate

inadequacy of the amounts awarded by the redundancy legislation, allow what is known sometimes as 'severance pay'. This is additional to redundancy pay and is usually calculated by using some formula that recognizes age, service and present earnings. Employers must recognize, however, that redundancies are sometimes the fault of their own lack of forward planning. If planning, and this includes human resource planning, is conducted thoroughly, many redundancies can be avoided by allowing natural wastage to reduce the labour force. But once it becomes apparent that redundancies are unavoidable this fact should be discussed with employee representatives so that plans for a properly phased run-down can be agreed.* This may include voluntary early retirements and compensation payments for voluntary terminations. In some cases it may be essential to keep employees working to a certain date in which case special 'incentive payments' to stay in the job will have to be agreed.

Retirement

The last type of termination is, of course, when a person goes into retirement and these days some of the more enlightened employers recognize that their responsibility extends beyond providing a pension and a gold watch. In fact, they provide some form of pre-retirement preparation that enables an individual to adjust to completely changed circumstances, because not only does he or she suddenly have greatly increased free time, but income may drop considerably and contact with friends and colleagues may be reduced. This may take the form of a steadily reducing working week with attendance at a pre-retirement course.

Exit interviews

The importance of interviewing employees when they leave was touched upon briefly earlier in this chapter, but it cannot be over-emphasized that the numbers and types of people leaving an organization are one critical indication of the success or otherwise of an employer's personnel and employee relations policy. Employees leaving can be a valuable source from which to learn where improvements in personnel practice can be made. With few exceptions, therefore, all employees should be interviewed before their departure, in order to:

1 Learn the real reasons for their departure (unless these are patently obvious).
2 Pin-point trouble spots and causes of irritation and frustration.
3 Inform employees of all their benefits and rights, such as pensions, and insurances. In the case of pensioners they will need to know what rights they retain such as insurances, holidays and discount purchasing facilities.
4 Explain the make-up of the final pay cheque including such items as holiday pay.

*This is laid down in Employment Protection legislation.

5   Hand over the P45 or obtain a forwarding address.
6   Collect any company property that may be outstanding such as cash advances, equipment, uniforms, protective clothing.
7   Part on friendly terms, if possible, so that ex-employees act as 'ambassadors'.

Who dismisses?

The question of who actually dismisses employees is a contentious one. Many line managers feel that they need to have this right as a support to, and indication of, their authority. Others, on the other hand, would dearly like to abdicate the responsibility to someone else such as a personnel officer. However, because line managers, in the last resort, are responsible for the results of their departments they should carry this burden and they should make the decision assisted and guided by specialists, where they are employed, such as personnel officers. In many circumstances it is best for the 'grandfather' principle to be applied to dismissals. This means that no person can dismiss subordinates without the approval of his own superior. Furthermore, in large organizations the approval of the personnel officer or department should also be obtained because they will know if any opportunities exist for an employee about to be dismissed or if legal consequences are likely. It has now become common practice in many companies for the right to dismiss to be held by the unit manager only, with the subordinate having the right to suspend and no more.

The industry: labour turnover

Many managers in the industry hold the view that the industry's high turnover rate is not as costly as some claim. Instead they maintain it has some beneficial effects.

First, some turnover is the inevitable result of the seasonal nature of the industry, although past patterns are now altering in many places as a result of such factors as increased tourism and conference business; for example, Brighton's season is very different from what it was twenty years ago and London has two peaks and two troughs.

Second, turnover, it is claimed, provides job variety and satisfaction for the industry's many semi-skilled and unskilled workers.

Because of the relatively low degree of skill needed in many jobs, and because many jobs are transferable between employers, the amount of training is minimal. Consequently the industry is able to accept a rate of labour turnover which in other industries, such as manufacturing, would probably be insupportable.*

The turnover of staff is one barometer of the success or otherwise of an

---

*See Angus Fisher of Reading University in *Catering Times*, October 1980.

employer's personnel management policies. Generally speaking, the higher the rate of turnover the poorer are his relationships with his employees and the lower the turnover, the better the relationships. High labour turnover often results in low levels of efficiency.

In most cases, when an employee leaves an employer, the employer should examine the circumstances very carefully to see whether he is in some way responsible for what is, after all, some degree of failure on his part. He may have failed the employee for a variety of reasons including wrong selection or placement in the first place, inadequate training, unsatisfactory conditions of employment or just poor management.

Further reading

Bevan, S., *The Management of Labour Turnover*, Brighton: Institute of Manpower Studies, 1987

Hornsey, T. and Dann, D., *Manpower Management in the Hotel and Catering Industry*, London: Batsford, 1984

Johnson, K., Labour Turnover in Hotels – Revisited, *The Service Industries Journal*, London: 1985

Mars, G., Mitchell, P., and Bryant D., *Manpower Problems in the Hotel and Catering Industry*, Farnborough: Saxon House, 1976

Wasmuth, W. J., and Davis, S. W., Managing employee turnover, *Cornell Hotel and Restaurant Administration Quarterly*, **23**, No. 4, 1983

Wasmuth, W. J., and Davis S. W., Why Employees Leave, *Cornell Hotel and Restaurant Administration Quarterly*, **24**, No. 1, 1983

Wasmuth, W. J., and Davis S. W., Strategies for Managing Employee Turnover, *Cornell Hotel and Restaurant Administration Quarterly*, **24**, No. 2, 1983

Questions

1 Describe how labour turnover may be measured, and discuss the different reasons for the termination of employment.
2 Discuss key ways in which labour turnover may be reduced.
3 Discuss what external factors may influence labour turnover.
4 Discuss the proposition that high labour turnover is not always a bad thing.
5 Using an employer you know well, evaluate their approach to managing labour turnover and terminations.

chapter 15

Industrial relations

The term 'industrial relations' has many different definitions. At one extreme are those who see industrial relations as being concerned with purely economic issues, that is the 'pay for work' relationship. At another extreme are those who see industrial relations as being concerned with politics and as an extension of party politics.

A useful definition of industrial relations, however, is that ' "industrial relations" describes the systems, formal and informal, public and private, for allocating rewards to employees for their services and regulating the conditions under which these services are provided' (Alton W. Craig, International Industrial Relations Association, Third World Congress, London 1973).

More simply the term industrial relations is generally used to describe the relationship that exists between the management of an undertaking and its work people, organized and represented often, but not always, within a trade union framework. In the hotel and catering industry the degree of organization of employees within trade unions varies considerably. At one end of the scale, industrial and institutional catering, more than sixty per cent of all employees' conditions of employment can be determined by collective bargaining; yet at the other end of the scale, hotels and restaurants, the number of trade union members is still comparatively low.

The attitude of management in the industry towards trade unions varies considerably too. Generally speaking, those managers with experience of trade unions accept their existence and believe that they have a useful role to play. On the other hand, most vociferous opponents of trade unions are to be found among those hotel and restaurant proprietors and managers who, by and large, have no experience of trade unions.

As stated earlier the degree of union involvement varies considerably from sector to sector, but, if examined carefully, it appears that, generally speaking, there are certain factors which either contribute towards, or militate against, strong union involvement. Bains and Price, in their book *Industrial Relations in Britain* (1984), identify a number of determinants concerning union growth or decline. These include:

1   Industrial structure.
2   Government action.
3   Business cycle.

Figure 15.1 *Factors contributing to low or high union involvement*

Low union membership	High union membership
Small units — small workforces Many part-timers and casuals 'Entrepreneurial' opportunities, e.g. tipping Ownership and management combined or closely related 'Secret' contracts Hostile ownership No other union involvement No tradition of union involvement	Large units — large workforces Few part-timers and casuals No 'entrepreneurial' opportunities Management distinct from ownership No 'secret' contracts Other unions involved in the enterprise Traditions of union involvement
Some examples: Restaurants, fast food, hotels, public house staff	*Some examples:* Hospital catering, university and college catering, school meals, Civil Service catering, public house managers

4 Composition of potential membership.
5 Employer policies.
6 Personal and job related characteristics.
7 Union leadership.

The level of union membership in the industry is looked at in Figure 15.3. Using some of the determinants identified by Bains and Price. It is possible to conclude that union membership is low for the following reasons:

1 The large numbers of small establishments that make it difficult for trade union officials to contact potential members and to organize meetings. (The average hotel has only about 25 bedrooms.)
2 The highly dispersed and departmentalized labour force, even in the largest establishments, resulting in the absence of cohesive groups of workers with common interests.
3 The large number of part-time employees who are not so interested in belonging to a trade union as full-time employees.
4 A large number of foreign employees who are in the United Kingdom for short periods of time.
5 Shift working which makes it difficult to contact and organize employees.
6 Tipping which introduces an 'entrepreneurial' element into work, which many employees fear a trade union would try to eliminate.
7 Individual and secret contracts made between the employer and the employee.
8 No tradition of trade union membership within some sectors of the industry.

9 Employers' resistance, because employers fear that they have more to lose than to gain from the trade union movement.

Development of the trade union movement

In order to see the hotel and catering industry's relations in perspective it is important to look at industrial relations generally and, in particular, to examine the development of organizations of work people and of employers.

The organization of employers and workers came about from the eighteenth century onwards with the emergency of modern industry. Before this time most conditions of employment had been regulated by the State, often through the local magistrate, and it was an offence in common law to do anything (even with the intention of improving one's own conditions of work) which might have been in restraint of trade. A combination of workers, therefore, to strike or to do anything else to improve conditions that adversely affected the employer's business, was a criminal act of conspiracy. But at the same time it was illegal for employers to form such combinations. As industry became more complex, the State regulations of wages fell into disuse and employers themselves were able to fix conditions of employment. Legislation followed banning combinations in one trade after another until the situation was made quite clear when the Combination Acts 1799–1800 provided for a general prohibition in all trades of combinations of employees or employers.

However, following the Napoleonic Wars there was an economic depression together with a movement to improve conditions which resulted in the repeal, in 1824, of the Combination Laws. The effect of this was to allow workers to enter into combinations for the purpose of regulating wages and other conditions without their committing the crime of conspiracy. This Act (the Combination Laws Repeal Act 1824) was followed shortly by another which somewhat circumscribed workers' rights, but it still preserved the right to withhold labour by collective action and this right has never been withdrawn although current legislation makes it more difficult to instigate certain types of industrial action without risk of penalties.

Subsequent acts, including the Trade Union Act 1871 and the Conspiracy and Protection of Property Act 1875, gave trade unions legal status and also permitted peaceful picketing. Then the Trade Disputes Act 1906 protected a trade union from being sued for alleged wrongful acts committed by it or on its behalf. Thus trade unions were freed of any risk of a *civil* liability arising from their actions. A variety of other legislation followed which repealed certain preceding legislation, covered the amalgamation of trade unions, and tied up some other aspects that were not satisfactory.

However, the most notable legislation to date was the Industrial Relations Act of 1971, which replaced most preceding legislation regarding trade unions and followed both the main political parties' examination of the increasingly complex and potentially disruptive industrial relations scene. This Act granted to an individual the right to belong or not to belong to a trade union. This was subsequently repealed with many other provisions by the Trade Unions and Labour Relations Act 1974. However, certain provisions particularly relating to 'unfair dismissal' remained to protect the individual, but have since been altered by subsequent employment legislation.

Present position

The trade union movement, along with other sectors of our society, is undergoing a period of mergers and rationalizations. At the end of 1972 there were about 480 trade unions whose members totalled about eleven million, in 1987 there were only 373 unions with 10.7 million members, in 1989 there were about 8.6 million members of unions affiliated to the TUC. Of course, a significant proportion of union members are outside the TUC, principally the Electrician's Union.

In some cases there is strong competition among unions for membership, and one notable case was in fact the hotel and catering industry where the Transport and General Workers' Union and the National Union of General and Municipal Workers came into conflict over recruiting hotel workers in Torquay. This competition is likely to increase as unions see their membership in the more traditional sectors (e.g. the Transport and General Workers Union membership fell from over 2 million in 1979 to 1.3 million in 1990) continue to decline and service industries and part-time women workers, in particular, become more important. The General, Municipal and Boilermakers Union formed a specialist union, the Hotel and Catering Workers Union, to meet this need. The National Union of Railwaymen has formed a specialist branch also, the National Union of Hotel and Catering Employees, whilst the Transport and General Workers Union formed a specialist section known as Hotels, Catering and Leisure.

The strength of the trade union movement obviously stems from its ability to present a united front, and therefore many individual unions join federations to further strengthen their movement. These federations are, however, in most cases rather loose, and the responsibility for action rests with the individual unions. There is no such strong federation in the hotel and catering industry.

The trade union movement comes together within the Trades Union Congress (TUC), the aims of which are:

To promote the interests of all its affiliated organizations and generally to improve the economic and social conditions of workers.

The TUC, as with the federations of unions, has little authority over individual unions, but it does oblige affiliated unions to keep its General Council informed of any trade disputes that may involve large numbers of work people.

In addition to the TUC there are two main groups of unions which are independent of the TUC. These are the Council of Managerial and Professional Staffs and the Federation of Managerial, Professional and General Associations. The government was reported to be supportive of these bodies as alternatives to the TUC and its more traditional values.

The role of trade unions

Trade unions are primarily concerned with representing their members in order to obtain what is considered by their members to be reasonable conditions of employment. Reasonable is, of course, relative; it may mean maintaining one's position in an 'earnings league' or it may mean preserving one's purchasing power.

Although unions are concerned with obtaining increased earnings they also strive to improve their members' other conditions of employment such as time off, holidays, safety and status. They do, in addition, show particular concern over job security and, very often, important political issues.

Their roles can be evaluated from a number of different perspectives.

Economic – Political

On the one hand unions may be concerned only with improving their members' conditions and, at the other extreme, unions may be an extension of a political movement. The Labour Party grew out of the British trade union movement. Some union leaders may use their unions in order to further their own political ends which may have little relationship with the wishes of the rank and file membership.

Capital – Labour

Another view is concerned with the relative rights of those who provide labour and capital. There are those who believe that ownership bestows certain inalienable rights, whereas others believe that those who provide their labour have equal rights to those of the providers of capital.

Democracy – Autocracy (Pluralist–Unitarist)

Related to the former is the argument about the degree of participation in decision making. There are those who believe that managers, because of training and experience, should be responsible for taking decisions, whereas there are others who hold the view that decisions should be shared by all who are affected by them.

Rank and file versus union leadership

An important discussion is the extent to which union leadership is really representative of the membership. It is argued that the very process of moving up the union hierarchy separates leaders from their members. Many of the Conservative government's measures in the 1980s were directed at reducing the power of senior officers of trade unions.

Individual rights versus group rights

An important discussion, particularly where 'closed shops' may be involved, relates to the rights of individuals to choose whether to belong to a trade union or not. On the one hand it is argued that the rights of individuals must be upheld; on the other hand it is argued that the majority has greater rights. Certainly this would appear to be what democracy is about.

In essence however, whichever perspective or perspectives are adopted, industrial relations is concerned, explicitly or implicitly, with the power of the participants to influence the distribution of the wealth they generate or the resources they have made available. Unions themselves claim to be democratic organizations, that the organization represents the wishes of the majority of its members. To what extent union leaders do represent their members', or their own, aspirations varies from union to union. However, Figure 15.2 shows how one large union, the parent union of the Hotel and Catering Workers' Union, is structured.

Types of union

Over the years unions have evolved into four main types.

Craft unions

These usually consist of members with specific trade skills.

General unions

These unions consist mainly of members with little or no specific trade skills and they have no skill or training requirements. The general unions constitute the largest unions in Britain today (e.g. Transport and General Workers Union).

Industrial unions

These unions consist of most workers in one industry (e.g. the National Union of Railwaymen).

White collar unions

These unions consist of administrative, clerical and managerial employees (e.g. MATSA, a subsidiary of GMBTU).

Figure 15.2　*Structure of a union*

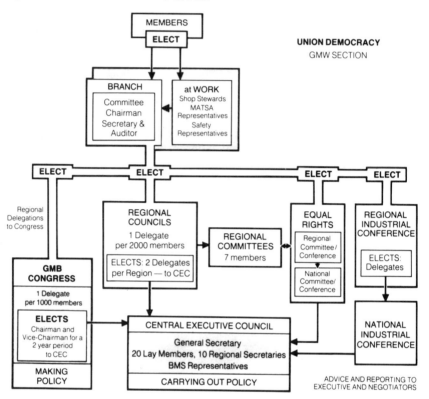

Employers' associations

The first employers' associations of any importance were probably the merchant guilds and livery companies which existed throughout Europe from the early Middle Ages. They dealt with a variety of matters that affected trade and labour.

With the repeal of the combination laws and because of pressure from the growing trade union movement, employers' organizations grew rapidly during the nineteenth century. Nowadays they are, generally speaking, organized on a trade or industry-wide basis and because of this they deal with matters of trade, such as encouraging government to take defensive measures against foreign competition, and with matters of employment, such as negotiating industry-wide conditions of employment.

These employers' or trade associations come together in various national bodies, the main one being the Confederation of British Industries (CBI), which has individual employers, trade associations, employers' organizations, and nationalized industries within its membership. In the private sector, the British Hotels, Restaurants and Caterers Association and the Brewers' Society are the hotel and catering industry's principal trade or employers' associations.

The conduct of negotiation and consultation varies considerably from employer to employer and from industry to industry. In some cases all negotiations will take place at national level between the trade union concerned and the employers' association. This is sometimes referred to as the 'formal' system. In other cases all discussions and negotiations will take place 'informally' at plant level, that is, between the local employer and his own employees.

Main types of agreement

There are three main types of agreement normally entered into between employers and trade unions.

Recognition agreements

These are usually the first type of agreement entered into. Under such agreements the employer normally agrees to recognize the union in certain instances, such as representing members in grievance and disciplinary matters.

Negotiating agreements

Under a negotiating agreement, an employer agrees to recognize a union's right to negotiate on behalf of its members and employees doing the same work as the union's members. As an example, one major hotel company has such an agreement with the Hotel and Catering Workers' Union. Although less than 20 per cent of the company's employees are members of the HCWU the negotiating agreement actually sets rates for virtually all the company's staff.

Substantive agreements

These contain the 'substance' of an agreement and include elements such as pay, hours and overtime rates.

Procedural agreements

These lay down the various procedures to be followed, such as dates for agreements to be made, procedures to be followed in the absence of agreements.

Industrial relations in the hotel and catering industry

Trade union membership within the hotel and catering industry, excluding local authorities, is, generally speaking, very low (see Figure 15.3). Estimates for 1990 were that, including industrial and institutional catering, there were about 100,000 members including the members of the National Association of Licensed House Managers. This means that probably approaching 6 per cent of the total labour force are union members. This shows hardly an increase on the estimated 5 per cent in 1978. Membership is relatively strong in the industrial and institutional catering sector (about 20 per cent of all employees) because the catering staff are frequently part of a large unionized workforce of another industry. Membership is also relatively high in local authority and hospital catering.

In the public sector the major bodies concerned with industrial relations are:

Hospitals – Whitley Council.
Education (e.g. colleges) – National Joint Council for Local Authority Service (Manual Workers).
School meals – officers – Soulbury Committee
            manual staff – National Joint Council for Local Authority Services (Manual Workers).

These bodies are negotiating bodies consisting of representatives of employers and trade union representatives.

Individual contracts

A major feature of the employee relationship in the hotels sector of the industry is the secret and individual nature of contracts (Mars and Mitchell, 1976). Because the vast majority of employers are small with only a few staff, contracts are made between the employee and the employer, who offers terms that will solve his immediate staff problem. These terms may be better than those currently enjoyed by other similar staff. Consequently, an element of secrecy is expected. This system of individual contracts is made easier because a considerable proportion of recruitment is informal, on a person to person basis and may involve undeclared cash payments. While managers believe that this individual and secret contract works to their advantage, it creates ambiguity and confusion which causes grievances and high labour turnover.

Wages Councils

In 1945 with the enactment of the Wages Councils Act and the creation of wages boards it was recognized that where employees were not organized there was insufficient pressure on employers to ensure that wage levels and other conditions kept up with those offered to other sections of the community. In this industry this had been recognized earlier and resulted in the Catering

Figure 15.3 The principal unions involved in the hotel, catering and associated industries

Sector of the hotel and catering industry	Principal unions involved	Approximate number of members					
		1973	1978	1980	1982	1986	1990
Hotels and restaurants	GMB*	20,000	25,000	30,000	31,000	33,000	N/A
	TGWU	3,000	9,000	9,000	7,750	6,000	4,000
	NUR	3,000	9,500	10,000	8,500	4,500	2,700
	TSSA					750	
	USDAW	4,000			2,000		2,000
Industrial and institutional	GMB		2,600				N/A
	TGWU	30,000	30,000	30,000	25,500	20,000	20,000
	USDAW	8,000	8,000	10,000	11,000		11,000
Public house managers	NALHM	10,000	15,000	17,500	18,000	15,500	13,000
	ACTSS	500	1,000		750	600	250
Motorway services	USDAW			2,500	2,500		2,500
	TGWU			1,500	2,500		2,000
Club stewards	USDAW		3,000	3,000	4,750		2,500
Bar staff	GMB						N/A
	TGWU		6,000	6,000		7,000	5,000
	USDAW				1,000		1,000
	NUCS					2,760	2,400
Local authority and NHS catering supervisors	NUPE	250,000	250,000	250,000		250,000	250,000
	NALGO				700		
	NUPE					2,000	2,000
	TGWU						5,000

*The GMB membership is now largely organized within their specialist union; the Hotel and Catering Workers' Union.

Wages Act of 1943 which created the Catering Wages Board. This board laid down minimum conditions of employment. However, this Act and others have since been superseded by the Wages Council Act 1959 which regulates wages and other conditions for employees in the industry through Wages Councils which include employer and employee representatives. Councils exist for the following sectors of the industry:

Licensed residential establishments and restaurants.
Licensed non-residential establishments and restaurants.
Unlicensed places of refreshment.

The rates laid down by the various councils, however, are considered by most employers and employees to be absolute minima and market forces generally oblige employers to pay above these rates. The value of Wages Councils nowadays is therefore questionable and it is hoped by many that these will be phased out. The Wages Act 1986 reduced the scope of Wages Councils to merely specifying a minimum wage for all employment within an industry and some hold the view that the Conservative government will eliminate some, if not all, wages councils in the 1990s.

'Manpower Policy in the Hotels and Restaurant Industry' – EDC report

Probably one of the most important reports on human resource management in the hotel and catering industry was 'Manpower Policy in the Hotels and Restaurant Industry' (NEDO 1975). Whilst this report was written over fifteen years ago it still contains much of relevance to the industry today.

The main findings of this report are summarized here and are discussed at greater length in appropriate chapters.

Social trends

Four main areas affect employment within the industry:

1 Increased employment legislation.
2 Increased demand for leisure, higher standards of living and social status.
3 More democratic forms of social control.
4 Increasing trade union membership. (In 1990 trade union membership was declining.)

If, therefore, the industry is to attract an adequate supply of the workforce, it must gear its management style and personnel policies accordingly. In fact, the EDC's research showed that the industry is more attractive to younger people than older people because of their needs (listed above in 1–4). Only those employers able to meet these needs will be able to retain the younger working people.

Fewer but larger companies

Over the last few years, the number of large companies has reduced. While this may provide opportunities for better work prospects and higher earnings (due to economies of scale), other problems, associated with administration and management of complex organizations, present themselves.

Labour costs

The difference between earnings of hotel staff and those in other industries has increased with the consequence that the industry is not viewed very favourably as an employer. As in so many cases, such comparisons can be misleading, however. Many of the staff receive board and lodging or board at least, so they are insulated somewhat from rapid inflation on such items as fares, fuel and food.

Employment policies

The EDC pointed to the need to improve staff retention so that pressure is taken off staff recruitment. Staff retention will only improve if employment policies are geared to the hotel employment market. Such policies will have to cover hours, pay, shifts, use of labour, management style and co-operation with the official agencies.

Senior management of companies

While the EDC research showed that deficiencies will not be corrected without new attitudes and approaches of unit managers, it is the responsibility of senior managers of companies to ensure that such changes occur through manpower planning which is integrated with the general company policy.

The trade associations

The image of the industry as an employer should be improved by co-operative effort of employers channelled through the trade associations.

These were the major findings of the EDC research and various detailed aspects of the report are referred to in other chapters of this book. The key to improvement probably lies in developing effective consultative machinery in the first place. Several other reports on manpower within the industry have also been produced, such as the BHRCA's *Manpower Problems in the Hotel and Catering Industry, Great Expectations,* and these largely confirmed the findings of the EDC report.

The larger employers claim that they are making considerable improvements to the industry's conditions and reputation and they claim their lead will be bound to set the pace for smaller employers. Such changes will take many years, however, because an industry employing about 2 million people has considerable inertia and change will not be easy. It is likely that its employees will remain, in 'take home pay' terms, amongst the lowest paid for a long time into the future or until productivity improvements make it possible to increase rates of pay. See also Chapter 19 on Labour Costs and Productivity.

Consultation

If good industrial relations are to be achieved, discussion must take place between management and staff on all matters related to conditions and methods of work. The size of the organization does not affect this principle; the only variation to it is one of degree, as the actual size and nature of the organization determines the type and degree of formality of discussions.

Within this industry there are probably three main types of consultative procedure. The first and probably the least formal will be found in the individually owned hotel or restaurant, managed by the proprietor who works in the establishment with his staff numbering up to about twenty. In this case any formal joint consultation or negotiation may be unnecessary as the employer is close to his employees and should be aware of their problems and views. It is his job to keep himself informed of their opinions and feelings and he may well hold informal meetings at regular intervals with all staff. Such meetings may already be held to discuss menus, special functions, etc., and from time to time they should be enlarged to cover methods of work and conditions of employment.

The next level may be found in a hotel or restaurant probably having groups of employees in several departments. Typically this would be a hotel or restaurant complex with from twenty to several hundred employees. In this case there may be small groups of people working together – each group with its own aims – often not the same as those of the organization as a whole. One only needs to think of the conflict between cooks and waiters in many hotels or restaurants to accept that this conflict exists. In this case each department should nominate a representative to meet management's representatives on a regular basis – probably between four and eight times a year. Some formality would be needed and agendas would have to be circulated beforehand and minutes produced afterwards.

The level after this would be in a company or organization with several large units. Each establishment would have its own joint consultative committee, and in addition it may find it worth organizing a company-based joint consultative committee with representatives from each establishment meeting head office management. This system would be most appropriate where a company is heavily represented in an area – London, for example – and because management would wish to discourage unnecessary movements between units caused by varying supervisory or personnel practices within the company's establishments. On the other hand it may not be necessary where an

Figure 15.4   *Industrial relations institutions*

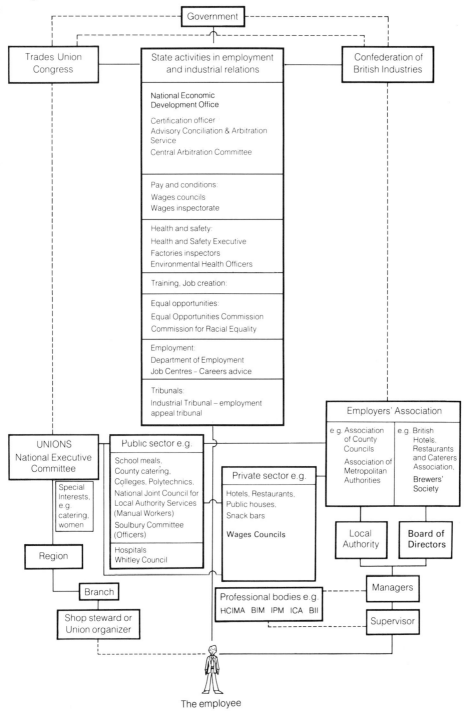

The employee

employer's establishments are located far apart in areas where conditions are different.

These are three examples of different levels of consultation (and possibly negotiation), but whether all three should be conducted with trade union representatives or not is generally for management and the employees to decide. The second and third levels, involving the larger employers, certainly could, and often do, involve trade union representatives.

Benefits of consultation

Managers may rightly ask what benefits can result from their taking the initiative in establishing joint consultation and even bargaining or negotiating procedures with their employees. First, and most important of all, it must be recognized that although employees may have no negotiating machinery they still push up rates of pay and win other concessions by 'voting with their feet'. They move from employer to employer continually looking for higher earnings and employers in turn have continually to increase their rates to attract replacement staff. Seasonal resorts will confirm that this practice is rife. The fear of 'runaway' wage increases consequently is generally exaggerated. Instead, because of continuous collective pressure from the employees their conditions would steadily improve, job security would become greater with the result that the staff turnover rate would almost certainly drop to reasonable proportions. There are many cases in those sections of the industry where trade unions are strong, where the annual staff turnover is not above 10% per annum, the school meals service is one such example. According to the Transport and General Workers' Union, the Penta Hotel at Heathrow which has the highest union membership of the twelve main Heathrow hotels, also has the lowest staff turnover rate. As a result the economies to be made through not having to recruit and train a steady flow of replacement staff are considerable, apart from the benefits of being able to maintain consistent standards.

A second benefit of consultation is a more willing acceptance of change. By nature most people oppose change, but if they have been involved in discussing changes that affect them and they understand the underlying reasons, they will almost certainly be more prepared to make the changes work. A further benefit is that many people have ideas that can improve working methods, and by consultation management can provide the opportunities for these to be expressed. A third view, however, is that whether these are measurable benefits or not, participation in decisions affecting working people is a right – not a privilege granted by management for instrumental reasons (see Chapter 20).

Disadvantages

On the other side of the coin there are disadvantages to be faced when entering into consultation with employees. First, management action will be open to question and discussion, with the consequence that management's decisions may take longer. Furthermore, even confidential information must be made available for discussion. Apart from this, it must be remembered that if trade unions are involved the possibility of industrial action such as working to rule, blacking, banning overtime and even striking must not be ruled out when agreement on such things as pay, working conditions, methods or procedures cannot be reached.

The industry's image

Of less immediate consequence to the individual employer, but of great importance to the industry as a whole, is the need to improve its image.

To improve its image the hotel and catering industry needs to offer conditions that satisfy the average working person's expectations, and this will only be achieved through regular, frank consultation and negotiation between both sides, as happens in many other industries. Without this dialogue and the consequent improvement in conditions the industry will not attract and retain the number of competent work people that are going to be needed in the future.

Establishing consultation

Once the decision has been taken to establish consultation within an organization, the scope of any discussions should not be limited, but should cover *all matters* of interest to both sides, including rates of pay, hours of work, fringe benefits, working methods, and company plans. It should be clear, however, that the purpose of these committees is consultation and not negotiation.

Setting up a staff consultative committee sometimes presents problems, because it is essential that the employees' representatives are chosen, and seen to be chosen by their colleagues and not by management. The outline of a constitution and rules for a staff consultative committee is illustrated in Figure 15.5.

Responsibility for good industrial relations

The responsibility for good industrial relations depends, within each undertaking, upon its management, and this can only result from frank discussion between management and staff. The Industrial Relations Code of Practice places the responsibility for stimulating this dialogue squarely on management. In the section on communication and consultation it says:

Management in co-operation with employee representatives should:
  i) provide opportunities for employees to discuss matters affecting their jobs with those to whom they are responsible:
 ii) ensure that managers are kept informed of the views of employees and of the problems which they may face in meeting management's objectives.

See also the end of Chapter 16 for information on union law.

Figure 15.5   *Staff consultative committee constitution (THF)*

1 Objectives

The object of the Staff Consultative Committee is to provide a means of communication and consultation between the management and staff of the hotel on all matters of mutual interest, including:

(a) Explanation on general information concerning Company activities, policies and procedures.

(b) Business plans for the hotel and current results, expressed in broad terms as percentages, etc.

(c) Ideas for improving sales, standards of performance, efficiency and productivity.

(d) Discussion on staff rules and regulations, and discussion on security matters.

(e) Terms and conditions of employment, staff amenities and welfare facilities. Wage rates/Wage reviews may be discussed in general terms only. The wages or status of an individual member of staff may not be discussed.

(f) Training activities.

(g) Health and Safety at work, including hygiene and welfare. (The hotel Safety & Hygiene Officer should be in attendance during discussion on these items.)

(h) Organising of social, sporting and recreational activities.

2 Membership

The committee shall consist of:

(a) **A Chairman** who shall be the General Manager.

(b) **Another Management Representative** preferably the Personnel Manager or Assistant Manager responsible for personnel.

(c) **A Head of Department or Supervisor:** normally a different Head of Department or Supervisor attending the meeting in rotation.

(d) **Elected Staff Representatives** from each Department of the Hotel (normally there should be between 6 and 12 staff Representatives on the Committee depending on the size of the hotel). They will also act as Safety Representatives for their Departments — *see Guidelines for the duties of Staff Safety Representative*.

(e) **A Secretary** to record the minutes of Meetings of the Committee. Staff Representatives shall be chosen annually by election, other members of the Committee being nominated by management. Should members of the Committee cease to be employed by the Hotel, then membership shall immediately terminate.

3 Attendance

Any member who is absent without adequate reason for two or more consecutive meetings may, at the discretion of the Committee, be disqualified from membership.

4 Co-option

The chairman may invite additional members of management and/or staff to attend meetings to provide special information.

5 Election of Staff Representatives

All staff over the age of 18 years who have been employed for over three months by the hotel shall be entitled to stand for election which shall be conducted annually by Departments. Elections which shall normally be by secret ballot, shall be organised by the Head of Department in consultation with the Hotel Manager, and shall be held normally in January or as required if a vacancy arises during a term of office. All staff on the payroll at the time of the election shall be entitled to one vote. Staff Representatives are entitled to wear a special Company badge whilst they hold office. These badges will be issued by the Hotel Managers and must be returned if the person concerned is no longer the Staff Representative.

6 Officers

The officers shall consist of the Chairman, a Management and Head of Personnel Representative as referred to in Paragraph 2 (a), (b) & (c).

7 Retirement

Staff Representatives shall be elected for one year and may be eligible for re-election every year. Management members shall hold office at the discretion of their superiors.

8 Meetings
(a) Ordinary meetings shall be held at least every two months during normal working hours if possible, and 14 days' notice of the meeting should be given. Items for the Agenda may be submitted to any member of the Committee and the Agenda should be distributed to members with a copy placed on the Staff Notice Board at least seven days before the meeting. Fixed items on the Agenda should be:
Minutes of last meeting
Matters arising
Training
Health & Safety
Business Results and Objectives
Security
Energy Conservation
Date of next meeting
(b) Special meetings may be convened at the request of any four members or the Chairman.
(c) The meetings shall conform to Committee procedure, members addressing the chair. Discussions shall be opened by the member in whose name the item on the Agenda stands. The first items of the Agenda should be the minutes of the previous meeting and matters arising.

9 Minutes
The Chairman shall ensure that accurate minutes of all meetings are kept which summarise the discussion and define clearly the action being taken and who is responsible for that action. (Minutes must always have an action column.) The minutes must be prepared and circulated within seven days of the meeting with copies distributed to all Committee members, all management and Heads of Department and all Staff Notice Boards.
Copies of the minutes are also to be sent to the Area/Operations Director, the Hotels Personnel Department and the Group Personnel Director.

10 Alteration of Rules
Additions or amendment to these rules may only be made by the Committee with the approval of the Company.

Source: Reproduced by courtesy of Trusthouse Forte Hotels.

Further reading

Armstrong, M., *A Handbook of Human Resource Management*, London: Kogan Page, 1988

Brewster, C., *Employee Relations*, Revised Ed. Basingstoke, MacMillan, 1989

Farnham, D. and Pimlott, J., *Understanding Industrial Relations*, 3rd ed. Eastbourne: Holt, Rinehard and Winston, 1986

Mars, G., Mitchell, P., and Bryant D., *Manpower Problems in the Hotel and Catering Industry*, Farnborough: Saxon House, 1976

Pratt, K. J., and Bennett, S. C., *Elements of Personnel Management*, 3rd ed., Wokingham: GEE. 1989,

Sisson K., (ed.), *Personnel Management in Britain*, Oxford: Blackwell, 1989

Thomason, G., *Textbook of Human Resource Management*, London: Institute of Personnel Management, 1988

Torrington, D. and Hall, L., *Personnel Management – A New Approach*, London: Prentice Hall, 1987

Questions

1 Describe the structure of industrial relations in the private (commercial) sector of the hotel and catering industry and also in the public sector of the hotel and catering industry.

2 Discuss the factors contributing to high or low union participation in different sectors or employers of the hotel and catering industry.

3 Discuss the external factors which influence the nature of industrial relations.

4 Discuss the positive and negative contributions made to employment relationships by trade unions.

5 Using an employer you know well, evaluate their approach to industrial relations.

chapter 16

Law of employment

The evolution and development of our complex industrial society has been accompanied by the need to regulate many of the activities of various groups of people. Without this regulation society would not be what it is today. In the case of industrial relations law, the activities of employees were long regulated by legal institutions such as magistrates who had, amongst a number of powers, the power to set rates of pay. More recently, the activities of employers became subject to increasing regulation in order to provide employees with greater protection in economic and physical terms. Factories legislation is just one example. Most recently the increasing power of trade unions, as distinct from individual work people, caused concern particularly to Conservative governments, with the result that the power of unions has been circumscribed by legislation. As stated above, until fairly recent times in our history responsibility for regulating conditions of employment rested largely on parliament and on local magistrates. This was relatively easy while the number of categories of workers was small. Gradually, however, as society became more industrialized it became increasingly difficult to exercise this control. The pendulum swung the other way. As was seen in the last chapter various laws were passed that made it possible for both workers and owners to combine into trade unions and associations in order to bargain, until the stage was reached where the State appeared to avoid any direct involvement in the relationships between employers and employees. The whole system of bargaining and negotiation then rested on voluntary understandings between the workers and their employers. However, as our industrial society developed even further the power of trade unions grew and the concentration of certain vital resources and services into what became vulnerable positions made it possible for many groups of people to disrupt supplies to the whole community.

The government therefore felt obliged to re-enter the field of relations between employers and employees by creating a legal framework for the conduct of what is now called industrial relations.

The government's responsibility rests with a senior cabinet minister, the Secretary of State for Employment. In addition, several other ministers have responsibilities that are related to employment and these include the Secretary of State for Social Services who is concerned with such matters as national insurance and pensions, and the Secretary for Trade and Industry who is responsible for such matters as regional development policy.

The law relating to employment is considerable now and it is only possible in this book to cover a small part of it. The major areas of employment law have been selected and summarized below.

Common law rights and obligations

Most aspects of the relationship between the employer and the employee are regulated by the contract of employment, much of which is now regulated by statute (i.e. Act of Parliament). The common law (judge made as opposed to Parliament made), however, also plays a part in setting minimum rights and duties.

The employer's duties are to pay the agreed wages, to provide work, to select and/or train competent workers, to provide adequate materials and to provide safe systems of work. Any breach of these common law obligations means that an employee could sue for damages, where an injury is sustained, or even to resign without notice and to sue for unfair constructive dismissal (where an employer creates circumstances in which an employee feels justified in resigning).

In turn the common law lays obligations upon employees as well. These include the duty to serve the employer according to the terms of the contract, to be obedient (i.e. to follow reasonable instructions), to work competently, to work for the employer in good faith which includes not taking secret profits or commissions, to keep confidential information and not to set up in competition.

Contracts of employment

A contract of employment is the basis of the working relationship between employer and employee and is subject to the general principles covered by the law of contract. There are seven essentials for a contract to be valid. These are:

1 *Offer and acceptance*; there must be an offer and an acceptance.
2 *Intention to create legal relations*; each party must intend to create a legally binding contract.
3 *Capacity*; each party to the contract must be legally able to make the contract.
4 *Consent*; must be genuine and freely given.
5 *Consideration*; something of value must be exchanged, e.g. money for work.
6 *Legality*; the purpose of the contract must be legal.
7 *Possibility*; it must be possible to perform the contact.

A contract of employment may be oral, written, or the terms may be merely implied. It consists of an offer by one of the parties and an acceptance by the other. A *consideration*, that is, an exchange of promises to perform certain duties and to pay certain wages and provide certain conditions, is necessary to create the contract. The *consideration*, as with all contracts, must have an economic value. The offer is usually (but not necessarily) made by the employer and should contain details of remuneration, hours, location and holidays. The offer may refer to other documents such as Wages Council publications. Not all conditions have to be included as some may be implied by custom and practice. The contract comes into existence when the offerer receives acceptance from the offeree.

Although, in common law, contracts need not be in writing, it is advisable that all offers and acceptances are in writing in order to avoid misunderstanding and possible problems. Furthermore, because most employees are entitled to a written statement of the main conditions of employment (see below) there is no real reason today for not preparing a proper, written contract of employment.

Employment Protection (Consolidation) Act 1978 – amended by the Employment Act 1980 and 1982

This Act provides the rights of employees, who work over a certain number of hours, to minimum periods of notice dependent on their length of service, and the Act also requires that employees are given written details of certain conditions of employment.

Where a contract provides for longer periods of notice the terms of the contract will apply, whereas contracts containing shorter periods are over-ridden by the periods laid down by the Employment Protection Act. Payment in lieu of notice may be made by the employer or the employee.

Written particulars

These must be given to people working for sixteen hours or more per week within thirteen weeks of employment commencing, or eight hours per week if employed for five years or more.

Written statements need not take any particular form but the contents are prescribed and they can refer employees to other documents such as manuals and booklets which must be reasonably available to them. There is no requirement in law for the employee or the employer to sign the statement. But it is advisable to issue all employees with a statement and to retain signed copies in the personal dossiers. The ideal way administratively is to design letters of offer so that they satisfy the Employment Protection Act requirements. An example is shown in Figure 6.2 (page 95).

Restraint on employees

In the case of some employees, such as chefs or managers, employers feel it necessary to include a clause in a contract restraining an employee from divulging trade secrets, entering into direct competition by operating his own business, working for another person in the same line of business or using lists of customers prepared in the course of employment in order to entice customers away.

In order to obtain protection against such eventualities any terms in a contract need to be clearly stated and not implied. It is important, however, to make such a term reasonable in the circumstances otherwise the right to any protection could be forfeited. At the same time such restraint clauses must be shown to be in the public interest and it is more unlikely that such a restraint clause will be upheld.

Searching employees

It is always advisable to obtain an employee's permission before attempting to search his or her person or property. To search a person without permission, and without finding evidence of theft, can result in the employer being sued for assault and battery. In those cases where the employer's right to search is considered to be vital, such as in hotels and industrial catering organizations, a clause to this effect should be written into every person's contract of employment. Even so an employee cannot be forcibly searched if he or she refuses. Such a refusal instead becomes the subject of disciplinary or dismissal proceedings.

Dismissals

Unfair dismissal

Under the Employment Protection (Consolidation) Act 1978 as amended by the Employment Act 1980 and 1982 there is protection for employees against unfair dismissal.

In the past, so long as an employer gave the agreed period of notice or money in lieu an employee had no recourse against the employer. The situation has changed and it is now necessary to show that reasons for dismissal were fair. Valid reasons include:

1 Lack of capability or qualification for the job for which an employee was employed.
2 Misconduct.
3 Redundancy, within the definition of the Redundancy legislation.
4 Unsuitability due to legal restrictions (e.g. loss of Justice's licence).
5 Some other substantial reasons (e.g. chronic sickness).

It should be noted that no complaint of unfair dismissal or of a worker's rights relating to trade unions will be heard by an industrial tribunal until a Department of Employment conciliation officer has looked into the circumstances to see if a settlement can be reached without a tribunal hearing.

Instant or summary dismissal

In certain instances an employer may be justified in dismissing an employee without giving the required period of notice or money in lieu. Although this may be permitted in such cases as an employee's permanent incapacity to perform his duties, in most cases it occurs where employees are guilty of serious misconduct. To dismiss a person instantly can have serious consequences for the employer, if a dismissed employee sues him successfully for damages, so it is not a step to be taken lightly. Reasons for instant dismissal include:

1 Serious or repeated disobedience or other misconduct.
2 Serious or repeated negligence.
3 Drunkenness while on duty.
4 Theft.
5 Accepting bribes or commissions.

The argument underlying instant dismissal is that the employee, through serious misconduct, has repudiated the contract, and the employer chooses not to renew it.

An employer can normally only dismiss an employee for misconduct committed outside working hours and away from the place of work if other employees were involved, which could have an effect on the employer's business, or if the employee is in domestic service.

Where an employer dismisses a person instantly it should be done at the time of the misdemeanour or when it first comes to the attention of the employer. To delay will imply that the employer has waived his right to dismiss. The reason for dismissal should be given at the time of the dismissal.

An employer may, in some cases, withhold money earned by an employee who has been instantly dismissed for good reasons, unless a contract states otherwise. However, legal advice should always be sought before taking such action.

Suspensions

In some circumstances, particularly involving alleged misconduct, an employer may wish to suspend an employee until the circumstances have been looked into and a decision has been taken regarding the employee's future. It is quite in order to do this so long as pay is not withheld – unless a contract specifically permitting the withholding of pay is in existence.

Payment of wages

The Wages Act

Generally speaking the arrangements for the payment of wages are regulated by the contract of employment. The Wages Act 1986, however, provides specific rules on deductions. These specify that an employer must not make deductions or receive payment (e.g. as a fine) unless:

the deduction is authorized by statute
the deduction is authorized in the contract of employment
the worker has agreed in writing to the deduction.

Certain deductions are exempted from the above conditions, such as the recovery of an over-payment.

In the case of the retail trade, including catering, employees can be required as a condition of the contract, to make good stock or cash shortages. However, such a deduction or payment must not exceed 10 per cent of the gross pay due for the period. On termination of employment, however, such deductions may exceed 10 per cent. They cannot be made retrospective for more than 12 months. Notice of intention to make such deductions has to be made in advance, and a written demand also has to be issued.

Payment of wages may be in a form agreed in the contract. This may be in the form of cash, cheque or credit transfer.

Most wages in the Hotel and Catering Industry are regulated by the Wages Council orders (page 176).

Attachment of Earnings Act 1971

This Act enables a court to order an employer to make periodic deductions from an employee's earnings and to pay the sum deducted to the collecting officer of the court. The court specifies the amount and can make *priority orders* for payment of fines or maintenance of dependants, or *non-priority* orders for the clearance of civil debts. The court will also specify the *protected earnings* which is the level of income below which a person's earnings should not be reduced by these deductions. Any consequent shortfalls in payments will be carried forward.

PAYE

Employers are obliged to deduct tax payable on money paid to any of their employees earning money falling under Schedule E (that is, emoluments from any office or employment). Some items are not subject to deductions: business expenses, and rent-free accommodation or temporary accommodation allowances which are provided because of the nature of the employer's business.

This responsibility covers service charge earnings and 'tronc' earnings where the employer is involved in the distribution. It is the duty of staff to declare tips where the manager is not involved in their distribution.

Employer's liability

There are two separate categories of liability that employers bear in relation to injuries suffered by their employees while in their employment. These are common law and statutory liabilities.

The common law responsibilities extend also to employees of other employers, such as contractors, while working on the employer's premises, and also to the employer's employees carrying out work for him on another person's premises, for example, an outdoor caterer's staff.

In common law employers are expected to provide protection that is reasonable in the circumstances. An employee will be compensated for injury if the employer was at fault in exposing the employee to unnecessary risk in the circumstances.

Unfortunately the common law is not able to provide for all developments in industry and therefore several statues exist to specify the nature of protection to be provided and to lay down certain other regulations covering the working environment.

Health and Safety at Work Act 1974

In 1975 the Health and Safety at Work Act 1974 came into force, which provides very flexible legislation protecting most employees at work. The Act in principle provides that employers are to ensure the safety of their employees (and also the general public) at the employer's premises, by maintaining safe plant, safe systems of work and safe premises, and also by ensuring adequate instruction, training and supervision. Other people, too, such as designers, manufacturers, installers, importers and suppliers of goods for use at work, are to ensure, in so far as they are responsible, that any health and safety risks are eliminated. Employees also are made responsible for the safety of others.

Office, Shops and Railway Premises Act

The Health and Safety at Work Act also re-enacted the Offices, Shops and Railway Premises Act 1963 which includes most catering establishments within its scope. This Act covers such aspects as cleanliness, overcrowding, lighting, temperature, ventilation and sanitary arrangements for work people.

Children (Employment of Children Acts 1933–1969)

Children are defined as being under the minimum school-leaving age. The principal Acts are concerned primarily with protecting the physical well-being of children and with specifying the hours which they are permitted to work. Children, for example, are not permitted to work during school hours and where a child is under 13 years of age the legal restrictions are particularly strict, for example, limiting their hours of work to no more than one per day outside of school hours.

The regulations are quite detailed but can vary in detail from one part of the country to another as they are administered mainly by local authorities.

Regulations cover the following points:

Hours of work
Hours on the employer's premises
Hours off duty
Frequency and duration of rest and meal breaks
Permitted overtime
Holidays
Medical examinations.

For details of the regulations as they apply to a particular area it is advisable to contact the local office of the Department of Employment.

The Equal Pay Act 1970

The purpose of this Act is to remove differences in terms and conditions of employment between men and women employed on the same or very similar work or work rated as of similar value. Industrial tribunals deal with any complaints and are able to award arrears of pay and damages. Job evaluation plays a part in determining pay differentials between jobs.

Sex Discrimination Act 1975

The Sex Discrimination Act 1975 was introduced in order to grant equal opportunities to both sexes in the fields of employment, education and training and to make it an offence to discriminate against a man or a woman on the grounds of sex alone. The main provision of this Act is that if a job can be performed equally well by a man or a woman it is an offence to discriminate against a man or a woman on the grounds of sex alone. This applies to recruitment of new staff and also to promotion.

There are certain exceptions, of particular relevance to the hotel and catering industry, such as cloakroom attendants or where limited staff accommodation has to be shared.

The Employment Protection (Consolidation) Act 1978 grants women the right to maternity pay, maternity leave and to reinstatement in the same or similar work when they return.

Social security

The Social Security Scheme provides a wide variety of benefits and welfare services such as benefits for unemployment, sickness, industrial injuries and also retirement. Most people over school-leaving age and under pensionable age are insurable. Persons who are insurable must register and obtain a National Insurance number.

Trade union legislation

The main legislation, covering trade unions currently, is contained in a number of Acts, including:

Trade Union and Labour Relations Act 1974 (as amended by the Employment Acts 1980 and 1982)
Trade Union Act 1984
Employment Acts 1980 and 1982

These Acts contain legislation concerned with 'collective' employment issues.

Recognition　To qualify for most rights under trade union legislation trade unions have to be certified as independent by the Certification Officer. Employers themselves need only recognize trade unions if they themselves wish to do so. 'Recognition' means that the employer recognizes the right of the union to represent employees in membership of the trade union. Issues covered in such recognition can include terms and conditions of employment, recruitment and termination procedures, work allocation, discipline, negotiating procedures.

Information　The Employment Protection Act 1975 imposes a duty on employers who recognize trade unions to disclose information which is necessary for collective bargaining.

Trade disputes and immunities　Trade disputes only attract immunity from actions for damages if they are disputes between employees and their employer and are concerned with matters central to their employment relationship. In addition, any action must have been approved in a ballot by a majority of those voting.

Picketing　Picketing is only lawful if carried out as part of a trade dispute and should be at or near the place of work.

See also Chapter 15 – Industrial Relations.

Further reading

Boella, M. J., (ed.) *Catering – Croner's Reference Book for Caterers* (up-dated every two months), London: Croner Publications
Pannett, A., *Principles of Hotel and Catering Law*, London: Cassell, 1989
Sweeney, S., (ed.) *Reference Book for Employers* (with regular up-dating), London: Croner Publications
Sweeney, S., (ed.) *Employment Law* (with regular up-dating), London: Croner Publications

Questions

1 Describe the main distinct areas of law affecting employment.

2 Describe the 'fair reasons' for terminating employment.

3 Describe a 'fair disciplinary' procedure. (See also Chapter 14.)

4 Discuss the proposition that a contract of employment is much more than the 'written statement' as required by the Employment Protection (Consolidation) Act 1978, as amended by the Employment Act 1980 and 1982.

5 Using an employer you know well, evaluate their approach to managing their labour force as the law requires.

6 Discuss the proposition that law has no place in the employment relationship.

chapter 17

Manpower planning, records and statistics

In recent years the importance of an undertaking's human resources has become much more apparent owing to the considerable costs of labour and the growing staff shortages in some sectors of the hotel and catering industry. The 'demographic time bomb', i.e. the reduction in the number of young people available for work in the early 1990s, will only contribute to the scale of the problem for many employers. The arrival too of new employers on the labour market, such as Eurodisney, will create new demands on a diminished labour market. Many hotel and catering operators are now recruiting actively in the United Kingdom and one estimate is that Eurodisney alone will be offering sufficient industrial experience placements at the Paris location to absorb a significant number of the UK's hospitality students. In many other industries and organizations these problems have led to much attention being paid to most aspects of human resource management. It has led, in particular, to accurate planning so that an employer has the right resources available when required and also so that labour costs are not unnecessarily high. Because of this, well-conceived human resource policies are now playing an increasingly important part in furthering many undertakings' business objectives. They translate the overall business plan, normally concerned in the private sector with competitiveness and profitability, into a detailed plan. Sound human resource policies can only be achieved through a thorough understanding of the organization, its objectives, its management, its operating style, and its social and political environment. Human resource planning can therefore be described as the process of interpreting the environment, predicting its effects on the organization, evaluating these effects, planning and controlling the appropriate measures in order that the right human resources are available when required.

Human resource policies must play a positive and creative role in the plans, developments and day-to-day activities of an undertaking. They must be designed to provide competent human resources when required. The need to plan on a sound basis of reliable information has been emphasized and much of a manager's work revolves around certain basic and fundamental information; for example, the need for precise job descriptions has been shown to be vital not only to recruitment, but also to training, performance appraisal, job evaluation and salary administration.

Human resource planning is divided into two separate and distinct parts:

strategic and operational. The strategic part of planning is concerned with ensuring that the right people will be available in the longer term, for example for hotels that are not even built.

Strategic human resource planning for larger organizations requires a good understanding of that organization and its environment. Figure 17.1 shows a 'systems thinking' diagram – how an organization's plan can be affected by its environment.

At the operational level management needs to know precisely what manning ratios are necessary. Each organization and each establishment will have its own, such as one waiter for ten covers and one room attendant for fourteen rooms (see Figure 17.2).

At the strategic level management needs accurate statistics in order to develop the undertaking's long-term plans. This is best illustrated by an example. If, for instance, a brewery company wanted to expand its number of managed public houses by 100 it would need to recruit at least 100 new husband and wife teams to run these public houses. In addition, if it had 100 managed houses already it would have to anticipate finding replacements for some of these existing 100 managers. If wastage rates are unknown, it is not possible to calculate accurately what numbers to recruit and train. On the other hand if the company has kept records, these may show that wastage among established managers is 20 per cent per annum and among trainees 30 per cent. It is then simple to determine how many to recruit in a year.

As 100 couples are required for new houses and 20 couples are required for existing houses, this indicates that a total of 120 couples are needed to complete training. However, as wastage during training is 30 per cent, the number to be recruited will have to be increased to compensate for this loss.

Thus: $120 \times \dfrac{100}{70} = 172$ couples (rounded up).

This then is the number needed for training.

The brewery, therefore, knows on the basis of past experience that it will need to recruit about 172 couples to fill 120 vacancies likely to occur in the next year. The actual phasing of this recruitment depends on other factors such as the length of training, the availability of new public houses, the policy for retiring or replacing tenants, etc. This illustrates that plans for the future are difficult to implement effectively without adequate records and statistics. However, as was said much earlier, the individual's needs, as well as the employer's, have to be recognized – consequently any records and statistical data must serve the individual as well as the employer.

Personnel information and records are required for several reasons:

1   To provide detailed operational information such as monthly strength returns and payroll analyses.
2   To provide ratios or data such as wastage rates, age analyses and service analyses for planning purposes.

Figure 17.1   *A 'systems thinking' diagram*

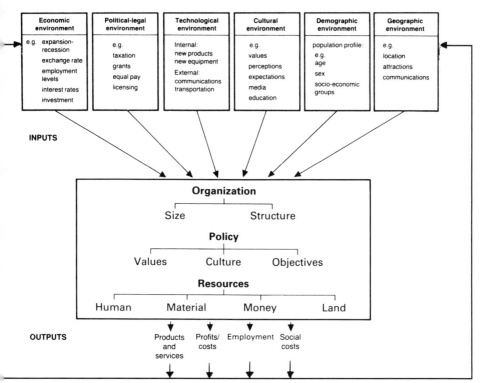

3   To provide information on individuals for administration purposes such as salaries and pensions and to provide information for career development purposes.
4   To provide information for statutory purposes such as National Insurance, Redundancy Payment or Registered Disabled Persons Act.
5   To provide information for re-employment and reference purposes.

The nature of records and statistics that may be maintained and produced by employers varies considerably. The largest organizations in this country will require highly sophisticated information possibly using computer-based systems, whereas smaller organizations will need only minimal information. However, the following are probably basic to most organizations employing more than a few people.

Personal record

This is the backbone of a good records system. If both the contents and the layout are designed carefully, it can provide valuable information quickly and

Figure 17.2   *Human resource planning – matching labour supply to demand*

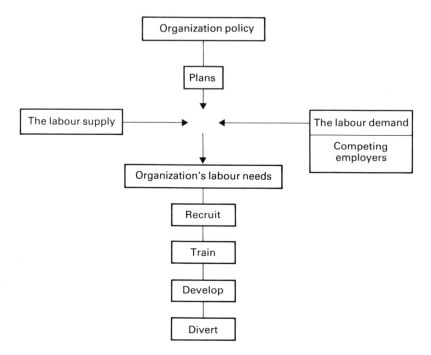

easily. Whether this record is a simple index card, a visible edge card, a computer file, depends on the number of employees and the amount of detail required.

The record should contain concise information which will be common to most employees such as age, education, qualifications, training, marital status. It is used primarily for statistical exercises or for the speedy retrieval of information; for example, the record may be used to produce an age distribution of all management employees in order to assist with management development plans, or, alternatively, the cards may be used to discover French speakers or all those with 'instructor' training. The personal record does not replace the need for a personal dossier for each employee. The nature and purpose of personal information kept by employers now has to be carefully considered for a number of reasons. For example, to keep information that could be used in order to discriminate on grounds of sex or race may be illegal.

A typical personal record card will look like the one shown in Figure 17.3.

Figure 17.3 *A personal record card. Source: Croner's Personnel Records 1/86, with kind permission of Croner Publications*

INDIVIDUAL HISTORY RECORD I

Personal

Surname	Forenames		Clock/Staff no.
Home address			Telephone no.
1st change of address			Telephone no.
2nd change of address			Telephone no.
Sex	Date of birth	Nationality	Ethnic origin
Marital status		No. of children	
Emergency contact (name, address, tel. no.)			Relationship

Employment

Work address			Telephone no.
1st change of address			Telephone no.
2nd change of address			Telephone no.
Start date		Work permit	Expiry date

Job History

Date	Dept.	Job title	Reason for change	Date	Dept.	Job title	Reason for change

Terms and Conditions

PT/FT	Temp./Perm.	Working hours	Shift pattern	Hours pw
Holiday entitlement		Co. sick pay entitlement	SSP qualifying days	Pension
Other				

Pay History

Date	Current salary	Increase	Remarks	Date	Current salary	Increase	Remarks

Payroll

Payroll no.	NI no.	Tax code
Bank (name and address)		Bank sort code
		Account no.

Figure 17.3 cont.

Health

RDP	Disability	RDP no.
Medical restrictions		

Pension Scheme/Insurance, etc.

Date	Comments	Date	Comments

Skills and Qualifications

Educational achievements

Work qualifications

Languages and proficiency

Test scores

Other skills

Management experience

Miscellaneous

Professional bodies

Public offices   Territorial army

Union membership   Check off   Union or safety representative

First aid certificate   Driving licence

Previous Employment

Dates	Company	Position	Reason for leaving	Dates	Company	Position	Reason for leaving

Termination

Due retirement date	Termination date	Termination code

Personal dossier

This should contain all documents relating to an individual employee. These may include:

Copies of letters of offer and acceptance
Application form
Copy of engagement form
Various reports and correspondence
Performance appraisals
Changes of conditions, e.g. salary increases
Records of company property issued to the employee
Disciplinary measures.

The dossier is usually left for a period of time (a year or two) after an employee has left, in case of queries.

Employment requisition

This is a document produced by the heads of departments (in larger organizations) requesting authority to recruit a replacement or an addition to staff. The nature of this form will vary considerably and will depend on the degree of authority of individual heads of departments. In some cases, for example, heads of departments will need no special authority so long as the person to be recruited will be within the laid down staff establishment or within authorized budget levels. On the other hand, there are chief executives even in some large organizations who insist on personally authorizing the recruitment of all new staff whether they are replacing leavers or exceeding the staff establishment.

In most of the larger well-organized undertakings, the personnel department will also have to authorize the salary or wage to be paid in order to ensure that anomalies are not allowed to creep in.

A typical form is shown in Figure 17.4.

Engagement form

This form should be completed when a new employee joins an employer. The purpose is to inform all the relevant departments so that appropriate action is initiated. These departments may include:

Wages
Training
Pensions
Insurance
Personnel records.

Figure 17.4 *Example of an employment requisition (THF)*

AUTHORITY TO RECRUIT

---

1. RECRUITMENT NEEDS ANALYSIS – Before completing the form:

a. Consider whether any of the following might provide a more cost-effective alternative to recruitment:
   — re-organisation of staff (duties/hours)?
   — contract labour?
   — mechanisation?
   — improved working methods?
   — revision of standards?

b. Consider whether business product changes might alter the situation.

c. Check whether recent exit interviews indicate a need to alter the job description, person specification or the reporting relationships.

Further guidance may be obtained from Personnel or by referring to the Recruitment and Selection Manual.

---

2. POSITION VACANT: ....

   ....

   DEPARTMENT/LOCATION: ....

   WAGE SCALE/SALARY RANGE: ....

   HOURS OF WORK: ....

   SPECIAL CONDITIONS: ....

   Replacement/New Position*

   Job Description

   attached/not attached*

   Person Specification attached/ not attached*

   *delete as appropriate

3. RECRUITMENT PLAN – indicate here which means of recruitment you intend to use or wish Personnel to use:

   tick

   internal applications

   career development scheme

   holding file

   job centre

   schools & colleges

   mail shots

   advertising

   agencies

---

4. NAMES OF AUTHORISED PERSONS

   To authorise recruitment......................

   ....

   To recruit: ....

   To select: ....

   To decide to make offer:.......................

   ....

FURTHER DETAILS – e.g. media to be used if advertising:

ESTIMATED RECRUITMENT COST:

5. I confirm that I have carried out a recruitment needs analysis and wish to recruit as above.	6. AUTHORISED
Signed.. (ORIGINATOR)	Signed....................................... (DESIGNATED MANAGER)
Date..	Date ....

Completed form to be sent to the recruiter responsible for action.

Source: Reproduced by courtesy of Trusthouse Forte Hotels

The information contained on the form will vary according to the system being used; for example, some employers may be able to use one engagement form for all departments and all levels of staff whereas other employers may need to use different forms for each. It is of prime importance, however, to ensure that the employee is paid and insured. Consequently information will have to include name, staff number, address, department, date of starting, rate of pay, bank address. Figure 17.5 shows one typical example.

Termination form

This form is necessary in order to fulfil several purposes:

1 To initiate documentation and administration procedures such as the preparation of the P45 and the final wages payment.
2 To provide statistical information regarding labour turnover.
3 To provide information for reference or re-employment purposes.

Other forms

There is a variety of other information that may have to be kept for contractual, statutory or other purposes. This can include:

Accident reports
Medical reports
Training reports
Absentee reports
Change of status, e.g. salary increases, promotions, transfers
Warnings.

From these various documents the majority of statistical information required for the satisfactory planning and control of most undertakings can be produced. This information may include the items given on pages 206 and 207.

Figure 17.5 *Example of an engagement form*

For H.O. use:_____ Log No. ST/HM*_____ Copies to: Salaries/Personal file/ Personnel input/Central	**CREST HOTELS** **New Employee/Transfer to Head Office Payroll** (Head Office Paid Employees)	Hotel_____ H/O Function_____ H/O Department_____

PERSONAL DETAILS

Surname_____   Home address_____
Mr/Mrs/Miss/Ms*_____   _____
Forenames_____   _____
Single/Married/Widowed/Divorced*___   _____
Date of birth_____   Postcode_____
National Insurance Number_____   Telephone number_____

New job holder's employment details   Salary p.a. £_____
Location where based_____   Live in/Live out*_____
Grade (if applicable)_____   Company Car Yes/No*_____
Department**_____   Crest Credit Card Yes/No*_____
Job title_____
Date from which employed/Transferred to H/O payroll_____
Position held before transfer to H/O payroll_____

Is this a new appointment_____   Yes/No*_____
If yes was this budgeted_____   Yes/No*_____
Application form attached_____   Yes/No*_____

Previous job holder's employment details (if applicable)
Name_____   Salary p.a. £_____
Job title_____   Live in/Live out*_____

Employees transferred from hotel to H/O payroll
Original date of commencement of company employment_____
Is the employee in the Retail Pension Scheme   Yes/No*_____
Frozen holidays   Yes/No*_____   No. of days_____
Deductions: BESSS Contribution Yes/No*_____£_____per month
Other deductions (please specify)_____£_____per period
Personal file attached   Yes/No*_____
If not attached give reason_____

*Delete as applicable
**For hotel employees enter department to be charged – Rooms, Food, Liquor,
Telephone or General etc.

Hotel Manager	H/O Dept Man/DDO*	Functional Director	Personnel Director
Signed	Signed:	Signed:	Signed:
Date:	Date:	Date:	Date:

To be completed at Head Office – Banbury

For Personnel Department use

BUPA Cover   Immediately/after 12 months/N/A*_____
                    Single/Married/Family*_____

BEPSS Yes/No_____   Roll number_____
BESSS Yes/No*   Scheme year_____   Scheme ref_____

Hotel deductions to:_____/19____Advised salaries_____/19_____

For salaries department use

Broken period paid on manual/computer* payroll period_____

Cheque Number:_____   Issued_____/19_____

First full period paid on computer payroll – Period_____

BESSS contributions from period_____   £_____

First BESSS deduction period_____   £_____

P45/P46/15* Sent to tax office_____   /19_____

*Delete as applicable

Signed_____ DATE_____ /19_____

Source: Reproduced by courtesy of Crest Hotels

Strength returns

This will show numbers employed by departments and should show changes in numbers. It may also incorporate 'establishment' numbers, that is the agreed numbers to be employed in each department. Any variation from 'establishment' will be shown.

Payroll analysis

This information (a development of the strength return) may be produced by a variety of departments including the wages department, and the cost or management accountant's department, or the personnel manager's department. It will include a breakdown, by departments, of labour costs. These may be shown in a large variety of ways including various ratios and percentages. The figures should always include a comparison of the actual and budget figures.

Both the strength return and the payroll analysis should be produced on a regular, periodic basis. Where there is strict control over wage and salary levels the 'strength return' will be sufficient for most day-to-day management purposes, since cost variances will only arise where there are variances from the laid down 'establishment'. In any case the labour costs should show up elsewhere – in particular on periodic operating statements.

Staff/labour turnover analysis

This has already been discussed in Chapter 14. However, it must be stressed that the regular production of this information can assist considerably in staff recruitment and retention by identifying the problem areas.

The turnover rate for each department and for the undertaking as a whole will make up part of this report. This can be arrived at roughly by the following formula:

$$\frac{Number\ of\ employees\ who\ left\ during\ period \times 100}{Average\ number\ employed\ during\ period}$$

Such data must be prepared and considered carefully, however. One company, for example, found that all in-company transfers had been included, thus distorting the turnover rate.

In itself the turnover rate may be of little value as it gives no indication, for example, of turnover among long-serving employees. It may, therefore, be necessary to supplement labour turnover figures with further breakdowns. This may be done in a variety of ways including showing numbers of leavers by length of service as shown in Figure 17.6.

Figure 17.6   *An analysis of leavers by length of service*

Analysis of leavers for 12 months ending 31 December 1990

Length of service	Number of leavers	Percentage
Years		
more than 5	4	5.0
more than 2 less than 5	8	10.0
more than 1 less than 2	10	12.5
up to 1	58	72.5
Total	80	100.0

Age and service analyses

For human resource planning and management development purposes it is important in the medium and larger-sized organizations from time to time to look at the make-up of the labour force and in particular at the age profile of the workforce and management team. If this is not done, an unanticipated spate of retirements and resignations can leave an undertaking without the necessary trained personnel. It is useful, therefore, to produce an annual age profile of management, headed by those due to retire. In some cases it may be desirable to link this with service as shown below (see Figure 17.7).

Figure 17.7   *An age and service analysis*

				Service						
Age	Under 1 year	1–5	6–10	11–15	16–20	21–5	26–30	31–5	36–40	41+
61–5			1		2		2			
56–60						1				
50–5		6	3	3		1				
46–50	3		2							
41–5	1									
36–40			1	1	2					
31–5	2	8	1							
26–30	8	7								
21–5	2	3								
under 21	1	2								

In examining the type of chart shown in Figure 17.7 one would hope to see the bulk of managers distributed fairly evenly through the chart, preferably with a slightly greater weight at the younger end. Where this is not the case the management team may not have the necessary combination of age, experience and inbuilt continuity. Consequently senior management may wish to take steps to put this right by promotion, transfers, recruitment and appropriate training.

Human resource audit

Some of the largest employers conduct detailed studies periodically which provide a complete breakdown of the labour force divided into various sections including job grades, age and service. They may also report on the quality of staff, their qualifications, performance and potential. The training plan, management development programme and manpower plan may be part of, or may be linked with, this audit.

Some organizations, the most sophisticated, may also set out to determine the 'economic' value of their human resources by placing values on the costs of recruitment, induction, training, development, wastage, etc. This is sometimes referred to as Human Asset Accounting (HAA).

Apart from the records and data discussed here, there are many more that may be necessary for effective planning and control. However, it is important to bear in mind that although the production and interpretation of information and statistics, in itself, can be an attractive occupation, only those data that serve a useful purpose should be produced. They should clearly be aids to line management in providing an effective service. If they do not satisfy this requirement, the information being produced is almost certainly unwanted and consequently it is a waste of resources that could be employed more fruitfully elsewhere.

Computers in personnel work

One of the more common uses of computers within organizations has been for the preparation of the payroll. This is because the payroll system was ideally suited to the earlier magnetic tape storage system. Personnel records can now be kept easily and relatively cheaply on computer because of the random access facility provided by disk-based systems. Such facilities lead onto the ability to produce a range of systems; for example, a spread sheet enables a manager to input a number of variables, such as revenue, labour costs, predicted increases, and to manipulate data so as to predict what labour costs, average wage rate, number on the payroll, etc., should be for the future. See Figure 17.8 for an example. Most personal data held on computer is covered by the Data Protection Act which restricts the use of such data.

Another system, 'Microprospect' (Institute of Manpower Studies, Brighton), is a model which examines the effects on groups of people within an organization. It deals with questions such as:

Number of trainees needed
Is the organization developing sufficient staff to meet its needs?
What are the promotion opportunities?
Effects of maintaining current promotion prospects
Effects of early retirement policy.

Microprospect looks at an organization using a manpower system illustrated simply in Figure 17.9.

Figure 17.8 *Example of a spread sheet applied to manpower budgeting*

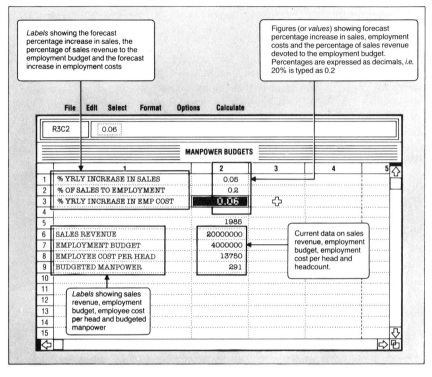

Source: Personnel Management, May 1986

Figure 17.9 *Example of a human resource system in an organization*

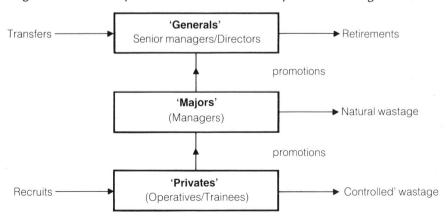

The effect of computers on employment levels

As the hotel and catering industry continues to grow there should be corresponding increases in levels of employment. In the whole of the tourist industry, this is estimated to be at the rate of about 50,000 new jobs per annum into the 1990s.

This expansion may be partially facilitated by the use of information technology where it enables organizations to provide new or improved services, such as faster counter service and check out, and to use the potential wealth of management information to maximize opportunities. This is referred to as the 'product effect.' There will also be some technological impact on the employment of clerical and administrative staff – known as the 'process effect'.

Table A5.1, page 323, shows the results of research into potential job losses and gains directly or indirectly attributable to the use of information technology.

Further reading

Armstrong, M., *A Handbook of Human Resource Management*, London: Kogan Page, 1988

Bramham, J., *Practical Manpower Planning*, 3rd ed., London: Institute of Personnel Management, 1982

Croner's Personnel Records, London: Croner Publications, 1986

Evans, A., *A Guide to Manpower Information*, London: Institute of Personnel Management, 1980

Pratt, K. J., and Bennett, S. C., *Elements of Personnel Management*, 3rd ed., Wokingham: GEE, 1989

Sisson K., (ed.), *Personnel Management in Britain*, Oxford: Blackwell, 1989

Thomason, G., *Textbook of Human Resource Management*, London: Institute of Personnel Management, 1988

Torrington, D. and Hall, L., *Personnel Management – A New Approach*, London: Prentice Hall, 1987

Questions

1 Describe the objectives of human resource planning and the various elements of an effective process.

2 Discuss what external factors influence the nature of human resource planning.

3 Using an employer you know well, evaluate their approach to human resource planning.

chapter 18

Organizing human resources

The preceding chapters have concentrated largely on the various management techniques which are concerned with obtaining, training, motivating and administering staff. In addition to these different steps, however, managers also have to organize staff, that is, to create groups of people who will meet the organization's objectives. This is normally one of the major responsibilities of line management who organize their work people into groups in the manner they think best, basing their organization usually on what they have observed or experienced elsewhere. Nowadays, however, there is a growing recognition that organizing people into the most appropriate work groups is a highly skilled and complex task often referred to as 'organization development', which is concerned with 'improving an organization's ability to achieve its goals by using people more effectively'.* A major aspect of the work of many management consultants now is concerned with examining organizations and recommending the most appropriate structures. A related development is the increasing involvement, albeit slowly, of human resource managers in the actual design of organization structures.

Organization development as a process can have a number of different goals. The most common are:

Improvement in organizational performance, e.g. profits or service levels
Improvement in decision-making processes
Improvement in group or team work
Responding to change
Changing value systems, attitudes.

A whole range of factors influence organization structures, each factor having some effect on the final type of structure, which may be either the result of careful design, the result of evolutionary development or merely expediency.

The main options open to organizations are:

Functional: where different individuals attend to the main management functions, i.e. finance, marketing, personnel, operations, research.

*D. French and H. Saward, *Dictionary of Management* (Pan 1977).

Product: where different managers manage different products, e.g. hotels or public houses or popular catering.

Geographical: where management attend to everything within a geographic region.

Project: where groups are set up for specific projects and disperse upon completion, usually relying upon existing hierarchical roles.

Matrix: a loose form of the above where individuals may be members of a number of different groups with leadership roles depending more on expertise than on hierarchical roles.

In the larger organizations it is possible to find a combination of the above. For example, many brewery companies are organized on both product and geographical bases.

Figure 18.1   *Organization structure and factors influencing it (see also Figure 17.1)*

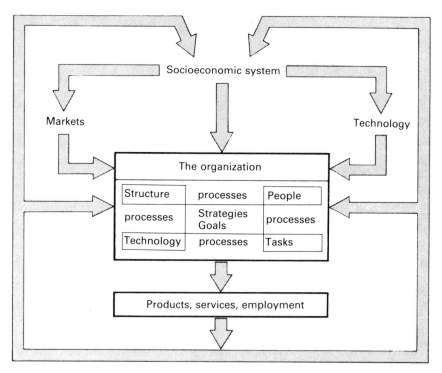

Power and the decision-making process

Underlying the process of organization will be the overall philosophy of senior management towards their workforce (see Chapter 2) and the principles of job design (see Chapter 3). Unitarist (or autocratic) style managers will tend towards concentrating decision making upon themselves, whereas a pluralist (or democratic) style manager will be prepared to share decision making. Public sector organizations tend to require committee-type decisions, made within a legislative or bureaucratic framework, whereas private sector organizations have far fewer legislative or bureaucratic restraints and decision making can be a simpler process, requiring fewer participants. Such differences in types of organization can influence quite considerably the formal and informal approaches to organizations.

The market

The single most important factor is probably the type of market being catered for. Obviously consumer demands determine the type of staff required but also the degree of seasonal fluctuation influences organization structure. A hospital with predictable and stable levels of demand, where the catering service is ancillary to other services, will have staffing needs very different from those required by a highly seasonal resort hotel or holiday camp where the accommodation and catering services themselves are the end product. The hospital will have a relatively stable and permanent labour force, whereas the seasonal hotel will probably have a small nucleus of permanent, key staff which is boosted by seasonal and casual labour as demand increases.

Technology

The technology of a particular sector is also important. One simple example is airline catering. In this sector of the industry space is at a premium, weight carries penalties, and constant supervision is not possible. These factors obviously influence the product offered, the equipment used and the staff selected; all having important consequences for the organization structure.

Centralization and decentralization

Likewise centralized purchasing and production affect the skill and knowledge needed, particularly at craftsman level. This has important consequences for such things as the number of craftsmen employed, their morale and attitudes to work and the quality assurance methods used. These, in turn, affect the organization structure.

Organizational objectives

Each type of organization has particular objectives. In some cases the objective is, first and foremost, to make a profit, while in others it is to provide a service. These obviously influence staffing levels because where profit is the main motive, staffing levels will normally be kept close to the most economic level, with attendant risks of occasional understaffing. Where service is paramount (e.g. on oil rigs), manning levels will normally be kept at safer levels because the cost of short staffing could be tremendous.

Size and diversity

Two other major influences on the structure are the size of the organization and its diversity. However, there does seem to be some agreement among the largest organizations that they need to devolve responsibility to smaller, readily accountable units. This may be done on a geographic basis. An example is the way in which breweries organize their public house districts. Their management may be responsible for all activities in an area, such as managed houses, tenanted houses, catering and entertainment. Alternatively, an organization may prefer to make its management responsible for particular types of products or services. An example is how some companies may concentrate their steak houses into one division, their licensed houses into another and leisure into yet another. For the largest companies both 'regional' and 'product' organization structures will be necessary.

At the individual unit level the degree of specialization is an important question and of particular importance is the degree to which certain specialists such as sales executives and financial controllers may be responsible to the unit manager and to the head office specialist manager. This is a constant problem in hotels in particular, where sales executives may see themselves as part of a sales team rather than part of the unit management. A consequence is that the sales staff often sell 'products' the unit has difficulty providing.

Span of control

Something else discussed in the organizational context is the question of 'span of control' (i.e. how many subordinates can each supervisor successfully supervise). While most will agree that 'one over one' is rarely, if ever, justified, beyond this all the factors listed above play their part in resolving the question of how many subordinates one person can control. There are situations where one supervisor can quite successfully control a hundred or more subordinates. Likewise, however, there are many other situations where one person can successfully supervise, at most, a handful of subordinates.

The products and services

Obviously shaping all these factors is the product being provided. At one extreme there is the *haute cuisine* meal experience involving an extensive range of technical, social and organizational skills which have taken many years of experience and training to acquire. At the other extreme nowadays we have fast foods and airline meals which involve very little craft skill but call upon management organization skills of a high order. In between these two extremes are numerous types and styles of product and service which make differing demands on capital, craft skill, social skill, training and organization ability. Each combination creates a particular set of organizational needs and constraints which should be reflected in the consequent organization structure.

Age and size

As successful organizations get older so they tend to become larger. Increasing size creates subdivisions and problems of co-ordination. Large size consequently creates conflicting effects. On the one hand size creates opportunities for economies of scale; on the other hand increasing problems of co-ordination and control can add to the administrative burden – the law of diminishing returns?

Objectives of organization development

In developing organizations a major consideration is the extent to which technical efficiency is pursued at the cost of job satisfaction or, at the other extreme, to what extent can organization structures sacrifice technical efficiency for job satisfaction. The objective should be to strike the balance between the technical and human demands so that an effective organization results.

Further reading

Armstrong, M., *A Handbook of Human Resource Management*, London: Kogan Page, 1988
Medlik, S., *The Business of Hotels*, London: Heinemann, 1989
Pratt, K. J., and Bennett, S. C., *Elements of Personnel Management* 3rd ed., Wokingham: GEE, 1989
Sisson K., (ed.), *Personnel Management in Britain*, Oxford: Blackwell, 1989
Thomason, G., *Textbook of Human Resource Management*, London: Institute of Personnel Management, 1988
Torrington, D. and Hall, L., *Personnel Management – A New Approach*, London: Prentice Hall, 1987

Questions

1 Describe the objectives of organization development and the various alternative approaches to organization structure.
2 Discuss the factors which influence organization structure.
3 Using an employer you know well, evaluate their approach to organization structure and development.

Figure 18.2 *Organization chart of a large hotel*

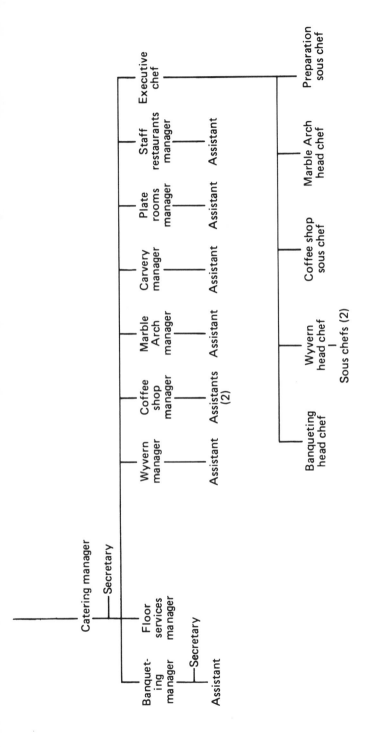

Organization chart of the Cumberland Hotel, Marble Arch, London W1. Number of rooms 910.

This organization chart shows the main management and supervisory positions.

It does not show operative staff, who number in the region of 500.

Reproduced by permission of the Management of the Cumberland Hotel and Trusthouse Forte.

Figure 18.3   *Organization chart of a medium-sized hotel*

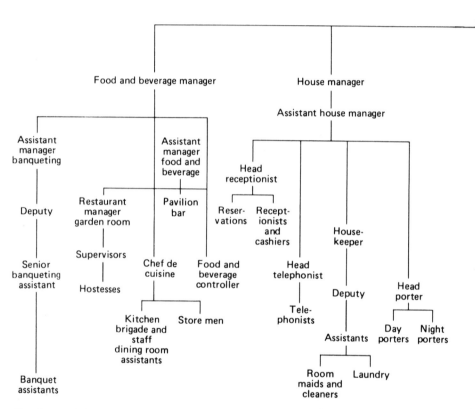

Organization chart of the Crest Hotel, Maidenhead.   Number of rooms 200.
Total staff numbers approximately 140.

Reproduced by permission of the Management of the Crest Hotel,
Maidenhead and Crest Hotels Europe

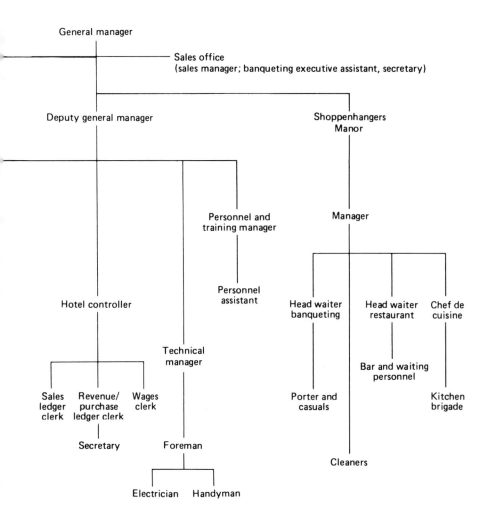

Figure 18.4   *Organization chart of a small hotel*

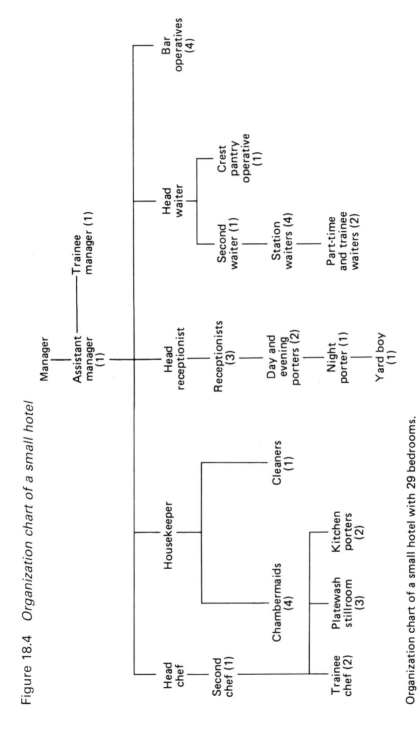

Organization chart of a small hotel with 29 bedrooms.

Reproduced by permission of the Management of the Royal Hop Pole and Crest Hotels Europe.

Figure 18.5 *Organization structure of a large hotel company with 30 hotels*

MANAGEMENT STRUCTURE FOR DE VERE & G W HOTELS

Reproduced by courtesy of the Management of De Vere Hotels

Figure 18.6   *Organization chart of a public house*

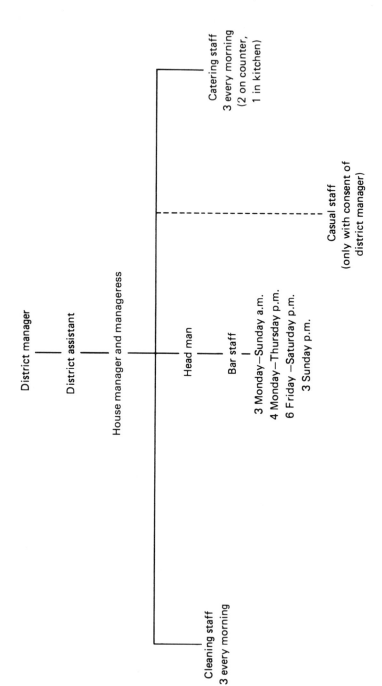

This is an organization chart of a typical public house with music and some catering, taking about £10,000 per week (net of VAT).

Reproduced by permission of Albion Taverns (Watney).

Figure 18.7 *Organization chart of a university catering department*

Organization chart of a university catering department serving about 1000 lunches, 1750 snacks, 300 dinners, private parties, functions and bars.

Reproduced by permission of Sussex University and Mrs Derin, Catering Manager.

Figure 18.8　*Organization chart of Brighton Polytechnic catering and bars division*

The Polytechnic has approximately 4000 full-time and 4000 part-time students and serves approximately 3800 meals per day. The catering department employed approximately 100 staff at the time this chart was produced.

Reproduced by kind permission of the Polytechnic, and with the help of Margaret Palmear

Figure 18.9 *Organization chart of a fast-food, take-away outlet*

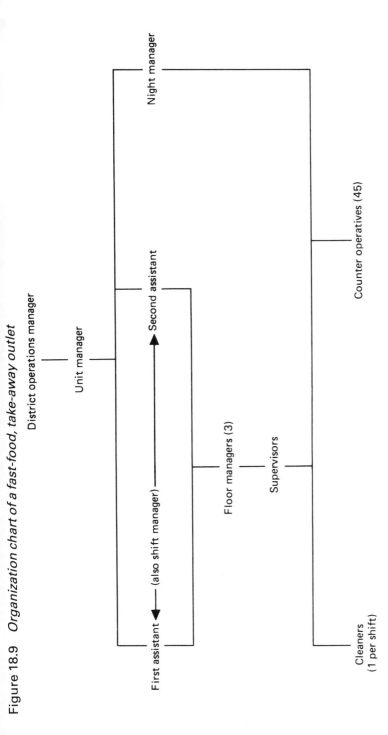

This organization chart of a fast-food, take-away outlet consists of French fries area, preparation room, counter, grills section and lobby. Turnover is in the region of £40,000 per week.

Figure 18.10 *Organization chart of the catering department of the Royal Sussex County Hospital*

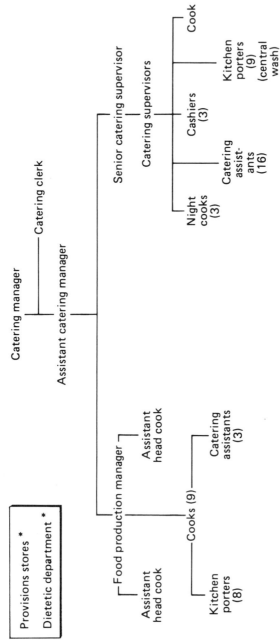

* Not directly responsible to catering manager but close liaison between departments.

The Hospital caters for approximately 900 patients and staff a day.

Reproduced by permission of the Royal Sussex County Hospital Catering Management and with the help of Mr Winter.

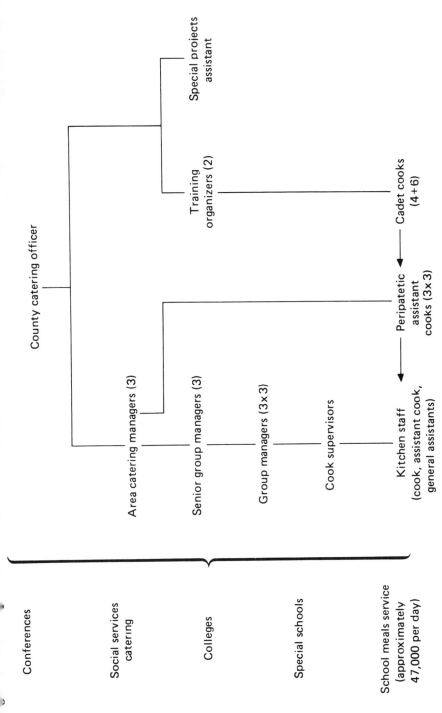

Reproduced by permission of the East Sussex County Catering Service and Michael Garrett.

chapter 19

Labour costs and productivity

In some industries it is reasonably simple to state with some degree of confidence what labour costs should be as a percentage of total costs, of revenue or of some other clear standard. However, because the hotel and catering industry often consists of a service to other industries, apart from creating an end-product in its own right, no such simple yardstick exists; for example, labour costs in a modern efficiently designed and well-managed public house may be as low as 10 per cent, whereas in many sectors of institutional and industrial catering labour may cost 60 per cent or 70 per cent of revenue. In some clubs labour costs can approach 90 per cent of trade done. In this case the apparently high labour cost is often caused by the very high level of subscription income not accounted for in the 'trade' revenue, and the low level of price charged for goods and services.

Factors influencing labour costs

The factors which influence labour costs are numerous but probably what determines labour cost more than anything else is the precise nature of the enterprise, and the employer's particular policy; for example, if it is to provide a subsidized service, with low selling prices to employees, then labour costs at a percentage of revenue will be high. If, at the other extreme, it is to maximize profit in the short term, by providing a product involving minimum service from capital-intensive plant, using unskilled staff, as in many fast food operations, then the labour costs will be low.

Another major factor will be the efficiency of the design. Modern, carefully designed hotels can now expect room-maids to service around seventeen bedrooms per section, compared with older hotels where sections often have to be much smaller.

Equally important of course is the level of service provided. A fast food take-away operation or a wine bar may operate with a labour percentage of around 15 per cent, whereas a high class restaurant offering skilled personal attention may need to operate at around 35 per cent labour cost. Likewise a modern three star hotel with minimal personal service can operate around the 18–20 per cent labour cost with the five star hotel needing to spend around 40 per cent on labour.

Figure 19.1 *Some factors influencing payroll costs*

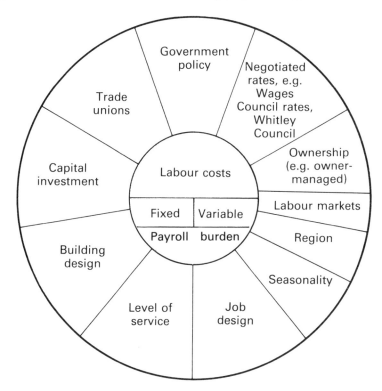

Trade unions

Trade unions influence rates and labour costs in a number of ways. In the public sector they negotiate on behalf of catering workers, along with many other workers. In the private sector they represent employees on the industry's Wages Councils and hence they influence the Wages Council rates which are either the actual rates paid by many employers or the rates are those used by other employers as bench-marks or guidelines in setting their own rates. Again, many catering employees' rates are determined along with those rates which unions have negotiated for another industry's primary workers such as motor manufacturers' or warehouse staff.

Owner managers

In establishments at the smaller end of the scale a vital factor influencing labour costs is whether an establishment is run by the owner or by an employed manager. Owners managing an establishment can influence labour costs in a number of ways. First, some owners 'pay themselves' unrealistic wages for a variety of reasons, not least to minimize tax liability. Second, owners generally are much firmer in controlling costs and, third, they avoid employing excess labour as 'cover' for themselves and for other employees.

The labour percentages in Figure 19.2 are intended to indicate the approximate level of labour cost (as a percentage of revenue) likely to be encountered in viable establishments. This does not mean that there are not successful establishments operating outside of these ranges. Likewise, it must be recognized that labour costs are partly fixed and partly variable so if trade drops dramatically there is a point beyond which labour costs can no longer be reduced to maintain them within the 'normal' percentages – a problem all too familiar to the management of seasonal establishments.

In some cases the wage percentage may well be reviewed on an annual basis. Most organizations however will monitor labour costs on a shorter-term basis, monthly or maybe even weekly, with many of the fast-food outlets now planning labour on an hourly basis.

Figure 19.2   *Labour costs as a percentage of revenue*

Type of outlet	Percentage range (as a percentage of revenue) per annum	Factors which can affect labour percentage	
		low	high
Hotels		efficient design,	inefficient design,
2–3 star	18–32%	limited menu,	extensive menus,
4–5 star	25–35%	living-in staff,	high level of
rooms division	12–20%	limited services	service, e.g.
food & beverage	30–45%		room service
Restaurants – waiter/waitress service	25–35%	as above	as above
Popular catering – waitress service	22–35%		
Self-service	15–25%	as above	as above
Wine bars	15–22%	as above	as above
Fast food take-away	11–18%	as above	as above
Department stores	20–25%	as above	as above
Kiosks, mainly confectionery and tobacco	around 6%	very high tobacco element	
Public houses	10–20%	efficient design, e.g. one bar, mainly liquor sales	high catering ratio, several bars/ restaurants

This table is intended to be a guide only, and it must be recognized that businesses may still operate successfully outside of these. These should be viewed as the range within which most viable businesses operate on a long-term (e.g. annual) basis. There can be considerable fluctuation on a short-term basis as labour costs are not a completely variable cost.

N.B. Contract catering is not included as results are totally dependent upon client policy.

Figure 19.3 Employees' work schedule

6 = 7 = 8 = 9 = 10 = 11 = 12 = 1 = 2 = 3 = 4 = 5 = 6 = 7 = 8 = 9 = 10 = 11 = 12 = 1 = 2

| Projected volume | 45 | 240 | 240 | 240 | 150 | 120 | 115 | 135 | 150 | 150 | 150 | 120 | 100 | 1955 | 180 |
| Projected labour | 2 | 2 | 9½ | 16 | 16 | 13 | 8½ | 12 | 14 | 14 | 14 | 14 | 13 | 8 | |

Day — Crew black line this side (Station / Hours worked):
Nadir, Robert, Edward, Rupert, Soraya, Steven, Michael, Paul, Selina, George, Barbara, Thomas, Dennis, Hammond, Chandra, Andrew, William

Night — Crew dotted line this side (Station / Hours worked):
Sandeep, Martin, Amina, Natasha, David, John, Sarah, Ashley

F R I D A Y

Figure 19.3 illustrates a format used by some fast food operators. The consequence of this precise hour-by-hour planning is that labour costs are planned and controlled accurately to precise percentages. One of the international fast food chains operates branches at around an 11.5% labour cost, with management costs ranging from 2% for the most efficient and busy branches up to 6% for others.

Payroll burden

There are other factors to take into account, however, which influence labour costs. In particular there is what is often referred to as the payroll burden. This consists of costs which are additional to the wages and salaries paid to labour and includes elements such as holiday pay, meals, uniforms, staff transport, etc. One key element is the extent to which an employer incurs tax or social security liabilities as well. In the United Kingdom the payroll burden can be around 11%, which is relatively low compared with some other countries such as France or Sweden where it can be as high as 40–50%.

Productivity measurement

One of the problems of using labour percentage as the main means of labour cost control is that it does not indicate whether the cost is the result of employing a large number of low paid people or of employing fewer people but paying them a higher wage. In addition, in many sectors of the industry such as the school meals service, the hospital service and employee meal services, labour costs cannot be expressed as a proportion of revenue because there may be little or no revenue, or because subsidies distort the picture. Other measures, therefore, become necessary. Basically these are concerned with relating labour input into the various forms of output. Such measures include physical and part physical/financial measures and they will vary amongst the different sectors and also within departments. These may be based on some constant (i.e. a factor unaffected by inflation) such as time. Some examples are shown in Figure 19.4. It should be borne in mind, however, that straight comparisons can be dangerous; for example, in one industrial catering situation a 'main meal' may offer each customer a wide choice, while in another situation there may be no choice. Other factors such as shift work and night work also play an important part, as do national and international work patterns; for example, in an Industrial Society survey (*Catering, Prices, Costs and Subsidies*) shows that for every individual catering worker employed, about 22 main meals were served. The author's own consultancy work shows that in some other European countries the number of meals served is frequently between 50 and 60 for each industrial catering worker employed.

The principal approaches to measuring productivity are described here.

Figure 19.4 *Some examples of productivity measures*

Department	Description of productivity measure	Some examples
Catering		
Employee meal service	(1) Number of meals served for each member of staff (full-time equivalent)	30 meals per day
	(2) Covers served per paid hour	4.5 covers
	(3) Paid minutes for each meal served	
	plate wash	7 minutes
	waiters	24 minutes
	cooks	15 minutes
	Coffee Shop	15 minutes
Hospitals	(4) Labour as a percentage of direct costs $\dfrac{\text{Labour + Materials}}{\text{Labour}} \times 100$	e.g. 52%
School meals	(5) Labour to materials ratio	£2 labour to £2 material
Hotels	(1) Employees per room	e.g. 0.9 per room
	(2) Number of guest nights for each member of staff (full-time equivalent)	21 sleeper nights for each member of staff
	(3) Number of rooms served for each member of staff on duty	17 rooms to 1 member of staff
	(4) Number of paid minutes for each sleeper night	
	room-maids	27 minutes per room (maids on duty only)
	reception	33 minutes per guest night
Public houses/bars	(1) Barrels and barrels equivalent per full-time equivalent	3.7 barrels per week

Number of units sold per employee

A commonly used crude measure of productivity is that of the number of units produced/sold for each employee. This measure is frequently used, for example, to compare car manufacturing productivity between nations. In hotels and restaurants one very simple measure is to relate the number of employees to the number of units of service, e.g. rooms, guests, meals served. These are usually extremely crude measures as comparisons are rarely like with like. Some rooms may be larger than others, some meals more complex than others, some guests may stay for longer periods than others.

Sales to payroll index

This is another way of expressing the labour cost as a proportion of revenue. It indicates the amount of revenue in pounds generated by each pound spent on labour. For hotels in Europe, for example, the index for *rooms* was $5.4 for every dollar spent on labour, while for *food and beverage* the index was £2.5 (source Worldwide Lodging Industry, Horwarth and Horwarth London;

Medlik, 1985). For hotels in the United Kingdom, for example, the index for rooms was £5.02 for every pound spent on labour, while for food and beverage the index was £3.41 (*The Business of Hotels*, Rik Medlik, 1989, quoting The Worldwide Lodging Industry 1985). There are other factors to take into account, however, which influence labour costs.

Sales and payroll cost per employee

Another way is to look at the sales per employee and after deducting the employee cost, the net sales per employee.

Added Value

This method assesses the value added by each pound spent on labour. It is calculated by representing the gross profit (sales less material costs) as a proportion of the labour cost. The Worldwide Lodging Industry survey showed the added value for rooms division in Europe was $4.6 for every dollar spent on labour, and for food and beverage the added value was $1.5 for every dollar spent on labour.

Materials to labour ratio

In many catering operations where there may be little or no revenue, or where there is a subsidy element (e.g. hospitals, schools, employee meal services, clubs) expressing labour costs as a proportion of sales is either not possible or it can be meaningless for comparative purposes. Other measures are, therefore, necessary – these can include the materials to labour ratio, i.e. how much labour is needed to process the materials required. In hospitals this can be around a 1:1 ratio, whereas in some school meals operations it can range from around 0.4:1.0 labour to materials in centralized production operations to as high as 2.6:1.0 in some labour-intensive, localized production systems. See Figure 19.5 showing comparisons of different forms of production in school meals.

Effective use of available labour is obviously one of the key measures to controlling labour costs. Other factors to take into account include considering alternative ways of getting work done which can reduce the payroll burden. For example, companies such as IBIS (part of the French Accor Group) use contract cleaners to service their hotel bedrooms. Whilst this may appear an expensive method short term, long term their labour cost is reduced and management can concentrate their efforts on the core business.

Good productivity measurement enables comparisons to be made between units or groups of workers on the same operations, or the same unit or groups of workers at different times and in spite of the many problems encountered in attempting to make comparisons, productivity measurement is a vital control tool for management, helping with budgeting, forecasting, human resource planning, incentive schemes and diagnosis of poor performance. Productivity measurement has the advantage over straight labour percentages of providing constant measurement which is unaffected by inflation and changes in wage rates.

Figure 19.5 *School meals data*

Productivity — School meals actual data referred to eight English local authorites

These figures were correct in April 1985

County	School meals produced per day 1000s	Staff required to produce 1,000 meals per day	Paid minutes per meal produced	Labour cost per meal £
Leicestershire	76.8	24.2	6	0.26
Kent	10.6	25.4	6	0.29
Lincolnshire	17.4	27.4	6	0.30
Staffordshire	82.3	27.3	6	0.29
Essex	81.5	28.0	7	0.31
Warwickshire	28.6	29.3	7	0.32
Cornwall	30.5	34.3	8	0.38
Bedfordshire	26.8	54.1	13	0.58
Average of group	56.6	26.7	6	0.29

Production methods — simple comparison

Production method	Labour costs	Materials	Transport	Total
Centralized production				
Individual meals	0.18	0.37	0.05	0.60
Bulk	0.15	0.37	0.05	0.57
Other forms of production				
Mainly local	0.26 – 0.58	0.22		0.48 – 0.90

Production Method	Labour to materials ratio in pence
Centralized production	
Individual meals	$\dfrac{\text{labour } 18}{\text{supplies } 37} = 0.48 / 1.0$
Bulk	$\dfrac{\text{labour } 0.15}{\text{supplies } 0.37} = 0.40 / 1.0$
Local production	
Division A	$\dfrac{\text{labour } 26}{\text{materials } 22} = 1.18 / 1$
Division B	$\dfrac{\text{labour } 18}{\text{materials } 22} = 0.82 / 1$

Further reading

Catering Prices, Costs and Subsidies, London: Industrial Society, annually
Medlik, S., *The Business of Hotels*, London: Heinemann, 1989
Jones, P., and Lockwood A., *The Management of Hotel Operations*, London: Cassell, 1989

Questions

1 Describe the objectives of and alternative approaches to labour cost and productivity measurement.

2 Discuss the differences between labour cost measurement and productivity measurement.

3 Discuss what external factors influence (a) labour costs and (b) productivity.

4 Using an employer you know well, evaluate their approach to managing labour costs and productivity.

chapter 20

Customer care

Most successful enterprises, one way or another, have arrived at the right approach to looking after their customers properly. Whether it is the 'up-market' restaurateur giving each lady a carnation or the road-side cafe giving speedy service, the successful operator has usually provided what it is the customers are seeking. The problems usually arise, however, with expansion. As a business becomes bigger, as more of the customers are dealt with by employed staff, frequently young and not well versed in social skills, and as competition becomes more severe the need arises for a systematic approach to ensuring that the 'target' customers receive the service they expect.

In setting out to provide customers with what the operator thinks they expect it is essential to recognise that the quality of the service is influenced by a number of different factors. Some of these factors are only noticed by the customer if the factor is wrong in some way, such as room temperature and noise levels. Other factors contribute positively to the experience, such as being recognized by the staff and being addressed by one's name. One can draw parallels with Herzberg's hygiene factors and motivators which relate to employees' perceptions of their work experience.

Over recent years there have been many different approaches to developing 'customer care' programmes but in many of these cases they do not recognize the full range of elements which go to making up the total 'customer experience'. Too many programmes concentrate on one element only – usually the staff training element.

Today the majority of the population now experiences a wide range of service 'products', be they fast food, medical care, leisure or education. And the expectations of these consumers have been heightened, and are constantly raised, by these self same 'service' products. Concomitant with this has been the increasing convergence of many products, be they motor cars, high street banks, airline flights or pub-restaurants.

In many cases the search for *product differentiation*, the process by which a provider of a generic product makes the product different from his competitors', has to be concentrated on the 'people inter-actions' involved. The classic example is the air transport industry in which companies compete on similar routes using similar aircraft. The main way by which they can increase their market share at the expense of their competitors is to obtain the best flight slots, after which the only extra dimension they can add is that of better service; speedier check-in, better waiting arrangements and better 'in-flight' food and cabin service.

Because 'customer care' has become fashionable many organizations decide it is something they have to do. The problem is that, as Herzberg and many others showed with regard to employment, 'customer care' is a highly complex issue. However, in looking at the range of customer care programmes it is evident that many employers make assumptions about what the problem is. Very frequently it is apparent that the employer believes 'social skill' training is either what is required or is all that can be afforded, whereas the fundamental problem may be one of design, the process of delivery or even product quality. What has not been done is to analyse the 'customer care' needs systematically.

There are, however, organizations which do this. The Sheraton Hotel Corporation, for example, runs a very sophisticated programme which involves regular assessment of the standards being achieved. Other organizations run customer care audits, some of which are carefully structured and some of which are not. One writer, Martin, has developed a two-dimensional diagnostic tool, similar to the Mouton and Blake Management Grid (see Chapter 21), which evaluates an oganization's customer care on two dimensions – procedures and conviviality. See Figure 20.1.

This need for diagnosis (part of the normal market research effort) is absolutely essential if the efforts put into 'customer care' programmes are to be properly focused and rewarded. To train staff in social skills when the under-lying problem is product quality may result at the least in resentment towards the management, whom the staff perceive as not recognizing the real issues.

The four 'Ps' of the 'customer care' mix

A careful analysis of most service operations and the wide range of customer care programmes will identify around four key dimensions. The elements are:

1 Product quality.
2 Process used to deliver the product.
3 Pricing and method of payment.
4 People inter-actions.

Product quality

In many service operations product quality may be similar to one's competitors – in retailing for example, a retailer may be selling products identical to his competitors' products. In other cases however, such as in catering, the organization may be creating unique products. In any event it is for manage-ment to develop ways and means for setting quality standards and monitoring the customers' perceptions of product quality. In the case of school meals the catering supervisors may need to spend more time talking with customers (children, parents, teachers) to determine the customers' expectations and perceptions of quality and preferences, i.e. they may need to become more

Figure 20.1 Martin's customer care evaluation grid

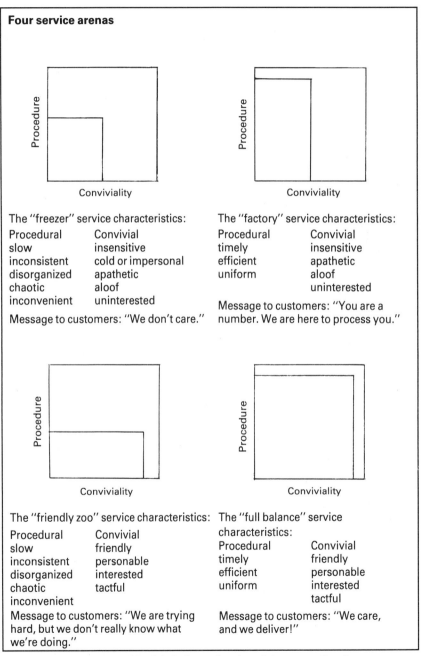

Four service arenas

The "freezer" service characteristics:

Procedural	Convivial
slow	insensitive
inconsistent	cold or impersonal
disorganized	apathetic
chaotic	aloof
inconvenient	uninterested

Message to customers: "We don't care."

The "factory" service characteristics:

Procedural	Convivial
timely	insensitive
efficient	apathetic
uniform	aloof
	uninterested

Message to customers: "You are a number. We are here to process you."

The "friendly zoo" service characteristics:

Procedural	Convivial
slow	friendly
inconsistent	personable
disorganized	interested
chaotic	tactful
inconvenient	

Message to customers: "We are trying hard, but we don't really know what we're doing."

The "full balance" service characteristics:

Procedural	Convivial
timely	friendly
efficient	personable
uniform	interested
	tactful

Message to customers: "We care, and we deliver!"

Source: Reproduced from Martin's 2-dimensional model – see reading list.

market oriented and less product oriented. At an organizational level the school meals' organization may need to be incorporated into schools councils, PTA meetings, etc.

Management must also recognize that effective 'customer care' may involve considerable expenditure. Cosmetic covering over of operational wrinkles with 'customer care' training may not be enough. In the case of school meals for example, the solution to cold food may not be 'customer care' training but an investment in proper equipment.

Process

In many service operations the overall 'process' by which people enjoy the service is often vital and complex. The process describes all the stages before, during and after, which contribute to the enjoyment of the service itself. In eating out or shopping, for example, a customer may attach considerable importance to being able to park a car close to the restaurant or shop.

The main elements of the 'process' may include:

1 *Access:* easy access, clearly identified.
2 *Information:* clear, friendly signing to the different services, avoidance of admonishing notices, such as 'keep out'.
3 *Products and services:* properly priced if necessary.
4 *Queueing:* A key element of the 'process', and a major dissatisfier in most service operations is queueing in one form or another. In many cases, particularly where customers have to make a choice between a number of queues, queueing is a lottery and a cause for considerable dissatisfaction. In other cases lengthy queueing causes irritation.
    Quite a lot is now known about queueing and this can be applied to reducing queueing related problems. For example, eliminating the lottery element from queueing by channelling all customers into one queue, with multiple service points, as is done in 'echelon' self-service restaurants and many banks, is one solution. Another is to issue customers with numbered tickets as is done for the serviced counters of many supermarkets. Another is to keep customers occupied whilst waiting. This could be by displaying attractive menus or, as is increasingly the case, by playing videos which may actually promote other services.

Another fact known about queueing is that if customers know the likely duration of queueing this reduces a cause for irritation. London Underground have recognized this issue and now display the approximate waiting time for trains in many of their stations. Likewise, customers do not feel that they are part of the process until they have been acknowledged by the staff or are clearly part of a queue – hence the considerable irritation felt by many pub customers.

Apart from the actual queueing there is also 'waiting time'. In a recent study (M. Anderson, D. Lengel, Yin Jian Zhou, 'Survey of Good Service in Fine-Dining Restaurants', Michigan State University – quoted in *Cornell Quarterly*, Nov. 1988) it was reported that customers were prepared to wait for two minutes to be greeted. However as *waiting* time is perceived as longer than *occupied* time the real time can be reduced dramatically to around 30 seconds according to Bonnie Knutson, *Cornell Quarterly*, Nov. 1988. Effective service operators manage this element of the process. In a restaurant for example, 'waiting time' may be occupied by customers looking at menus, drinking an *aperitif*.

In many cases service providers actually complicate the process unnecessarily. For example the use of foreign language menus may do something for the atmosphere of a restaurant but little for the efficiency of order-taking if they are not translated. There are still many restaurants, ethnic restaurants particularly, who do not translate their menus, causing order-taking delays in busy periods and even deterring many potential customers.

Price and payment

In many service operations both the price and the method of payment play crucial roles in the customer's perception of the experience. The method of price display is crucial also. Most supermarkets make price comparisons relatively easy and supermarkets give their customers a degree of control over the amount spent. It is possible to select many items at a price one can afford because of the range of products, package sizes and prices. THF hotels have recognized that a major determinant of wine choice is price so their wine list is organized by price as well as by wine type.

Many service providers, restaurants for example, still have supplementary charges, such as service charge and cover charges, which may deter some potential customers who want to know the exact price.

The actual *process* of payment is also crucial to the service experience. Supermarkets have invested considerable amounts in improving their check-out procedures but it still remains a key problem in their operation. In many restaurants guests have to queue to pay after their meal. In many hotels checking out can present serious problems and delays and these have to be eliminated wherever possible. A good customer care programme might identify these as problems needing to be resolved rather than training the staff in how to handle the complaints of the dissatisfied customers.

Alternative methods of payment may also be crucial to the perception of the service experience, apart from possibly increasing the 'spend per head'. For example, some customers may wish to use credit or bankers' cards and establishments which do not accept this form of payment may be disadvantaging themselves relative to their competitors.

People

The last element in the 'customer care' mix is concerned with the people, the staff, who provide the service. How such people are selected and developed will vary considerably from one situation to another. In this respect it is necessary for staff to recognize their interdependency on other staff and the need for all staff, including those who do not deal with customers directly, to recognize the importance of their role relative to the customer.

Some forms of training concentrate on teaching the staff certain 'scripts', such as 'good day, how may I help you?' and teaching staff to use a customer's name. Others may be less prescriptive but may still require certain rituals to be observed. Sheraton for example set a variety of 'Sheraton Guest Satisfaction Standards'. Figure 20.2 shows one such standard.

Figure 20.2　*A Sheraton Guest Satisfaction Standard*

Meeting 1: "Greet the Guest"

HANDOUT 1–1

Sheraton
Guest Satisfaction Standards

1. Every time you see a guest, smile and offer an appropriate hospitality comment.

2. Speak to every guest in a friendly, enthusiastic and courteous tone and manner.

3. Answer guest questions and requests quickly and efficiently, or take personal responsibility to get the answers.

4. Anticipate guest needs and resolve guest problems.

Specific *selling* skills may also be developed. For example, one of the leading fast food chains trains staff to attempt to 'up-sell' one item more than the customer has ordered but never two or more.

Other training will be concerned with developing attitudes and skills based on certain schools of psychology such as the famous 'transactional analysis' often described as TA (see *What Do You Say After You Say Hello?*, Eric Berne, Corgi, London 1974) which sets out to develop a person's ability to recognize a customer's personality state and to respond with an appropriate one. TA has been used over many years as a form of 'customer care' training by a wide range of organizations including British Transport, Scandinavian Air Services and Crest Hotels.

Transactional analysis

Transactional analysis sets out to analyse the nature of the individual personality states involved in transactions between people and the nature of the transactions themselves. Each normal individual's personality consists of three separate but interacting personality states or elements, the *Parent*, the *Adult*, and the *Child*.

The *Parent* is derived from experiences of authority figures including parents and parent substitutes such as teachers, the police, etc.

The *Child* part of the personality draws upon the person's experiences, particularly the feelings and emotions of childhood. For example the trepidation felt by many employees when the boss says 'I want to talk to you', may be to do with the memory many people have of how worried they were when their own father said just these words. There may be nothing to worry about but certain phrases and situations recall involuntarily certain experiences.

The *Adult* part of a person's personality functions rationally. It does not mimic parental attitudes nor does it react emotionally.

The Adult part of the personality receives information from outside, from the Parent part of the personality, and from the Child part of the personality as well. It questions the validity of the information from each source and it then attempts to produce a rational result. This is based neither on what is expected by the Parent or wanted by the Child.

A person with a strong Adult is often described as mature or well-balanced. One with a strong Child may be described as immature and one with a strong Parent as too rigid.

When two people meet therefore the three parts of each person's personality are involved and the outcome of the meeting or transaction will be dependent entirely upon which part of each person's personality is involved. Every transaction is a two way affair – with one person communicating in the first instance (providing the stimulus) and the other responding (making the response).

In the simplest transactions the arrows are parallel and these are called *complementary transactions*, as shown in Figure 20.3. If the arrows remain parallel – that is when the transactions are complementary – communication may proceed indefinitely.

Figure 20.3 shows a simple example of a Parent type communication

Figure 20.3 *A complementary transaction*

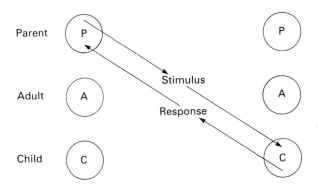

receiving a Child response. An illustration of such a transaction would be a domineering executive booking in at a reception desk manned by a receptionist who reacts in an obedient, submissive childlike way to the 'parental nature of the executive'. The interaction or transaction, as such processes are called, could continue for some time.

Figure 20.4 shows a *crossed transaction* – the type of transaction which apparently causes most trouble. An example of this is when a waitress asks (in Adult fashion) for the meals for a particular table and the chef replies that everyone is in a rush and that he needs more staff in any case, replying much as a child often does when irritated by a parent.

The transaction breaks down because the chef raised issues which were not relevant to the rational request of the waitress. It was not an Adult reply but a Child reply to an Adult request. The only probable solution to this Child response is for the manager (a Parent figure) to order the chef to produce the goods. This then keeps the second part of the transaction upon parallel lines. These complementary and crossed transactions are simple one-level transactions.

Figure 20.4   *A crossed transaction*

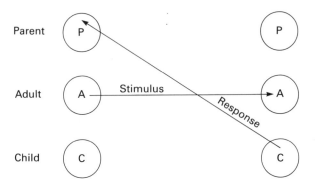

Figure 20.5   *A two-level transaction*

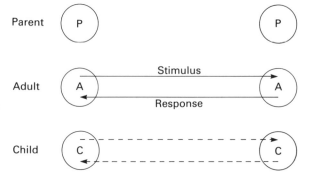

But beyond these there are two types of ulterior or 'two level' transactions. On the surface we see a complementary Adult to Adult transaction but the stimulus may be 'a sales hook' appealing to the Child in the respondent. For example, to offer sweets from the sweet trolley or, at the other extreme, an executive jet to a chief executive, can be made to sound very Adult, with Adult reasoning put forward in justification. But all along the offer – the stimulus – may really be appealing to the Child. In this case the Respondent may respond to the stimulus in a Childlike way 'I want it and I will have it'. (See Figure 20.5.)

Types of transactions

The principal interactions or transactions which take place between people are divided into several basic types:

Procedures
Rituals
Activities and work
Pastimes
Operations
Games.

Procedures

The 'procedure' is a series of transactions between two people at an Adult level, and is concerned with achieving objectives as effectively as possible, which are normally understood by each person. Booking a hotel guest into a hotel under normal circumstances is a 'procedure' because one person wants a room and the receptionist wants to sell the room.

Rituals

'Rituals' consist of a series of stereotype transactions which may be informal or highly formalised. An informal ritual takes place when two close friends meet, shake hands and ask about one another's families. A more formalised ritual takes place between complete strangers and in many commercial transactions, for example when buying something in a shop. Rituals are the safest form of transaction because the outcome is predictable.

Activities or work

Activities or work transactions are programmed by the work itself, for example by the material or the system. During the activity there is no need for involvement with others – there may be a need, but it is not essential. The outcome again is predictable and therefore work is the next safest form of interchange between individuals.

Pastimes

After activities or work come pastimes. Pastimes are like social skirmishing, getting to know more about the other person in order to decide whether the next step – games – can be taken.

Operations

An operation occurs when one person states his needs frankly and the other person, the respondent, satisfies these needs without taking advantage of the situation. Operations, no matter how often they are repeated, are to be distinguished from games and also rituals and pastimes.

Games

'Games', although appearing to be operations, are ulterior transactions between people, which have psychological pay-offs or rewards. They are normally repetitious but repetition in itself does not make the transaction a Game. There must be a payoff. For example, if an employee regularly seeks reassurance that he is doing his job satisfactorily and when reassured, goes away content then there is no ulterior motive and therefore a Game is not being played. But if after receiving several reassurances he were to say 'in that case I want an increase in pay' then there was an ulterior motive and he has 'conned' his boss. He has played a 'Game' with his boss who probably now feels aggrieved that a normal human response – to give reassurance where it was merited – has been used against him for an ulterior or unexpected motive.

Within the hotel and restaurant world, where personal transactions are the very essence of the business, all of these types of transactions are possible and in many cases guests or staff will move rapidly from the ritual stage to the games stage. Once games are being played unfortunately either guests or a member of staff can suffer. As a consequence and to ensure that this does not happen particularly to the socially inexperienced staff, such as the young or the newcomers from a business with less public contact, it is wise to build up a defence of 'Rituals' which will direct their social contacts with their guests. Some will argue that this will result in too much uniformity and lack of individual personality showing through.

This could be the case if taken too far, but in the absence of rituals there is far too much 'game playing' between guests and staff, leading to one or the other being hurt, so if rituals are designed carefully to meet all the more common, workaday transactions between staff and guests a good deal of the hurtful 'game playing' that takes place will be eliminated.

Generally, the rituals need to be simple. Many socially aware managers have recognized the need and have ensured that the staff are trained to use them. There are, within a hotel context, two main types.

Firstly a regular ritual is one used when something normal and routine occurs. For example when a guest arrives to book in, a strictly laid down script could be followed, which covers the various alternatives such as:

A guest with a confirmed booking
A guest with a booking but no confirmation
A chance guest.

The second ritual would be one developed to deal with non-routine events which, however, occur from time to time – such as dealing with an over-booking or an incorrect booking.

In both cases one has to design a ritual which is acceptable to the Adult part of a person's personality. Most frequently, particularly in the case of dealing with complaints, everything immediately 'switches on' . . . the Child or the Parent in a personality. The Child who has not got what he wanted. The consequence is that – as with dealing with young children – reason will not prevail in any event. And only when something 'switches on' the Adult again will reason prevail. Frequently this occurs only after there has been a change of personalities involved, and the receptionist who has failed to placate an irate guest is surprised to see the manager deal with the situation very smoothly. It is not necessarily because of the manager's extra skill but only because the change of personalities enables the irate guest's Adult to be 'switched on' again.

Different approaches to customer care

Frances Sacker, of the Industrial Society, in her article 'Customer service training in context' (*Personnel Management*, March 1987) separated training into two main types, the 'evangelical' and the 'exploratory' styles. The evangelical style is aimed at creating 'a high degree of excitement and enthusiasm' whereas the exploratory style is concerned with giving individuals 'the opportunity, through discussion, video, etc. to make decisions about their own behaviour and about practical actions they can take to improve their own performance.

The organization's needs and the resources they have available for training as well as the calibre of their staff will all contribute towards the decision regarding the most appropriate approach to training. Obviously the question arises as to which is more important – the ability to select well or to train well. Many personnel specialists take the view however that training is only likely to be effective if the right calibre of person is recruited in the first place.

Selecting and motivating staff

In looking at the 'customer care' mix it is apparent that there is considerable dependence between the four separate elements of the mix. In addition however it is vital that the approach to staffing is correct as well, including

Figure 20.6   *The Sheraton customer care cycle*

recruiting staff with the correct attitudes, training them and rewarding them appropriately. In the case of the Sheraton programme employee recognition features as a key element (see Figure 20.6).

In the case of Barclays Bank the fourth declared objective of their programme is 'to reinforce the objectives with accountability and recognition'. If an employer claims that customer care is so crucial to the success of the enterprise then the employer must demonstrate that commitment by developing proper reward systems. This could be in the form of bonuses but many programmes involving rewards appear to use other forms of employee incentive. Several of the large hotel groups and airlines for example, select the 'employee of the month' from the workforce and reward accordingly. Sometimes these are selected by management, sometimes by customers. Unfortunately, many are known by the staff to be manipulated – the award going to each department in turn. It could be argued however that such approaches to motivation are external or extrinsic to a proper customer care programme. Instead a proper programme, which is also concerned with recruiting the right staff, itself engages the interest of the staff and of itself provides the necessary motivation.

The need for a policy and diagnosis

As stated earlier many 'customer care' programmes start without a properly defined 'customer care' policy or a proper audit or diagnosis of what the organization's needs are. Typically many concentrate on solutions to problems which have not been identified. Some however do contain 'diagnostic' elements – Sheraton Hotels, for example, have a regular customer rating process (see Figure 20.6) which provides each unit with its own customer rating index and its rating relative to other similar Sheraton hotels.

Figure 20.7   *A Customer Care Evaluation Scheme (Cross Channel Ferries)*

A. The questionnaire

	Positive +	Neutral	Negative −
Food temperature			
Signposting			
Value for money			
Sensitivity towards customers			
Drink temperature			
Menu information/explanation			
Payment system			
Ability to adapt			
Presentation			
Queueing			
Bill clarity			
Cleanliness of uniform			
Aroma of food			
Waiting time			
Price display			
Appearance			
Freshness			
Service			
Exchange of money			
Skill			
Taste			
Opening time			
Methods of payment (cheque, cash)			
Language			
Value for money			
Hygiene			
Usefulness			
Courtesy			
Appropriateness of dishes			
Ambience			
Dealing with a problem (payment)			
Understanding problems			
Product range			
Comfort			
Resolving complaints			
Shipboard knowledge			
Portion size			
Heating			
Budget control			
General knowledge			

Figure 20.7   *A Customer Care Evaluation Scheme – cont.*

B. Score Sheet

		P		P		P		P
	1		2		3		4	
	5		6		7		8	
	9		10		11		12	
	13		14		15		16	
	17		18		19		20	
	21		22		23		24	
	25		26		27		28	
	29		30		31		32	
	33		34		35		36	
	37		38		39		40	
TOTAL	(product)		(process)		(price/ payment)		(people)	

C. Improvement Target

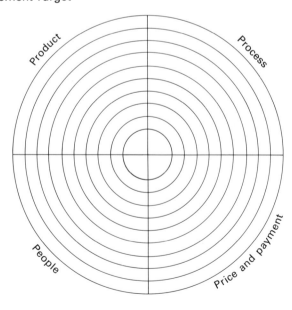

A diagnostic tool

One integrated approach (developed and used by the author), entitled 'Bullseye', provides a flexible instrument designed specifically for each customer care situation. It consists of a number of separate elements:

1 The initial research which identifies the organization's expectations. This research may include management, operative staff and, of course, customers and potential customers of the organization.
2 Preparation of a questionnaire to be used for evaluation of the existing level of customer care (see Figure 20.7).
3 A 'Bullseye' scoring sheet which determines the actual level of achievement for each of the key elements (see Figure 20.7).
4 An 'improvement plan' which could be based on an MbO and/or Quality Circles approach.

Figure 20.8   *Elements of a Customer Care Programme*

What the customer wants	What the caterer or hotelier should do	How
INFORMATION	Inform the customer	Use positive, friendly helpful notice, **not** warnings and admonishments
FAIRNESS	Design ordering procedures and queues to eliminate unfairness	Ensure that customer perceives ordering procedures and queues as fair, i.e. first come, first served
ACTIVITY	Keep customers actively involved in the 3 phases of a meal 1 pre-queuing 2 queuing 3 the meal	Involve customer as much as possible in the process, e.g. looking at menus
ATTENTION	Greet and/acknowledge customer, top-up glasses, remove used plates	Use scripts, eye-contact, body language, develop perception skills
'STROKES'	Make each customer feel special	Use customer name, compliment
REASSURANCE	Keep customer informed	Devise scripts and/or procedures
TIMELY SERVICE (and an idea of the time he/she will have to wait)	Provide timely service and keep customer informed	Set standards, control standards, informing customers of waiting times
COURTESY	Provide courteous staff and service	Personal grooming, deportment, devise systems and routines and train staff. Develop attitudes and empathy
FEEDBACK SYSTEM AND ABILITY TO COMPLAIN	Design an effective procedure for customer feedbacks, particularly complaints	Devise a policy and procedures provide training

Typically this approach fits well into Frances Sackers' 'exploratory' style – because it provides the basis for the participants to develop their own solutions to the problems they themselves have identified. Of course if an organization moves down the MbO or Quality Circles route other issues emerge such as the need to train all management and the operative staff in the effective operation of such an approach.

It should be evident from the above that effective 'customer care' consists of a number of interdependent elements, some quite complex, some simple in themselves. In most cases effective 'customer care' is likely to involve senior management commitment and the involvement of the whole workforce. It can also involve major investment in 'hardware' such as buildings, equipment, etc. A simple outline of what can be involved is shown below in Figures 20.8 and 20.9.

Figure 20.9   *The customer care process*

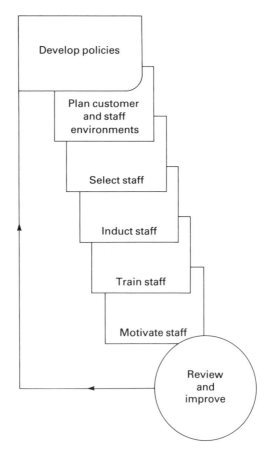

Reading list

Berne, E., *What Do You Say After You Say Hello*, London, Corgi, 1975

Berne, E., *Games People Play*, London, Penguin, 1976

Jones, P. and Lockwood, A., *The Management of Hotel Operations*, Cassell, London, 1989

Martin, W. B., 'Defining what quality service is for you', *Cornell HRA Quarterly*, February 1986

Peel, M., *Customer Service*, Kogan Page, London, 1987

Shames, G. and Glover, W., *World Class Service*, Intercultural Press, Yarmouth, USA, 1989

Questions

1 Describe the key elements needing to be considered relative to 'customer care'.

2 What is meant by the four 'Ps' of customer care? Discuss each.

3 What can be done to minimize dissatisfaction caused by queueing?

4 Discuss the value of Transactional Analysis to a work organization.

5 Evaluate the effectiveness of the customer care approach of an employer with whom you are familiar.

6 Design a customer care programme for an employer with whom you are familiar.

7 What issues will need to be considered in designing customer care programmes in the future?

chapter 21

Managing people

Within the hotel and catering industry virtually everybody works in groups of interdependent individuals. A key feature of much of the industry is the fact that most work people are very dependent, in an immediate sense, upon the work of colleagues. It is this working of interdependent individuals, brought together as groups, which determines the success or failure of many enterprises. The success of the group in turn is dependent upon the ability of some individuals, the *managers* or *leaders*, to lead such groups to achieve desired results.

What makes such a person a successful manager or leader of others has, no doubt, been a subject of discussion since the time people began to live in organized societies. At one extreme are leaders who are in positions of power and leadership as a direct result of their personalities. This is referred to by some as 'charismatic' leadership. At the other extreme are managers who rely on strict procedures and peer support in their approach to management. This is often referred to as 'bureaucratic' management. In addition, as mentioned in Chapter 2, there are other approaches as well.

Figure 21.1 identifies some of the more common approaches.

Figure 21.1 *Some of the more commonly described approaches to management*

Charismatic, Paternalistic, Bureaucratic	(Weber)
Theory X ————— Theory Y,	(Douglas McGregor)
Exploitive authoritative, benevolent authoritative, consultative, participative group,	(Rensis Likert)
Autocratic processes, consultative processes, group processes	(Vroom)
Relationship motivated – task motivated	(Fiedler)
Concern for people – concern for production	(Mouton and Blake)
Socio-technical system	(Trist et al)

Note: all of these are described in more detail in *Writers on Organizations*, edited by Pugh and Hickson; details in the reading list to this chapter.

With such a variety of different approaches it is not surprising that people are constantly asking which of these is the most likely to be successful and it is not surprising either that there is no clear cut answer. What may be successful in one situation may well prove a failure in another set of circumstances. For example, the type of leadership or management needed on the flight deck of an aircraft coming in to land will be very different from that needed in leading a team of architects designing a new building. Likewise the management skills needed to manage a fast-food outlet will be very different from those needed to manage a small directors' dining room.

Figure 21.2 illustrates some of the many factors which interact in any group/leadership situation.

Figure 21.2 *Leadership interactions*

Individuals and leadership

Considerable research has been carried out in order to identify which traits contribute to an individual being a leader or a follower. One example is the work of the armed services who subject applicants for officer status to a series of tests lasting several days. The work of J. Munroe Fraser (5-point plan for interviewing) and the National Institute of Industrial Psychology (7-point plan), discussed in Chapter 5 sets out to evaluate both genetic and social or cultural factors, some of which may contribute to leadership abilities.

In looking at these different approaches it is apparent that a range of different characteristics or traits are evaluated when individual potential is being considered. But in spite of there being a range of different methods of assessing leadership skills many employers continue to devise their own methods of identifying and measuring management potential and performance (see Chapters 7 and 9). One of the outstanding points, however, is that the majority of employers continue to develop their own methods. If, in fact, a single set of personality traits or characteristics did make for successful management or leadership, it is probable that by now some agreement would have been reached, as is more the case with single and maybe simpler personality traits such as 'intelligence'. It would appear therefore that successful management or leadership may not be the result of a simple set of characteristics but is more likely to be dependent or 'contingent' upon a whole range of interacting elements.

In looking at the many different contexts in which leadership functions, including business, government, the military, the church, etc. it is not surprising that many different types or approaches to leadership may be necessary. It is also not surprising that attempts to measure and to identify 'leadership' characteristics have been so difficult and largely fruitless. Some of the key elements in Figure 21.2 are discussed more fully here.

The individual

At the individual level there are two main aspects which have to be considered – each consisting of many different elements.

Firstly there are the 'innate' characteristics such as intelligence, height, gender. Secondly there are the culturally acquired characteristics such as beliefs, attitudes and values. These are illustrated in more detail in Figure 21.3 below.

Figure 21.3   *Some individual characteristics*

Genetically determined characteristics	Culturally determined characteristics
Physical characteristics	Values, beliefs, attitudes,
Gender, race, size, build	expectations, self-image
Psychological characteristics	language, accent,
Intelligence	behaviour, manners
Introvert–extrovert (after Eysenck)	perception of role, self-image
Stable–unstable (after Eysenck)	
Creative	

The above division between *genetic* and *cultural* personality traits is illustrative only. There are conflicting opinions about many of the above traits, for example, introversion and extroversion may be as much culturally influenced as genetically determined.

Genetic characteristics

What is inherited genetically may contribute to leadership in a number of different ways. These include characteristics such as intelligence, gender, height, physical build, even the ability to be persuaded (Open University *Evolution, Genetics and Social Behaviour*, 1976). For example, some research has shown that successful managers generally tend to have above average intelligence and to be above average height. Also males generally are more likely to hold senior management positions than females (see Figure 1.5) even when females make up the majority of the workforce. Whilst the reason for this may be more cultural than genetic a person's gender (which is genetically determined) plays a significant part in determining whether a person will be more or less acceptable as a leader or manager.

It may also be that male 'aggression' or assertiveness contributes to male success in leadership in cultures where competitiveness is a key element in organization culture. Cattell identifies one factor, factor E, which is concerned with *assertiveness*, which, to some extent, may also be genetically influenced.

Cultural characteristics

Apart from the inherited characteristics, a society through 'socialization' equips people with a whole range of beliefs, values, attitudes, prejudices and related behaviour patterns. For example, an individual's attitudes towards punctuality, honesty, work, the opposite sex, minorities, superiors and subordinates, are all part of an individual's make-up and stem from the social context in which the individual has developed. For example, certain schools and types of schools, build specific career expectations into their pupils, as do most higher education courses.

Groups

In any discussion on management or leadership it is essential to consider the nature of who or what is being managed. In most cases managers manage a range of resources including equipment, buildings, land and a number of individuals, usually organized in a group or groups. Groups are the basic building blocks of society. Groups come in all shapes and sizes and have many different purposes and there are many different definitions of groups. At one extreme are definitions which require face-to-face relationships (e.g. Robert Bales, *Readings in Social Psychology*, 3rd edition, New York, Holt, Rinehart and Winston 1958) whilst at the other extreme are those that define a group as a number of people with 'concrete, dynamic interrelations' (Kurt Lewin, *Readings in Social Psychology*, 3rd edition, New York, Holt, Rinehart and Winston 1958).

For the purpose of this book however this author is defining a group as: *two or more people interacting together in order to achieve a common goal or goals.*

Such a definition can include as few as two people working together and it can include an organization of many thousands of employees. *For the purpose of this book the definition includes both the small group and the larger group, sometimes referred to as an organization*, although some differences between groups and the organizations will be looked at later. The reason for this definition is that management, even that of large organizations functions through groups. Most chief executives of large organizations do not manage the organization, they manage a group of senior managers who in turn manage other groups.

Types of groups

The two most commonly distinguished groups are primary groups and secondary groups.

Primary groups
Primary groups, of which the family is the best example, have few, if any clearly written rules. The individual members are kept together through feelings for one another. Friendship groups are another example of a primary group. Objectives of primary groups generally are concerned with relationships between the members.

Secondary groups
Most other groups are formed for social and economic reasons, e.g. profit, education, employment. In general they are more formal than *primary* groups. As a consequence they have clearly articulated rules and procedures. Typical examples may include schools, employers, sports clubs and professional associations.

Primary groups, such as friendship groups, may form as a result of membership of secondary groups, such as attending the same school, college or employer. In some cases primary groups will devolve into secondary groups.

Reference groups
A reference group (rather like a 'role model') is a real or imagined group which has attributes attractive to an individual who may aspire to becoming a member of such a group. Supervisors, for example, may aspire to becoming a member of the management group. The concept of the 'reference group' can be used in a very manipulative fashion. Advertisers, for example, will show that the use of certain products will admit users to their 'reference' group.

Figure 21.4　*Some examples of groups*

	Socio-economic	Affiliative
Primary groups	A family	A group of friends
Secondary groups		
Formal	A Trading Company	A sports club
	A District Council	A professional body
	Trade Union	A Charity
Informal	A neighbourhood protest group	A group of fellow workers

Individuals may have several reference groups. Apart from the many different definitions there are also many different features of groups which can be isolated for discussion, such as why do groups form, how do they form, what effect does group membership have on the individuals making up the group? In order that a number of individuals may be described as a 'group' there has to be a number of elements present to a greater or lesser extent. Again, for the purpose of this book, only some key issues are to be discussed. These follow.

Features of groups

Shared goals

Ideally all members of a group share common goals. In work organizations the primary goals are likely to be task-oriented with the making of profits and/or the provision of services as fundamental. The group is created or develops because it is likely to be more efficient than the individuals working independently. In non-work organizations, such as clubs, the goals are likely to be of a personal affiliation/fulfilment nature. In some situations, however, shared goals may hardly be present. In the work situation for example, the sharing of goals can sometimes be minimal. Some trade unionists certainly do not share the same goals as their employers. Etzioni (see Chapter 2) writes that some managers have a coercive attitude to their workforce and that the workpeople in such a situation are likely to have an alienative attitude to the management. In such a situation the only shared goal is likely to be to exploit one another to the full. At the other extreme, Etzioni identifies managers with a 'normative' attitude to their workforce who in turn have a 'moral' attitude to their work. In such cases there is a sharing of common values.

Common values or norms

Ideally members of a group should hold similar values. Employee selection and induction, in fact, is largely concerned with identifying and developing individuals who share or will share the same values as the employer. To what extent, however workpeople share values with their employers may be very questionable, particularly as a considerable proportion of the total workforce may be peripheral, i.e. drawn from the secondary labour market (see Chapters 1 and 2).

This question of the members of an organization needing to share common goals or values and all that follows from this, constantly recurs as a major preoccupation of organizations. Writers such as Drucker suggest that MbO (see Chapter 3) is one means. Other writers (e.g. Lawrence and Lorsch) show that different types of company and technology create different needs for integration and different means of achieving it.

Interdependence

People with common interests and values alone do not make a group. The readers of a national newspaper, whilst probably sharing many interests and values, can hardly be described as a group. Cooks working thousands of miles apart, for the same fastfood chain can hardly be described as members of the same group. For a group to exist, there needs to be a common purpose, activity and interdependence.

Communication between members

In order that individuals can work together, in order to achieve their common goals, there will need to be communication between some, if not all the members.

Group size – larger or smaller

Group size is a key feature affecting management. The smaller the group, the easier it is generally to coordinate its activities and, as membership increases, so do the problems of coordination and control. Larger groups potentially, of course, can perform more work and have more skills available.

In employing organizations, because each member incurs costs, there is strong pressure to keep groups to a minimum size whilst setting out to have the number of individuals and skills necessary for the tasks to be performed. In other cases, such as trade unions, the pressure will be the reverse, to increase membership size, because this increases economic and political power.

Group structure – formal versus informal

Because some individuals in a group will need to communicate, the leaders to exercise control, and because the individuals are interdependent, a structure will be developed. This may be very apparent and formal or it may be very loose, informal and changing.

Whilst larger organizations will set up *formal structures* which they believe will be most efficient from a task achievement, group maintenance and control point of view, other forces will be at work within the organization. As Charles Page (*Man and the Organization*) writes, the informal side of an organization 'consists of rules, groupings and sanctioned systems of procedures . . . they are never recorded . . . they are just as real and just as compelling on the membership'.

So, in any consideration of groups the two faces – the 'formal', as laid down by senior managers and the 'informal', as determined by the emotional needs and the practical working circumstances, have to be considered.

Figure 21.5   *Different channels of communication*

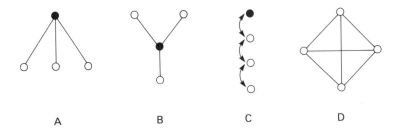

A   B   C   D

Group orientations

Groups, in the main, consist of both leaders and those being led and each develop their own orientations or attitudes to work as well as towards those who work or organize their work. Etzioni (also Chapter 2) describes both managers' attitudes to their workforce and the workers' corresponding attitudes to work. These are:

Managers' power	Worker involvement
Coercive	Alienative
Utilitarian	Calculative
Normative	Moral

McGregor (see also Chapter 2) describes Theory X managers who tend to expect the worst from their workers and Theory Y managers who expect the best. Schein (see Pugh and Hickson) goes further than McGregor and suggests four main assumptions that managers make of their workpeople;

rational-economic:	workers motivated by money
social:	workers motivated by work-group relationships
self-actualization:	workers motivated by need to fulfil potential
complex:	other models are too simple; workers are motivated differently at different stages of life.

From these models of attitudes to workers and to work it is apparent that attitudes may be dynamic in the sense that managers can create policies, working environments and styles of supervision which shape the nature of the workers' own attitudes to work and the employer. Furthermore, one of the problems of attitudes (not just to work) is that they may persist long after the reasons that created them have ceased to exist, a phenomenon at the basis of much prejudice . . .

Communications

Groups exist because communication is possible between individuals. The communication process has important effects on group behaviour and leadership because, if *information* itself is seen as a valuable asset, it is possible to use that asset as a means of exercising control. If, for example, groups are structured as illustrated in Figure 21.5, A, B, or C, one person can easily monopolize information whereas in D, all have access to everyone in the group. The person can choose to pass it on or not. There are two consequences of such a situation. Firstly the person with the information can automatically acquire the role of leader or secondly a person with certain personality traits, recognizing the power of the position, will move into the focal position.

Group management

Where large groups of people have to be managed, as is the case with large enterprises, it is most likely that management will be, to a greater or lesser extent, of a *bureaucratic* nature. The word *bureaucratic* is not meant in a perjorative sense but describes a particular approach to management, first described by Max Weber. Procedures will be formalized. Decision making is more likely to be a shared responsibility. Treatment of individuals will be based on clearly defined rules (as has been described in many chapters of this book). The key features of a *bureaucratic* approach to management include:

vertical authority structure
maximum specialization
close definition of duties, privileges and boundaries
decisions based on expert judgement, technical competence and disciplined compliance with directives of superiors
impersonal administration of staff
employment consisting of a lifelong career.

(After Max Weber, reproduced from International Dictionary of Management, Kogan Page, London, 1975.)

The problem with Weber's view of bureaucracy is that it tends to imply that organizations are rational entities or systems, independent of the people who are the organization. Another view, that of Silverman, is that to understand organizations, it is necessary to view them from an 'action frame of reference', that is, as the product of the actions of the people who are the organization, pursuing their own objectives. This perspective, when contrasted with Weber's, indicates that organizations are not the rational system that many would like to believe they are but are the results of the decisions of the leaders or the organization, pursuing their own ends.

Technology

Within an economy many different technologies are used to create goods and services. Different technologies create different organization structures and situations for managers. Joan Woodward, in examining manufacturing industries, identified nine technologies grouped into three broad categories: unit and small batch, large batch and mass production, and process production. Each of these creates different management needs and structures.

Whilst hotel and catering operations, in the main, do not fit into these categories, the industry does have many different market sectors with different technologies ranging from the small, low volume, top price country house hotel through to high volume, low price fast-food outlets. Each of these creates different situations for management.

The nature of the task

In addition to the individuals and groups being managed the nature of the task also has to be considered. In some situations, for example, the reception/cash desk of an hotel at 8.30 am or a busy kitchen at 1.00 pm, there is little room for debate about how things may be done differently and therefore a strict hierarchical structure may be vital to success. Some of the variables concerned with the task itself include:

Pressured – unpressured
Self-paced – externally paced
Skilled – unskilled
Hi-touch – lo-touch (e.g. level of customer contact)
Creative – non-creative
Difficult – simple
Group work – individual work
Perishable – non-perishable (e.g. if not sold today can it be sold tomorrow?)
Low risk – high risk.

Different combinations of the above variables should lead to different forms of management. Skilled tasks will need more investment in training. Group tasks will need more co-ordination. Perishable tasks (e.g. bedrooms unsold tonight can *never* be sold again) may need more complex communications and control. High risk tasks (e.g. preparation of large numbers of 'in-flight' meals) will need very strict systems of supervision and control.

Environment

As the leadership function can only function within groups of people so too groups can only function within a wider environment. Groups are not closed, isolated systems. They draw from the environment. The environment factors influencing management of the workforce are listed below. See also Chapters 17 and 18.

Economic factors	– demand for products, more or fewer jobs
Politico-legal	– employment legislation
Technological	– capital investment, educational attainments of employees
Cultural	– employee expectations
Demographic	– labour supply
Geographical	– demand for products, labour supply

What is a successful management or leadership?

Successful leadership should consist of the ability to achieve specified goals through the proper use of the resources available. For most managers this contains at least two key elements.

Firstly there is the achievement of the specified goals, e.g. of a financial or service nature. To some extent the specification of goals and their achievement occurs through job design, performance appraisal and approaches to management such as Management by Objectives (see Chapters 3 and 7) and budgetary control.

The other key responsibility is the *group maintenance and development role* which has been the subject of most of the chapters of this book. Again the achievement of this dimension of management can be measured, but usually with more difficulty, through approaches to management such as performance appraisal and Management by Objectives.

Within the hotel and catering industry it could be argued that there appears to be more effort directed at the former goal than the latter, if the industry's high labour turnover is used as an indicator of the industry's managers' concern with the 'group maintenance and development' goals.

Many believe that successful management consists of achieving a balance between task achievement and concern for the group. This has been expressed by Blake and Mouton (see Pugh and Hickson) who developed the concept, illustrated in Figure 21.6.

Other writers on management, including Fiedler, suggest 'that a group's

Figure 21.6 *The managerial grid*

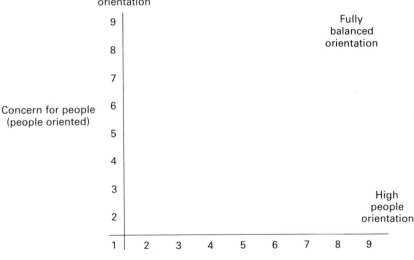

performance will depend on, or be 'contingent' upon the appropriate matching of leadership style with the group and the extent to which the situation provides the leader with influence over the group' (A. Lockwood and P. Jones, *People in the Hotel and Catering Industry*, Holt, Rinehart and Winston, Eastbourne, 1984).

The process of managing groups

The process of managing groups at work has been analyzed by many management writers in the past. The first, Henri Fayol (see Figure 2.2, Chapter 2) identified five key steps. These are:

1 To forecast
2 To organize
3 To command
4 To coordinate
5 To control.

Other writers include Peter Drucker. Today it is possible to describe the process as a continuous, self-perpetuating process. Figure 21.7 illustrates the process.

Figure 21.7 *The management process*

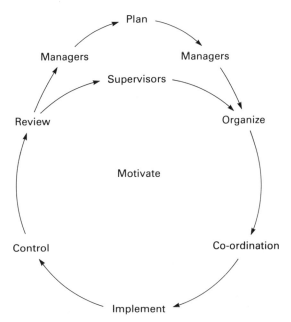

Managers and supervisors

Some argue that managers and supervisors are basically concerned with the same process and that there is no real distinction, apart from location in the hierarchy. However, in looking at the above diagram, it can be seen that the main distinction and an important one, is that managers are concerned with the planning function. Another way of illustrating differences between levels of supervision and management in the hierarchy is as follows.

Figure 21.8   *The management hierarchy*

High level of involvement		
Supervisors	Managers	Directors
Low level of involvement		
Routine tasks, e.g. supervising	Organizing controlling	Non-routine tasks, e.g. planning reviewing

Differences between groups and organizations

Both *groups* and *organizations* share many features in common. In order to be effective members of both should have common goals and values. In many ways organizations are extensions of groups. Where groups consist of inter-dependent individuals, organizations consist of interdependent groups with overlapping memberships. Whilst all the individuals are members of the organization, they are also members of smaller groups. The board of directors of an hotel company, for example, makes up the group concerned with the overall direction of the company. Each director in turn is a member, maybe the leader or manager, of specialist departments or groups. Figure 21.9 illustrates this.

From this it is apparent that whilst the most junior members may be members of their own work group and of the organization overall they are not

Figure 21.9   *Organization and group membership*

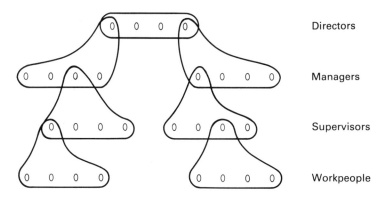

members of 'similar interest' groups; most workpeople who share most in common, from a work point of view, are not members of a wider workpeople's group. One of the reasons for the emergence and development of trade unions was a response to the need for workpeople to form a group or organization with common interests. Some enlightened employers also set out to develop ways and means of making every employee feel an integral part of the wider group or organization. Such techniques include induction, internal transfers and pro-motions, joint consultation, staff exchanges, company newspapers, staff parties and dances, staff guilds, inter-unit competitions of a work or social nature.

Some differences and similarities between groups and organizations may be summarized as appears below in Figure 21.10.

Figure 21.10   *Groups and organizations compared*

	Groups	Organizations
SIMILARITIES	Members may share common goals and values	
DIFFERENCES	Small	Large
	Simple structures	Complex structures
	Informal	Formal
	Emotional bonds	Economic/social bonds
	Simple decision-making	Complex decision-making
	Short lived	Long lived?
	All members know one another	All members do not know one another

Conclusion

Most of this book has been devoted to the various processes used by employers to attract, retain, develop and motivate their workforces. This chapter has focused on considering what is involved in actually managing the workforce and what influences the process. It has suggested that managing work people successfully depends upon a complex consisting of the make-up of the individuals involved, the nature of groups which is different from the sum of their members, the nature of the work performed by the work people and finally, the environment in which the performance of the work takes place. The conclusion of this author is that there is no simple explanation of successful management or leadership but, using an analogy which it is hoped will be meaningful to most readers, it is more like a successful meal. The component parts should always be of good quality but the recipe can be different for different situations.

Reading list

Blake, R. R. and Mouton, J. S. *The Managerial Grid*, Gulf, Houston USA, 1964

Drucker, P., *The Practice of Management*, Harper, New York, 1954

Handy, C. *Understanding Organizations*, 3rd edn. London: Penguin 1986

Jones, P. and Lockwood, A., *Management of Hotel Operations*, London: Cassell, 1989

Koontz, H., O'Donnell, C. and Weinrich, H., *Principles of Management*, New York: McGraw Hill, 1988

Lockwood, A. and Jones, P., *People and the Hotel and Catering Industry*, Eastbourne: Holt, Rinehart and Winston, 1984

Pugh, D. S. and Hickson, D. D., *Writers on Organizations*, 4th edn., London: Penguin, 1989

Wilson, D. and Rosenfeld, R., *Managing Organizations*, London: McGraw-Hill, 1990

Questions

1 Describe what you consider to be the key features which contribute to effective management of people at work.

2 Discuss the proposition that leadership is an 'innate' characteristic.

3 What relevance does the 'informal' group have to the manager?

4 What effects does the 'nature of the task' have on the management of groups and organizations?

5 What effects does the 'environment' have on the management of groups and organizations?

6 Design a procedure for selecting individuals with management potential.

7 Describe the 'process of managing' and discuss how a manager should relate this to the task and to the people being managed.

8 Compare and contrast *groups* and *organizations*.

chapter 22

Managing in an international context

Many sectors of the hospitality industry have, for many years, been international by nature. Most de luxe hotels and many top restaurants anywhere in the world expect that a significant proportion of their visitors will be foreign. Much of the industry in Britain, as it is today, has been significantly influenced by overseas managers and staff. Some of Britain's top hotels and restaurants of the last one hundred years, such as the Savoy and the Ritz, were designed and run from over the Channel – such as Cesar Ritz. Trusthouse Forte, one of the world's top hotel companies, was formed largely by Lord Forte, of Italian origin. Significant companies in the hotel, restaurant, brewery and take-away sector, such as Sarova hotels, Edwardian Hotels and the Park group, are run by people of Asian origins. Furthermore, many of the managers and staff in certain sectors of the industry are of foreign nationality or origin. One notable point about the industry which has made this possible is that the knowledge and skills necessary are readily exportable. Consequently most people joining the industry can anticipate working with people of nationalities different from their own – be they customers, staff, managers and, increasingly, owners.

The establishment of the single market within the European Community will accelerate this process further through increased cross border ownership, increased cross border competitive tendering for public sector contracts such as hospitals, and increased worker mobility. In addition, the growth of tourism, estimated to triple around the Mediterranean basin alone over the next twenty-five years, for example, will increase the demand for staff with international capabilities, i.e. those with 'cultural awareness'. As a leading authority on intercultural management, Geert Hofstede states: 'cultural awareness is one of the subtle features of competition in world markets, and firms which are better at it have a distinct advantage over their competitors' (*European Management Journal*, 1989).

Cultural awareness is much more than the ability to speak a foreign language or two, although this in itself will be vital. Cultural awareness is the ability to recognize and to respond to cultural differences. This will include the ability to communicate with customers or potential customers in both written and spoken form. In Britain now, efforts are being made through the national curriculum and the design of many higher education courses to improve the overall foreign language ability of the British. In this respect Britain compares unfavourably with some of our continental partner/competitors. In Belgium, for example, it is estimated that around 90% of their hotel managers can work in four languages. In several European countries it is a requirement of all higher education courses, and the Baccalaureat ('A' level equivalent), that at least one foreign language is studied.

Other than language there are many other differences which exist between cultures. These can include differences in values, attitudes, behaviour, communication, personal space, technical differences, dress, etc. Geert Hofstede, in a study of over one thousand IBM employees employed in over seventy countries identified four key dimensions which help to distinguish one culture from another. These are shown in Figure 22.1 below.

Figure 22.1   *Dimensions for comparing cultures*

Dimension	High	Low
Power-distance	Supervisors are distant from their staff	Supervisors are close to their staff
Uncertainty-avoidance	High risk taking is encouraged	Risk taking is discouraged
Individualism	Individual initiative/ and private life valued	Individual initiative discouraged, collectivist culture significant
Masculinity	Assertiveness valued	Warm, caring values significant

The *power–distance* dimension sets out to differentiate to what extent a country's organizational culture encourages supervisors to exercise power. France, for example, was found to have a high power distance culture. This explains to some extent why many British students, accustomed to relatively close relationships with English managers or lecturers, when on industrial placement in France have difficulties with French managers. Conversely, French students sometimes have difficulty adjusting to the relatively relaxed, 'first name' style of lecturers in English colleges.

The *uncertainty–avoidance* dimension is concerned with the degree to which people in a country prefer structured or unstructured situations. Where uncertainty–avoidance is strong (e.g. Japan, Greece) people need clear guidelines and support. In weak uncertainty–avoidance cultures structures and rules are less important.

The *individualism* dimension is concerned with the degree to which people in a culture learn to act as individuals as opposed to as members of a group. Britain, along with most of the 'old commonwealth' and the United States, are described as being high on individualism. This encourages personal initiative and achievement and a right to a private life. Countries low on the individualism dimension tend to have 'collectivist' cultures where the extended family and the clan are significant to the individual.

The *masculinity* dimension is concerned with values such as assertiveness, performance and success as opposed to feminine values such as warm personal relationships, quality of life, caring for others. Countries high on the masculinity dimension include Italy and Australia, whereas those at the other extreme include Scandinavia and Holland.

Hofstede analyzed each country using these four main dimensions and then grouped countries with similar sets of dimensions into eight clusters which tend to have historical developmental similarities rather than simple geographical connections. These are shown in Figure 22.2.

Figure 22.2   *Country clusters and their characteristics*

I: More developed Latin high power-distance high uncertainty-avoidance high individualism medium masculinity	II: Less developed Latin high power-distance high uncertainty-avoidance low individualism whole range on masculinity	
BELGIUM FRANCE ARGENTINA BRAZIL SPAIN	COLUMBIA MEXICO VENEZUELA CHILE PERU PORTUGAL YUGOSLAVIA	
III: More developed Asian medium power-distance high uncertainty-avoidance medium individualism high masculinity	IV: Less developed Asian high power-distance low uncertainty-avoidance low individualism medium masculinity	V: Near Eastern high power-distance high uncertainty-avoidance low individualism medium masculinity
JAPAN	PAKISTAN TAIWAN THAILAND HONG KONG INDIA PHILIPPINES SINGAPORE	GREECE IRAN TURKEY
VI: Germanic low power-distance high uncertainty-avoidance medium individualism high masculinity	VII: Anglo low power-distance low to medium uncertainty-avoidance high individualism high masculinity	VIII: Nordic low power-distance low to medium uncertainty- avoidance medium individualism low masculinity
AUSTRIA ISRAEL GERMANY SWITZERLAND SOUTH AFRICA ITALY	AUSTRALIA CANADA BRITAIN IRELAND NEW ZEALAND USA	DENMARK FINLAND NETHERLANDS NORWAY SWEDEN

Reproduced by courtesy of G. Hofstede.

Whilst IBM is not a 'hospitality' company it has many features which are similar to multi-nationals operating in the hospitality sector, including THF, Accor, Sheraton, Holiday Inns, Marriott and Hilton.

The main conclusion from this research is that even if business practices within one type of business or company may be similar across international boundaries there may be significant differences in values. It follows that if countries have different values, then similar management styles across different cultures will not necessarily work. For example, MbO, which involves managers negotiating targets and taking personal risk, may well succeed in Britain or the USA but not in France, Spain or Portugal.

Cultural differences, however, should not be seen as being confined to differences between nationalities. Obviously each country has its own cultural inheritance which differs to a greater or lesser extent from other countries' cultures. However, cultural differences also exist within national cultures. Different socio-economic groups from different countries have more in common, in some respects, than with different demographic or socio-economic groups from their own country. For example, twenty-year-olds from Britain are more likely to share tastes in music, clothes and leisure with twenty-year-olds from other countries than with forty- or fifty-year-olds from their own country.

How individual hospitality companies demonstrate or develop *cultural awareness* varies considerably. In many cases nothing whatever is done to accommodate the needs of other cultures. For example, no staff may be able to speak another language and menus may not be translated even where significant numbers of foreign customers are served. At the most basic it may be that brochures, tariff displays, menus, etc. are translated. At the next level employers may translate important signs or at least use internationally recognized symbols. They may employ staff of appropriate nationalities, or who are able to speak appropriate languages. Some employers will actively promote acquisition of language by paying 'language bonuses' and/or paying or providing language tuition. Good language education not only equips people with basic communication skills but it also introduces key cultural issues such as forms of addressing others. Some employers may go further by researching key cultural issues concerning potential and actual customers and setting out to meet these needs, such as the provision of a copy of the Koran in the bedroom rather than Gideon's Bible. Finally some employers train staff through role play, etc. in how to meet the needs of people from many different cultures.

The purpose of this chapter is not to produce a list of cultural differences. Instead it is intended to create the awareness that cultural differences exist, that they are important, and ignored at risk of giving offence at the very least and of losing business at worst. When working with people of other cultures, whether as managers, employees, customers or owners, the relationship is likely to be more successful if cultural differences are anticipated and accounted for. Figure 22.3 is intended to illustrate some of the areas where significant differences are likely to be encountered.

Figure 22.3 *Examples of cultural differences*

Aspects of culture	*Some dimensions*
Values, e.g.	
individual's place in society	autonomy valued ....collective effort valued
social status	material wealth.................social contribution
	ascribed at birth................acquired through personal effort
concern for others	caring ....unconcerned
Attitudes, e.g.	
towards work	economic necessity..........personal identity
towards authority	formal, respectful ....informal, unconcerned
attitudes towards those in subordinate social roles	demanding, superior ....relaxed, egalitarian
towards the other sex	strong gender...................weak gender role role differentiation differentiation
towards alcohol	alcohol consumed as ....alcohol consumed in adjunct to a meal order to get drunk
towards food & meals	important, symbolic.........unimportant, functional
Behaviour, e.g.	
relationships at work	formal...............................informal
manner of dressing for work	formal...............................informal important unimportant
personal space	close ....distant
forms of address	very formal ....informal important unimportant
non-verbal communication (e.g. gestures)	important..........................unimportant
meals, eating habits	very formal ....informal important unimportant

Figure 22.4 *Some examples of cultural differences of interest to the hospitality industry*

Forms of greeting	Continentals tend to be much more formal than people from the UK or USA, and may address one another by Mr or Mrs throughout their working lives. First name terms may be reserved for genuine friends or family. The familiar 'tu' in France, and its equivalents in other countries, is avoided.
	Some continentals tend to shake hands the first time they meet each day.
Meals	In some cultures meals are extremely important; some cultures 'eat to live whilst others live to eat'.
	Staple elements of diet, e.g. rice, pasta, potatoes, vary between cultures.
	Courses may be in a different order. The French take cheese before dessert.

Figure 22.4   *cont.*

	Meals may contain different items. A Nordic breakfast may contain cheeses, hams, salami type sausage.
	Meals may consist of more courses, each of one item.
	Table 'lay-ups' may be different. The French may eat continental breakfast, using large cups, with no plate on the table.
	Side-plates may not be used at other meals either. The same cutlery may be used throughout a meal.
	Many ingredients have local characteristics which can be important, e.g. the Latins drink much stronger coffee than Anglo-Saxons.
	Meal times may be different – e.g. the continentals tend to eat for a longer period and later than the British.
	Children are not only tolerated but are welcome in most Continental restaurants.
	Children tend to eat meals at the same time as their parents.
Drinks	Attitudes may be very different towards drink – some cultures view alcohol as an accompaniment to a meal, other cultures may see drinking as an end in itself, with status connotations, e.g. a 'macho' thing to do.
	Drinks may be used differently, e.g. port may be used as an aperitif, whisky as a digestif/liqueur.
Accommodation	Some nationalities prefer twin beds to doubles, showers to baths, duvets to blankets.
	Some races prefer the Koran to the Bible in the bedroom.
Complaining	Some nationalities complain readily but are satisfied if the cause is rectified – others, e.g. the British, tend not to complain but do not return.

Questions

1 Describe, with examples, various ways in which one culture may differ from another.
Apply your answer to the hospitality industry.
2 Describe different aspects of the hospitality experience which management need to consider when providing for people from different cultures. Consider first customer needs then staff needs.
3 Give examples of lack of 'cultural awareness' you have observed. Choose a particular setting such as at work, on holiday, at college.
4 Describe the measures which you believe would be necessary in order to develop an effective cultural awareness programme for a group of employees with whom you are acquainted. (You may find it useful to refer to Chapter 19 on Customer Care.)

5 Discuss how cultural differences may lead to the need for different approaches to management styles.
6 Discuss the proposition that cultural differences may be greater between socio-economic groups within a country than between similar socio-economic groups from different countries.

Reading list

Hofstede, G., 'Organising for Cultural Diversity', *European Management Journal*, Volume 7, No. 4, 1989

Hofstede, G., *Culture's Consequences: International Differences in Work Related Values*, Sage Publications, 1990

Open University, *International Perspectives* (Unit 16), Open University, Milton Keynes 1988

Pugh, D. S. and Hickson, D. J., *Writers on Organizations*, 4th Edn. Landau: Penguin, 1989 appendix 1

A review of personnel management in the private sector of the British hospitality industry

This article, written by the author of this book, is reproduced from the *International Journal of Hospitality Management*, 5, No. 1, pp. 29–36, 1986 with the permission of Pergamon Press Ltd.

In setting out to present a review of the literature of a particular subject area or discipline it is essential that the objectives are absolutely clear because, even within a relatively immature subject area such as personnel management in the hotel and catering industry, there is, potentially, a considerable amount of work to review. The objective of this paper has been to select material which is considered to be of value to the understanding of the development of personnel management in the private sector of the hotel and catering industry in Britain. It is confined exclusively to texts published in Britain, leaving colleagues elsewhere the task of reviewing their own literature. Also works which (in the author's opinion) are of general sociological (or similar) concern and which merely had their locus in the hotel and catering industry, with two exceptions, have been avoided.

Most people, in reviewing the management literature of the hotel and catering industry, tend to start with the work of W. F. Whyte (1948), which was based on Whyte's research into human relations in a number of hotels and restaurants in the United States. The other work which tends to be regularly cited is that of George Orwell (1969) which gave valuable insights into the nature of menial work in hotels. It was based on Orwell's experience of working in hotels in Paris in the 1930s.

The purpose of this paper, however, is to review the British texts which have contributed to the development of the personnel management function in British hotels and restaurants, and the relevant starting point appears to be later than Whyte's and Orwell's work.

In fact it appears that it was legislative change in the 1960s, which radically altered the practice of personnel management, particularly where unions were not strong. Until the early 1960s the employment relationship was governed mainly by the law of contract. Employers could dismiss any employee including long-serving staff merely by giving notice which was the same as the pay period (weekly-paid staff received 1 week's notice) even after years of service. No written terms and conditions were required and employers could modify their expectations of their employees arbitrarily, given that they had the 'divine right of dismissal'. Obviously employment practices in a fragmented, small unit, industry like hotel and catering differed vastly from the concentrated industries (such as manufacturing) where unions had already been responsible for creating the need for a professional personnel management function.

In the industry – outside the public sector – the number of managers concerned entirely with personnel work in the whole of the United Kingdom was probably in the region of 20. Most of these devoted their time to recruitment, with some companies beginning to show interest in the training activity. These included J. Lyons who had trained staff very effectively for many years, Trust Houses who ran a training centre at the Berystede Hotel in Ascot, and Forte's, who with a considerable nationwide expansion programme, employed a small team of recruiters and trainers. However, changes were imminent because in 1963 the Contracts of Employment Act created the right of employees to receive a written description of their main terms of employment. So started the need to create written contracts and records, in addition to pay records, and with it the need for staff to attend to these 'personnel' issues. In 1964 the Industrial Training Act became law, an event which probably had more impact upon manpower management, in large sections of the hotel and catering industry, than any other single influence.

It was at this time also that the first personnel management courses for the hotel and catering industry were organized by Philip Nailon and some of his colleagues at the Battersea College of Advanced Technology – soon afterward to become the University of Surrey. Also the first college graduates who had studied in Britain specifically for management started to make an impact on the industry. The formation of the Graduate and Student Management Society in the early 1960s brought together a number of young, aspiring managers, who started to question the industry's practices, running meetings on such topics as the need for a Code of Ethics. Interestingly, there were no texts of direct interest to managers, and particularly to the aspiring personnel and training specialists, about the industry's manpower or manpower practices.

It was at this point, largely as a result of the Industrial Training Act, that the Hotel and Catering Institute (one of two bodies subsequently to merge, creating the Hotel, Catering and Institutional Management Association) formed its own Hotel and Catering Industry Committee and pressed for the formation of a training board for the hotel and catering industry. The efforts of the Institute were successful. The Hotel and Catering Industry Training Board was formed in 1966 and the Institute's Secretary was seconded to the newly-formed Board.

The first Industrial Training Act was responsible for long-term changes in employment. For the first time many companies examined carefully what their employees did and, in order to provide comprehensive training programmes, companies needed to develop job descriptions, training manuals, standards of performance, etc. They also needed to develop scores of supervisors and senior staff as on-job trainers – in other words, to develop their communication skills. This was done by many employers initially in order to recover grants rather than because of any intrinsic belief that it was the right thing to do.

Towards the end of the sixties growing awareness began to develop of the crucial importance to Britain of the hotel and catering industry (as a major ingredient of the tourist product). As a consequence the government-sponsored National Economic Development Office created the Economic Development Committee for the Hotel and Catering Industry. Interestingly, at its first meeting it set up a manpower working party. Its task was to 'identify the manpower problems of the industry . . . not only how to recruit more, but also . . . how to do with less' (NEDO, 1967), p. iii). The book, one of the earliest concerned with the industry's personnel, was devoted almost entirely to presenting data derived from the 1961 census. One interesting conclusion, a reflection on the personnel management of the time, was that 'The industry has nothing approaching the information about labour turnover [found] in manufacturing industries.' (NEDO, 1967, p. 40). As a result the EDC commissioned a report on the industry's labour turnover 'to identify the causes, the cost of high labour turnover and the action that can be taken to reduce it' (NEDO, 1967, p. 40).

Two years later in 1969 the results of the study into labour turnover were published. The research had been carried out by the Tavistock Institute on behalf of the EDC for Hotel and Catering. The study, as anticipated, discovered that the industry's turnover was generally high compared with most other industries, canteens having the lowest rate and hotels the highest. The importance of this study, however, was that it went beyond a quantitative analysis of labour turnover. Approximately half the report (about 24 pages) was devoted to conclusions and recommendations. Probably most important (but missed by many in the industry?) was the statement, 'The study findings support the view that there is a *management style* that tends to attract and retain entrants.' (NEDO, 1969, p. 44). The recommendations were made with the full knowledge of the tremendous difficulties likely to be encountered and 'that the changes recommended in the study will not be universally welcomed . . . Some managers will find their acceptance psychologically difficult while others will be inclined to shrug the problem off as being of little practical significance.' (NEDO, 1969, p. 47).

In 1972 the Industrial Relations Act 1971 came into force which provided, for the first time, the right of protection from unfair dismissal. This granted the individual a permanent right to his or her job – so long as the contract was fulfilled and there was a need for the job. No longer could a boss dismiss an employee arbitrarily. The consequence of this removal of 'the divine right of dismissal', linked with the Contracts of Employment Act's requirement for a properly recorded contract, started the process of putting employees in a protected position – which only those protected by powerful unions had previously enjoyed.

The obvious development was that many employers, particularly the larger ones, now removed hire and fire decisions from junior managers and adopted at the least the 'grandfather principle', that is, any dismissal had to be authorized by the dismissing manager's own superior.

The beginning of the 1970s also saw the publication of two reports by the Manpower Research Unit of the Department of Employment; Manpower Studies No. 10, *Hotels* (Department of Employment, 1971) and Manpower Studies No. 11, *Catering* (Department of Employment, 1972). The objectives 'were to analyse current manpower . . . to forecast requirements in five years time . . . both in terms of numbers of employees and in the nature of their work' (Department of Employment, 1971, p. 5).

The manpower problems of the industry were now becoming very pressing as a consequence, largely, of a growth in demand encouraged by the Development of Tourism Act which stimulated the building of no fewer than 250 new hotels between 1970 and 1973. The report concluded that 'little attention was being given to forward manpower planning even by companies committed to opening new hotels' (Department of Employment, 1971, p. 41).

Concurrent with these reports were two reports published by the Commission on Industrial Relations. The Secretary of State for Employment and Productivity recognized the lack of formal negotiating machinery in the hotel and catering industry and referred the industry to the Commission in order to 'report the functioning and the development of voluntary collective bargaining in the hotel and catering industry with particular reference to the securing of any improvements in industrial relations that appear necessary and desirable' (Commission on Industrial Relations (CIR), 1971, p. iv). The two reports concerned themselves with the hotel and catering industry (Report No. 23; Commission on Industrial Relations, 1971) and with industrial catering (Report No. 27; Commission on Industrial Relations, 1972).

The first report identified clearly the lack of formal negotiating machinery (i.e. involving trade unions) and recommended 'that the hotel and restaurants industry should acknowledge the contributions which it can make to better industrial relations . . .' (CIR, 1971, p. 57). The report also formally recorded the formation in April 1970 of the Hotel and Catering Personnel Managers' Association. The objectives of this new association were to carry out research in areas such as 'recruitment, management development, staff structuring, training attitudes, improving job image . . ., a five day working week and the reduction of labour turnover' (CIR, 1971).

Here, therefore, was probably an important milestone in the industry's personnel activities. For the first time, managers responsible for personnel matters were to get together to share knowledge on matters of mutual concern.

Interestingly, the other report, on industrial catering, concluded that collective bargaining and the determination of conditions of employment were so well organized that the Commission of Industrial Relations recommended the abolition of the sector's Wages Council.

In addition, these reports gave considerable insight into the workings of the industry and the nature of those working in the industry, referring for example to 'This individualistic, competitive outlook of the hotel employee . . . supported and extended by the degree of isolation of many employees and the independent nature of a number of working tasks' (CIR, 1971, p. 36).

So was the industry beginning to come of age from a personnel management point of view? Certainly there was the emergency of a group of personnel specialists in hotels and restaurants. In another major sector the determination of conditions was such that the Wages Council could be abolished.

It was shortly after this that the first book devoted entirely to personnel management in the hotel and catering industry (Boella, 1974) was published. It was not an evaluation of the industry's personnel management. However, in looking at the contents, and bearing in mind that at the time of writing the author had had recent experience with two of the industry's leading employers and was a member of the Hotel and Catering Industry's Personnel Management Association, it evidences much of the industry's attitude to its workforce. In all, about 98% of the book was concerned with personnel techniques: how to recruit, how to train, etc. Less than 2% was concerned with underlying research findings or theory – for example, why people work.

The mid-seventies, however, appeared to be an important turning point. Whilst the Department of Employment studies of 1971 and 1972 into the Manpower of Hotels and Catering were quantitative in nature, in that they set out to produce manpower forecasts, the NEDO report, Manpower Policy in the Hotels and Restaurant Industry (NEDO, 1975) produced the first detailed qualitative report designed 'to assist the industry to recruit the labour it requires, to improve staff retention, and to make the fullest and most efficient use of its available manpower' (NEDO, 1975, p. xi). The report drew many critical conclusions on the industry's style of managing its workforce.

In essence it was really saying that the best recruitment and training techniques were worth nothing unless managers adopted new attitudes and new approaches. A range of detailed recommendations was made which was directed at developing a professional approach to managing the industry's personnel.

In the mid- to late-seventies the HCITB levy exemption scheme provided an important impetus to improving the management of manpower resources. Previously many companies had set out to maximize their grants, irrespective of their real training needs. Under the new levy exemption scheme however, companies could avoid paying the statutory training levy (around 1% of the payroll) by demonstrating that they were meeting their real needs. The consequence was that many companies, including some of the country's largest, who had still done little in the way of realistic (needs-driven) training, now faced a financial penalty unless they set about training adequately. For many companies this meant professionalizing the training function and, because of the interdependence between training and the other personnel activities, the whole personnel function. A number of personnel professionals were recruited from outside the industry, and this had the effect of importing effective personnel practices into the industry, at least into some of the larger companies.

In 1977, Magurn's book, *A Manual of Staff Management in the Hotel and Catering Industry* (Magurn, 1977), was published. This was concerned, as the title implies and the author intended, with personnel techniques. Nothing of significance appears on underlying theory, the peculiar nature of the industry or personnel policy.

The industry's first two specialist textbooks appeared, therefore, to suggest that the personnel manager's task was to find staff for the operators, evidenced possibly by the statement – 'they [personnel managers] assist management to find the best possible candidates and to provide training for the successful candidates' (Boella, 1974).

Neither book tackled the issues of 'attitudes and approaches' identified by the NEDO report. They reflected the industry's own management perspective of the role of personnel management – which could be encapsulated as 'get us the staff but don't expect us to change anything.'

Throughout this time the HCITB was publishing booklets, research papers, etc., which in the main were of a quantitative nature. Little important work concerned with the industry's underlying issues, apart from the NEDO and CIR reports, was made public until Mars (1973) wrote on hotel pilferage, Mars and Mitchell (1976) published their study *Room for Reform*, their report on low pay in the industry (Mars and Mitchell, 1977) and Mars *et al.* (1979) published 'Manpower Problems in the Hotel and Catering Industry'. They too recognized that 'the vast majority of the industry was really asking for . . . a short practical guide to managing human relations at the level of the individual' (Mars *et al.*, 1979, p. vii). Certainly the industry has received plenty of guidance on techniques from the HCITB, Boella and Magurn. Mars and his colleagues, instead, using a variety of different sources, examined the underlying issues by looking at causes, not merely the symptoms. They looked at, amongst other things, the work of the American W. F. Whyte, which included the examination of 'labour turnover, factional strife, interdepartmental friction, autocratic supervision, unclear lines of authority, and union grievances' (quoted from Mars *et al.*, 1979, p. 21). As a result of their examination of seven case studies Mars *et al.* drew conclusions and made recommendations concerning the changes in the use of manpower. In essence they found that:

(i) 'The style of management in the industry . . . can be best characterised as "fire fighting" '.
(ii) 'The money earnings of hotel and catering workers are universally low'.
(iii) 'Such earnings are nonetheless *supplemented* in a wide variety of ways, some recorded, many illegitimate, and most involving a high degree of local management collusion' (Mars *et al.*, 1979).

Nineteen seventy-six saw the publication of Angela Bowey's book *The Sociology of Organization*. The aim of the book was 'to present a model of behaviour in organizations . . . for the practising manager it will be an aid in the search for relevant management policies for influencing human behaviour in organizations' (Bowey, 1976, p. 15).

Essentially the book, whilst based upon the study of behaviour in a number of Manchester restaurants, is of more interest to organization theorists than practising personnel managers. However, for students of management in the restaurant industry it provides valuable insights into the socio-technical culture of restaurants.

It was during the seventies that the trade union movement became more active in the industry. In the public house sector, because of the threat by the Transport and General Workers Union to organize public house managers, the brewers had fostered the formation of the National Association of Licensed House Managers which quickly moved to a position of virtual monopoly of public house managers. The General and Municipal Workers Union formed the Hotel and Catering Workers' Union and, as a consequence, a spate of industrial relations training was started and a small number of industrial relations experts were employed by major companies. Another consequence was that middle and senior line managers were now needing to use, and rely on, specialized personnel techniques concerned with job evaluation and salary administration.

In 1980 the second edition of Boella's work *Personnel Management in the*

Hotel and Catering Industry was published. It reflected in a small way the underlying concern of many that personnel techniques, however well practised, were not enough. What was needed was an understanding of people's behaviour at work. This was evidenced by the inclusion of a chapter on personnel policy and an attempt to enlarge the understanding of the employment relationships by including a page on Etzioni's work in addition to continuing with the, by now, 'old hat' and well tried, Maslow and McGregor.

In the introduction to this paper it was stated that only those works which could materially assist in a greater understanding of the practice of personnel management in the industry would be considered. One such work, whilst not a 'mainstream' personnel text, is that by Conrad Saunders, *Social Stigma of Occupations* (Saunders, 1981). Its contribution is that, in the same vein as Mars *et al.*, he gives insights into the very nature of the work of many of the industry's labour force, with recommendations for reducing some of the industry's manning problems. For example, about kitchen porters he writes, 'We found little evidence of . . . use of mechanical or technological aids that could take the drudgery out of this work . . . but established that no fewer than 85% of the sample highly value proper tools . . . and that these would be conditions to do this work more permanently' (Saunders, 1981, p. 148).

By 1983 Boella's book *Personnel Management in the Hotel and Catering Industry* came to its third edition and the two additional chapters are of interest because they reflect the growing expectations of personnel management. The first of the new chapters, 'Organizing Manpower', without being explicit introduces the concept of organization development from a contingency theory viewpoint and its inclusion demonstrates that senior managers in the industry were now beginning to look to personnel managers to be their 'organization' specialists.

The other chapter emphasized that personnel managers should be in the front line of organizational effectiveness by concerning themselves with labour costs – something their colleagues have done for many years in other industries.

The two chapters taken together, therefore, indicate that the personnel specialist could find himself in the crucial decision-making locus of the company – no longer just the 'hirer and firer' or the 'do gooder'.

In 1984 two further books specifically concerned with manpower matters were published. One was *Manpower Management in the Hotel and Catering Industry* by Hornsey and Dann; the other was *People and the Hotel and Catering Industry* by Lockwood and Jones. Both books were certainly important additions to the literature because, for the first time, textbooks were available which set out to relate theory and practice. The books by Boella and Magurn were largely concerned with personnel techniques, leaving aside the underlying theory. They described the 'what and how' of personnel management but largely omitted the 'why'. The books by Mars *et al.*, Bowey and Conrad based on their own research gave interesting insights into the idiosyncratic nature of the industry, whilst Hornsey and Dann, and Lockwood and Jones set out to relate academic theory about people and work to the practice of manpower management in the hotel and catering industry.

So what can be said of the current state of personnel management in the hospitality industry? There is no simple answer. All industries and many sectors of individual industries are, to a greater or lesser extent, idiosyncratic. To suggest that one industry has good personnel management practices when compared with those of other industries, in the final analysis, is a value judgement. If, however, an attempt is to be made to evaluate the personnel practices of an industry one approach is to compare its practices against what are considered to be the expected practices generally. Where does one find a résumé of such expected practices? The answer probably lies, if anywhere, in the personnel practitioner's professional body, as indicated by what the professional body considers to be its current corpus of knowledge and professional ethics. The professional body for personnel management in the United Kingdom is the Institute of Personnel Management which has a corpus of knowledge as contained in its examination syllabus. In addition, the Institute publishes a range of texts, the most important of which, because it sets out to look at the full scope of personnel management, is Thomason's *Textbook of Personnel Management* which sets out 'to produce a coherent summary of the position we have now reached in "personnel management" ' (Thomason, 1981, p. xi). In this a clear definition of personnel management emerges. He writes, 'the personnel function has come to be regarded as distinct from the technical and financial functions . . . and as having its own "technology" . . . and its own "ideologies" (generally bifurcated between the welfare of the individual employee and the welfare of the undertaking as a whole)' (Thomason, 1981, p. 49). So here we see that personnel management should be concerned with the welfare of the employer and the individual employee. Thomason then details the scope of personnel management demonstrating the major activities and how each relates to the employer and the employee.

Torrington and Chapman (1984), in their book *Personnel Management*, asserts that personnel work has three elements:

(i) Determining the expectations that employees have of their organisations and the expectations that organisations have of their employees.
(ii) Setting up a series of contracts or agreements between organisation and employee that describe the mutual expectations.
(iii) Servicing the contracts to ensure that the expectations are fulfilled (Torrington and Chapman, 1984, p. 4).

They justify their assertion by drawing on work of a number of authorities, including Mumford, Dubin, McCarthy and Ellis.

They point out that, whilst there is still a great deal of 'unilateral decision-making' as opposed to 'management by agreement', there is a clear trend away from unilateral decision-making' in *all* aspects of the employment of people' (Torrington and Chapman, 1984, p. 6). They summarize this position: 'Personnel management is a series of activities enabling working man and his employing organization to reach agreement about the nature and objectives of the employment relationship between them, and then to fulfil those agreements' (Torrington and Chapman, 1984, p. 12).

Armstrong defines personnel management as:

● obtaining, developing and motivating the human resources required by the organisation to achieve its objectives;

● developing an organisation structure and climate and evolving a management style which will promote co-operation and commitment throughout
the organisation;
● making the best use of the skills and capacities of all those employed in the
organisation;
● ensuring that the organisation meets its social and legal responsibilities
towards its employees, with particular regard to the conditions of employment and quality of working life provided for them (Armstrong, 1984, p.
13).

Armstrong's book is divided into the five main areas, as laid down by the
Institute of Personnel Management.

Taken together, these three texts, together with the examination syllabus,
may be considered to present a current over-view of the scope, but not
necessarily a common perspective, of the personnel management function.
Table 1 shows the coverage of personnel management topics by the main
British textbooks devoted entirely to personnel issues in the hotel and catering
industry. The topics listed by chapter numbers in the top of the table (Part A)
are those identified by Thomason (1981) in his review of the general personnel
texts. The lower part of the table (Part B) identifies topics which have been
covered specifically in the textbooks written for the hotel and catering industry
and which do not appear to fit easily with Thomason's list. The texts show that
the nature of interest in personnel management in the industry has changed
considerably in the eighties. Many of the areas formerly considered either
unnecessary to the health of an organization, such as organization development, labour costs and productivity now feature as subjects of concern in the
literature.

In the mid-1970s Boella and Magurn were concerned almost entirely with
personnel techniques. The NEDO publication 1975, followed by Mars and
Mitchell (1976, 1977, 1979), consisted of more thorough examinations of
management practice as it affected the industry's workforce. By the 1980s,
however, Boella (1983) had added organization development and labour costs
to the scope of personnel management, whilst Lockwood and Jones (1984) and
Hornsey and Dann (1984) had selected a considerable range of material from
the behavioural science and showed its application to the industry's
manpower.

The 1980s has been a period of consolidation and possibly of maturation.
There are now hundreds of managers with major or total responsibility for
personnel matters. Their responsibilities now go well beyond those of the few
personnel managers of twenty years ago. Many more are now recruited from
outside the industry, as senior managers recognize the value of employing
professional personnel managers rather than making one of the new junior
managers responsible for personnel. The fear of the middle and late seventies
that trade unions would ride rough-shod through the industry did not
materialize as the unions attempted to confront a highly-fragmented, individualistic and entrepreneurial workforce.

If, however, questions are to be asked about the present and the future of
personnel management in the industry they could well concern themselves
with the decision-making process. Torrington and Chapman suggest that there

are trends towards a more pluralistic approach. They write 'that there is a clear trend away from unilateral decision making in *all* aspects of the employment of people' (Torrington and Chapman, 1984, p. 6). If their contention is correct then this could prove to be a fruitful area for exploration.

Figure A1.1   *Coverage of personnel management topics†*

	Boella (1974)	Magurn (1977)	Mars & Mitchell (1979)	Boella (1980)	Boella (1983)	Hornsey & Dann (1984)	Lockwood Jones (1984)
Part A							
Objectives							
Policy				2	2	2	
Organization							
Function							
*Manpower							
Planning	16			17	17	2	
Employment							
Recruitment	3, 4, 5	1, 2		4, 5, 6	4, 5, 6	3	
Wage							
Determination	9, 10	9	1	10, 11	10, 11		
Termination	13	16, 17	7	14	14		
Employee records	16	5, 6		17	17	2	
Promotion							
*Employee services							
Welfare		13					
Health/safety		12, 14					
Employee development	7, 8			8, 9	8, 9		
Interviewing/counselling	4, 6	2, 10, 15		7	7		
*Resource control							
Standard setting	2			3	3		
Appraisal	6	10		7	7		
Training	7, 8	4, 11		6, 8, 9	6, 8, 9	5	
Discipline/rules		15, 16					
Motivation/incentives	11, 12	9		12, 13	12, 13		4
Wage and salary administration	9, 10			10, 11	10, 11	9	
Supervision							
*Industrial relations	14	18		15	15	8	
Negotiations	14	18, 20		15	15	8	
Joint consultation	14	18		15	15	8	
Procedures	14	19		15	15	8	
Organizational development			5				
Job analysis	2						
Work groups							
Organizational analysis							
Communication							
Organization development					18		
Environment							
Part B							
Social science issues							
The individual		7				4	2
Groups, interpersonal relationships			4			4	6, 7
Perceptions							3
Communication		8					5
Leaderships		7	6				8
Organizations			5				10
Managing change				8, 9		7	
Productivity			9				
Law	16	3	16	16			
Structure of the industry		1		1	1		
Labour costs					19		10

*Chapter headings as identified by Thomason (1981).
† Numbers indicate chapter numbers.

References

Armstrong, M. (1984) *A Handbook of Personnel Management Practice*, 2nd edn. Kogan Page, London.

Boella, M. (1974) *Personnel Management in the Hotel and Catering Industry*, Barrie & Jenkins, London.

Boella, M. (1980) *Personnel Management in the Hotel and Catering Industry*, 2nd edn. Hutchinson, London.

Boella, M. (1983) *Personnel Management in the Hotel and Catering Industry*, 3rd edn. Hutchinson, London.

Bowey, A. M. (1976) *The Sociology of Organisations*, Hodder & Stoughton, London.

British Hotel, Restaurant and Caterers Association (1975) Manpower Problems in the Hotel and Catering Industry, BHRCA, London

Commission on Industrial Relations, U.K. (1971) *Hotel and Catering Industry. Part 1. Hotels and Restaurants*. Report No. 23, Cmnd. 4789. H.M.S.O., London.

Commission on Industrial Relations, U.K. (1972) *Hotel and Catering Industry. Part II. Industrial Catering*. Report No. 27, H.M.S.O., London.

Department of Employment, U.K. (1971) *Hotels*, Manpower Studies No. 10. H.M.S.O., London.

Department of Employment, U.K. (1972) *Catering*. Manpower Studies No. 11. H.M.S.O. London.

Hornsey, T. and Dann, D. (1984) *Manpower Management in the Hotel and Catering Industry*, Batsford Academic and Educational, London

Lockwood, A. and Jones, P. (1984) *People and the Hotel and Catering Industry*, Holt-Saunders, Eastbourne.

Magurn, J. P. (1977) *A Manual of Staff Management in the Hotel and Catering Industry, Heinemann*, London.

Mars, G. (1973) Hotel pilferage: a case study in occupational theft. *The Sociology of the Workplace*, Warner, M. (ed.). Allen & Unwin, London.

Mars, G. and Mitchell, P. (1976) *Room for Reform? A Case Study of Industrial Relations in the Hotel Industry*. Unit 6, Industrial Relations Course, P881. Open University Press, Milton Keynes.

Mars, G. and Mitchell, P. (1977) Catering for the Low Paid: Invisible Earnings. Low Pay Unit Bulletin No. 15, June.

Mars G., et al. (1979) *Manpower Problems in the Hotel and Catering Industry*. Saxon House, Farnborough.

National Economic Development Office (1967) Economic Development Committee for Hotels and Catering. *Your Manpower: a Practical Guide to the Manpower Statistics of the Hotel and Catering Industry*. H.M.S.O., London.

National Economic Development Office (1969) *Hotel and Catering EDC: Staff Turnover*. H.M.S.O., London.

National Economic Development Office (1975) Economic Development for Hotels and Catering. *Manpower Policy in the Hotels and Restaurant Industry – Summary and Recommendations*. NEDO, London.

National Economic Development Office (1975) Economic Development Committee for Hotels and Catering. *Manpower Policy in the Hotels and Restaurant Industry – Research Findings*. NEDO, London.

Orwell, G. (1969) *Down and Out in Paris and London*. Penguin Books, Harmondsworth.

Saunders, C. (1981) *Social Stigma of Occupations*. Gower, Farnborough, Hants.

Thomason, G. (1981) *A Textbook of Personnel Management*, 4th edn. Institute of Personnel Management, London.

Torrington, D. and Chapman, J. (1984) *Personnel Management*, 2nd edn. Prentice-Hall, London

Whyte, W. F. (1948) *Human Relations in the Restaurant Industry*, McGraw-Hill, New York.

The IPM Code of Professional Practice in Personnel Management

Introduction to the Code

Personnel management is that part of management concerned with people at work and with their relationships within an organization. Its aim is to bring together and develop into an effective organization the men and women who make up an enterprise, enabling them to make their best contribution to its success.

This Code is a guide to those engaged in personnel management on the essential principles and practices appropriate to the profession. The object of the Code is to establish high standards of practice and publicly declare them. While the Code is directed primarily to members of the Institute of Personnel Management, it is commended to all those working in this field.

The Institute of Personnel Management

The IPM exists to promote and develop the professionalism of personnel management and in particular the development and application of policies governing:

Industrial relations.

Manpower planning, recruitment, selection, placement and termination of employment.

Education, training and development.

Organization development and the effect of change in organization and methods of working.

Terms of employment, methods and standards of remuneration and employee benefits.

Working conditions, health and safety.

Formal and informal communication and consultation between representatives of employers and employees and with employees at all levels in the organization.

The Institute adopts a positive and initiating role, seeking to influence the occupational and social environments, legislation and management thinking – locally, nationally and internationally. It aims to be a leading authority in the field of the management of human resources and the guardian of high standards in the practice of personnel management.

A member of the Institute commits himself to its aims and objects. He is interested in the establishment of good practice within the profession as a whole and in the development of younger members. He is mindful of his responsibilities to his employer and the special nature of his relationship with the employees. At the same time he is concerned that those engaged in personnel management who are not members of the Institute should adopt its standards and understand its objects. In his relationships he should conduct himself with due regard to the high standards of integrity and behaviour demanded by the particular responsibilities of the profession, and will not knowingly take any action which may be liable to bring the good name of the Institute or its members into disrepute.

The personnel manager

While the management of people forms part of every manager's job, the personnel manager provides specialist knowledge, advice and services for other members of the management team so that they may be assisted to make the most effective use of the human resources of the organization. He should have a clear understanding of the economic factors affecting the success of the organization, particularly the cost-effectiveness of manpower and associated expenditure.

A personnel manager is concerned with the long-term success of the organization both as an industrial, commercial or public enterprise, and as a social entity. He has, however, a special involvement in the livelihood of people, their working conditions, security of employment, reward and development, and is also a privileged recipient and guardian of personal information and confidences.

Responsibility to the employer

A personnel manager's primary responsibility is to his employer. He should conduct himself as a responsible member of the management team committed to the achievement of the organization's objectives with the optimum use of resources. He will:

1 Advise on good personnel practice concerning: terms and conditions of employment, staffing and the labour market, the organization of work, training and development, employee benefits, welfare facilities and the working environment.
2 Seek to establish and maintain good working relationships with trade unions and employee representatives.
3 Encourage the development of effective consultation and communication at all levels in the organization.
4 Respect the employer's requirements for the confidentiality of information entrusted to him during the performance of his duties, including the safeguarding of information about individual employees.
5 Promote non-discriminatory employment practices, and common

standards of justice in the treatment of individuals by the corporate employer.

6 Constantly update his professional skill and knowledge in respect of new learning and legislation in the personnel field and the impact of technological, economic and social change on people at work.

Responsibility to employees and potential employees

By his conduct and good practice a personnel manager will establish confidence in himself and understanding of his role and thus resolve the conflict which must sometimes exist between his position as a member of the management team and his special relationship with the workforce in general and with individual employees. In particular, he will:

1 Be available to act in a counselling role to individual employees and to advise them about their personal development and career opportunities.
2 Seek to achieve the fullest possible development of the capability of individual employees commensurate with the opportunities available and the needs of the organization.
3 Ensure the privacy and confidentiality of personal information to which he has access or for which he is responsible, subject to any legal requirements and the best interests of the employee.
4 Ensure that existing and potential employees are given full and accurate information concerning employment with his organization.
5 Observe the Institute's Codes of Practice and use his best endeavours to ensure they are applied throughout his organization.
6 Be concerned with the welfare of pensioners and the dependants of deceased employees.

Relationships with other organizations

In his relationships with other professional bodies, government departments, institutions, employer and trade associations, trade unions and other employee associations, a personnel manager will use his best endeavours to enhance the standing and good name of his profession. He should not disclose information about an employee to external bodies without the agreement of the individual concerned, except where this would conflict with his public duty, or when responding to legitimate requests for references.

Notes

1 The use of masculine throughout this Code is deemed to include the feminine.
2 The term personnel manager is used to include all those working at an executive level in the personnel function whether specialized or not.
3 The terms 'enterprise' or 'organization' are used to include the industrial, commercial or public service sectors.

The IPM Recruitment Code

Introduction

In the spring of 1977, Michael Dixon's Job Column in the *Financial Times* highlighted the resentment felt by many job applicants against recruiters. It made no difference, it seemed, whether the recruiter was a company personnel manager, a small company managing director or a selection consultant. All were guilty of meting out callous injustices to the innocent and defenceless applicant. What was needed, said Michael Dixon, was a *candidates' charter* so that the much-abused applicants were protected with a minimum standard of behaviour by the recruiters. This must have caused many readers with experiences of recruitment and selection to shake their heads with a tired sigh. It is, after all, well-known that a satisfied, rejected applicant is almost as rare as a man who believes his dismissal was justified. Fortunately some recruiters decided to take issue with the *Financial Times* and Michael Dixon's column echoed with demands for a *recruiters' charter* to protect them against the thoughtless, the unreliable, the rude and the downright dishonest who surface in any large batch of job applicants. In an inspired compromise Michael Dixon suggested a 'two-way agreement' giving simple, basic guidelines which, if followed by recruiters and applicants, would eliminate the causes of the complaints. The Institute of Personnel Management was suggested as an appropriate national sponsoring body.

The IPM's National Committee for Pay and Employment Conditions (under the then Vice-President and Chairman, Robert Fleeman) took up the challenge and meetings with Michael Dixon and other interested parties followed. Ideas were aired and a draft code published in the *Financial Times* and the IPM *Digest*. The response revealed an unexpectedly high level of support for the venture and brought many ideas for embellishments and additions. All of these were carefully examined and some found their way into the final document, *The IPM Recruitment Code*. The Code is above all simple and brief. Those who have had experience of such things will know how much easier a longer document would have been.

What it is

The Code aims to set down briefly and clearly guidance on those matters which most commonly cause resentment to recruiters and applicants. The faults are most often the result of inexperience or thoughtlessness, rarely the result of deliberate intent. Many well-run personnel departments will believe that they have nothing to learn from the 'recruiters' obligations', but experienced recruiters know how necessary it is to check regularly that good procedures are not being bypassed. Even in the best-run organization therefore, the Code might be a helpful prompter. Small companies, which want to do their occasional recruitment well – and which are conscious of their public image – will find that the Code provides a useful check list.

Considerable time was spent in refining the Code and making it as short as possible. A crisp, concise, compact Code has a better chance of acceptance and survival. Furthermore, if it is a short document, organizations might be tempted to issue it to applicants, thus reminding them of their obligations (which also are more often casualties of thoughtlessness than intent).

The IPM would like to see the Code mentioned in recruitment advertisements and literature and publicized by trade associations, professional institutions, employment agencies and other bodies. In other ways the IPM will be doing all it can to encourage the use of the Code. It will follow up apparent breaches and seek the co-operation of the 'offending party' in at least avoiding a repetition. Most lapses are unintentional and most companies are unaware of the damage being done to their public relations. For these reasons it is expected that most organizations will respond positively to a carefully phrased and polite approach. Perhaps we can then look forward to the day when the Code has to be revised – because some of yesterday's common faults are no longer common.

What it is not

No one associated with the development of the Code would lay claim to its being revolutionary or even highly original: it does not seek to repeat or replace the laws of the land. Those who support the Code are, in any case, unlikely to ignore the law deliberately on (say) sex or race discrimination, recruiting people under the age of 16, or charging employment agency fees to applicants. The absence of a list of illegalities does not mean that the IPM condones them; it means that the need for the Code did not arise from breaches of the law. Nobody complained to Michael Dixon or the IPM of illegalities; they did complain in volume of the common discourtesies, the inefficiencies and the simple lack of thought that bedevils so much of the recruitment process. Certainly the IPM wants people to act within the law and anyone in doubt about the legality of some matter connected with recruitment should seek professional advice or turn to one of the IPM's publications on the subject. For instance the IPM's Joint Standing Committee on Discrimination has made a special study of the problems of discrimination in recruitment and anyone experiencing difficulties of this type should study the Committee's Report *Towards Fair Selection: A Code for Non-Discrimination* which is obtainable from the IPM Publications.

The IPM Recruitment Code is not a mandatory document. How then will its aims be enforced? The answer is that if we tried to force it on people we would negate its effect. There are examples enough of this happening in the legislative field. Far better to encourage the adoption of the Code voluntarily and although there is no thought of coercion the IPM will take every opportunity of reminding people of the Code and will follow up any alleged breaches which are reported to it or which come to its notice.

The recruitment code – 4th edition

The aims of the code

The Code seeks to promote high standards of professional recruitment practice by encouraging recruiters and applicants to adhere to common guidelines.

The IPM hopes that employers will adopt the Code throughout their organizations on the grounds of common courtesy. The way in which candidates are treated also reflects on an employer's public relations image. Poor publicity can result from bad recruitment practices. Many organizations have excellent recruitment standards, but the Institute accepts that the current levels of unemployment result in large numbers of applications for most vacancies, and other organizations may be unable to meet these standards at all times. The Code, therefore, sets out the basic elements of a professional recruitment policy, which should be implemented in practice wherever possible.

Although some parts of the Code may apply more to white collar employment, the IPM believes that the spirit of this Code should apply to all recruitment. Common courtesy is the right of all applicants, whether for a shopfloor job or for the position of managing director.

The Code aims to provide guidance on those matters that most commonly cause difficulty to recruiters and applicants. Faults usually arise from inexperience or thoughtlessness, and rarely from deliberate intent. Many well-run personnel departments will have little to learn from the Code, but experienced recruiters know that it is necessary to check regularly that procedures are being followed. Even in the best run organizations, the Code should prove helpful as a basis for auditing and updating recruitment practices. Small companies should find that the Code provides a useful checklist and training device for line managers.

Unsolicited applications/Keeping interview appointments

A major concern of recruiters is that of unsolicited applications and how best to deal with them. Large employers can receive many thousands of such applications every year, and the IPM believes that it is unreasonable to expect them to bear the cost of reply. Where, however, the hopeful applicant has enclosed a stamped addressed envelope the recruiter should, at least, acknowledge receipt of the application.

Many recruiters also mention the problem of applicants who fail to keep interview appointments or who do not notify changes of circumstances, such as accepting a job elsewhere.

The Institute accepts that it is difficult to enforce adherence to the Code among applicants and can only remind them that they too have obligations, particularly to help the recruiter. A list of the courtesies that the IPM expects applicants to show appears at the end of this appendix.

Expenses

From the applicants' point of view a number of irritations still, unfortunately, seem to arise, of which the payment of expenses is a significant one. The IPM believes that recruiters should be prepared to pay reasonable and significant expenses incurred by applicants in attending interviews. However, it must be recognized that some recruiters have determined not to do so. In these cases it is reasonable to expect that the recruiter's policy concerning expenses is clearly explained to applicants when they are called to interview and not, as is often the case, at the interview or even afterwards.

Taking up references

The practice of taking up references before making a job offer is largely restricted to the public sector. **Employers should make it clear that they will not approach current or previous employers without the candidate's permission.** Employers should also bear in mind that the high level of company liquidations in recent years means that personnel records may be incomplete for some applicants and it may be impossible to obtain references from some of their previous employers.

Selection techniques

Many complaints are received that the selection techniques of some organizations fall short of professional standards. Employers are urged to bear in mind the damage done to their image in the eyes of both successful and unsuccessful applicants by poor recruitment and interview methods.

Similarly, psychological tests should preferably have been scientifically validated and should always be interpreted by qualified staff. Recruiters should beware of the results of non-scientifically validated tests. Personality tests, in particular, require sensitive handling and interpretation.

Employer: employer relationships

The institute has received complaints from employers about the practice of other employers approaching existing staff at their place of work. Potential and existing employers do have a responsibility towards each other, which is primarily one of trust (e.g. in respect of references). This relationship is considerably damaged by activities amounting to the recruitment of employees in their existing employer's time and at their existing employer's expense.

Discrimination

Sex and race

Unless employers have appropriate employment policies and procedures, discrimination on grounds of race and sex will continue to be practised. This point is particularly important with regard to indirect discrimination. Any requirement which excludes a high proportion of ethnic minorities or women, and is not a realistic requirement of the job, creates indirect discrimination and is unlawful.

Methods of recruitment exist other than advertising such as executive search, recruitment consultants, agency introductions and 'word of mouth'. Whichever is chosen, care must be taken to ensure that the method is fair to applicants and potential applicants and does not effectively screen out minorities or members of one sex. In particular, the 'word of mouth' approach can be unfair and discriminatory, since it will tend to perpetuate a workforce from the same sources as at present.

Keeping records of sex and ethnic origin of job applicants is recommended by the EOC and CRE in their Codes of Practice. A record of the sex and racial origin of all candidates for employment, the jobs applied for, their qualifications and whether or not selected, would provide a means of analysing in detail the recruitment experience of different groups.

It is generally best to obtain these data from the application form, but it is also advisable when asking questions about ethnic origin to include an explanatory note that the information is needed for monitoring purposes and to explain why monitoring is necessary.

Recruiters are also advised to avoid the use of questions at interviews which might be construed as discriminatory, for example, a tendency to inquire into the marital and domestic circumstances of female applicants and not of males.

Disabled applicants

Another form of discrimination operates against disabled people. It is important to get disability into perspective. It does not necessarily affect a person's ability to do the work, although sometimes it may affect the manner or the place in which they perform it. When interviewing the rule should be to test the ability for the job first, discussing the disability only if adjustments need to be made to allow the applicant to do the job.

The MSC has produced a Code of Good Practice on the Employment of

Disabled People which is supported by the IPM. Copies of the Code and further information and advice can be obtained from the MSC's Disablement Advisory Service through Jobcentres.

Rehabilitation of offenders

Naturally, employers will have regard to the provisions of the Rehabilitation of Offenders Act 1974 and not discriminate against or dismiss the applications of candidates with spent convictions. The Act has implications for the design of application forms and interview methods. Guides to the Act are available, published by HMSO.

Recruiters' obligations

1 Job advertisements should state clearly the form of reply desired, in particular, whether this should be a formal application form or by curriculum vitae. Preferences should also be stated if hand-written replies are required. Many applicants complain of labouring to produce a detailed application letter, only to receive an application form asking for the same information. Stating the form of reply saves the time of both the recruiter and applicant. Closing dates should give a reasonable length of time for return of applications. Advertisements should reflect the job as truthfully as possible and preferably carry some indication of remuneration. A number of people complained of bogus advertisements by some employment agencies which were replenishing their files of available candidates. There were also instances of advertisements which appeared largely because of bureaucratic procedure and not because any outside applicant was really wanted. The Institute condemns both practices.

2 An acknowledgement or reply should be made promptly to each applicant by the employing organization or its agent. If it is likely to take some time before acknowledgements are made, this should be made clear in the advertisement.

Applicants should understand that unsolicited applications may not always be acknowledged without receipt of a stamped addressed envelope.

3 Applicants should be informed of the progress of the selection procedures, what these will be (e.g. group selection, aptitude tests), the steps and time involved and the policy regarding expenses.

Employers should bear in mind that attendance by the applicant of interviews will usually involve expenses and they should therefore have an explicit policy in respect of the reimbursement of expenses. The policy should be set out clearly when inviting applicants to interview.

Employers should also make every effort to keep to interview times. Applicants who put themselves forward for interviews are entitled to careful consideration whether or not they are ultimately successful. Unsuccessful applicants should be sent a courteous rejection letter.

Employers using confidential box numbers may have difficulty in meeting this obligation while remaining anonymous. This can be achieved by such means as using blank notepaper and either postal franking without an advertising slogan or ordinary stamps.

4   Detailed personal information (for example religion, medical history, place of birth, family background) should not be called for unless it is relevant to the selection process.

It is not intended that this should bar any request for personal details. There will be some jobs in which it will be necessary to know certain information at the initial application stage. With many others some personal details may never be required. It is not intended that interviewers should be hamstrung. It is the interviewer's job to get to know the applicant, and incidental reference to personal details is inevitable: this is unlikely to offend anyone. What candidates object to is answering an exhaustive list of personal questions on an application form at a very early stage of the selection. Few will, however, object to being asked for certain personal details if the reason is given (or is obvious); for instance, employment agencies should state when asking for nationality that they are statutorily required to do so.

Recruiters must take every care to keep within the guidelines of the codes of practice on sex and race discrimination and should be ready to explain why certain information is required.

5   Before applying for references, potential employers must secure the permission of the applicant.

It still happens that the applicant's current employer is approached for a reference without the applicant's knowledge. If a rule is made that *all* reference approaches must be approved by the candidate, this situation (and others which could be equally embarrassing) will be avoided. If the candidate raises any apparently unreasonable objections, the recruiter will need to know why and may properly take this into account in making the selection.

A further problem is the practice of some organizations of requiring reference names before the shortlisting stages which entails unnecessary approaches to potential referees.

6   Applications must be treated as confidential.

Complaints of breaches of confidence are usually connected with indiscriminate reference checks. It also still happens that an applicant's details are passed to another organization without the applicant's approval.

Applicant's obligations

Just as the code aims to reduce the irritations often felt by applicants, and to give them the right to certain courtesies, it also imposes certain obligations on them. Their main obligation is to show respect and courtesy to employers and to assist them in recruitment. As a minimum, therefore, the Institute believes it reasonable to expect applicants to show the following courtesies.

1   Advertisements should be answered in the way requested (for example telephone for application form, provide brief details, send curriculum vitae).

It is common to receive lengthy details in response to a request for brief initial replies or for people to turn up on the doorstep. Such actions are likely to be remembered to the applicant's disadvantage, and they do hinder a carefully arranged selection procedure.

2   Appointments and other arrangements must be kept, or the recruiter be informed promptly if the candidate discovers an agreed meeting cannot take place.

About one in every five candidates is late. One in ten never shows up.

3   The recruiter should be informed as soon as a candidate decides not to proceed with the application.

This decision presumably is the commonest reason for one in ten failing to attend an interview and the explanation for countless letters from recruiters which are not answered.

4   Only accurate information should be given in applications and in reply to recruiters' questions.

Deliberately supplying inaccurate information may be a cause for terminating any subsequent employment contract. A skilled interviewer will usually detect any inacurracy.

5   Information given by a prospective employer must be treated as confidential, if so requested.

Applicants need a lot of information to decide about a job. To encourage recruiters to give as much information as possible, it will be evident that confidences must be respected.

appendix 4

Effective staff training

An abridged version of the publication *How to Get the Best from Your Staff: An Introduction to Staff Training Skills* by Michael J. Boella.

Author's note

This book sets out to cover the basics of staff training. It covers in a simple, step-by-step process, each of the main areas of knowledge and skills required by senior staff, supervisors and managers responsible for training. Because it is a partially programmed text it enables those who do not have the opportunity to attend a course to study and practise the basics. It also helps more senior managers to know just what is expected of their supervisors and staff trainers. Third, it can be used as a refresher for those who may have already attended a staff trainers' course. Finally, for those who themselves run staff training courses this makes a concise, easy-to-use guide and hand-out.

This book is not however to be seen as a substitute for attendance at a proper course.

Acknowledgements

My thanks are due to many people, known and unknown, who over the years have contributed the knowledge, experience and material which have made this short book possible. Regretfully, I cannot acknowledge everyone personally. However, I would like particularly to record my gratitude to the Tack Organisation and the Industrial Society whose courses I attended and to the HCITB with whom I have collaborated on many occasions.

Introduction

The success of every business depends upon its staff and it has been found that people work most satisfactorily when they have confidence in their employer, in their surroundings and particularly in their own performance of their job.

Obviously no single factor contributes to creating this sense of confidence.

But possibly more than anything else, effective induction, that is, the introduction of everything surrounding a person's job, and through training in the knowledge and skills necessary to do the job, are responsible for creating the confidence which can lead to a person doing his job in a competent and satisfactory manner. Unfortunately however there are those who feel that systematic training is unnecessary, is too costly, and is beyond their capabilities – or they feel that the ability to train others is something that one is born with. Yet most managers know that a person such as a secretary or a chef, who is skilled in his or her job, is more efficient than an unskilled person. This principle applies equally to the *skill of training* which is distinct from, and additional to, the *job skills* to be passed on. The skilled trainer trains more effectively than the unskilled trainer and, in contrast to the myth that there is not enough time to train, the skilled trainer makes training opportunities throughout the normal working day and will help to create a well-trained employee in a shorter time than an unskilled trainer.

Training others is a skill which can be learned by many normal staff and it makes sound business sense to train key staff, particularly the heads of departments, in this essential skill.

Benefits of training

Training, as with all other activities of an organization, should benefit the organization in the short or long term. These include:

1 Increased customer satisfaction
2 Increased customer demand
3 Better use of time
4 Safer working methods
5 Reduced waste
6 Reduced damage
7 Reduced staff turnover.

Hence – more efficiency.

However, because the staff are the people being trained they should also benefit in some way. These include:

1 Increased efficiency
2 Increased earnings
3 Improved job security
4 Improved job prospects.

Hence – increased job satisfaction and confidence in the job.

Planning training

If you are to train staff efficiently it will need to be properly planned and in order to do this four main elements have to be considered:

Who is to do the training?
What is to be taught?
How is it to be taught?
How is it to be judged?

Who is to do the training?

We all know that some people can do a job very efficiently themselves but when it comes to teaching others they are no good at all. This is because to teach others requires certain characteristics which are additional to being able to do the job well.

Anyone who is selected to teach others consequently will need to have certain characteristics. These include:

1 Wish to help others
2 Sympathetic and patient manner
3 Competence in the job
4 Understanding of trainees' needs and problems
5 Systematic approach to work
6 Knowledge and skill of teaching techniques
7 Ability to be self-critical.

From this description it is apparent that most trainers will be more mature people, generally employed at some supervisory level. However, this is not always the case as many craftsmen and even more junior staff make excellent trainers; they enjoy the responsibility and often they are in the best position to train their colleagues, and the task of training others can be a valuable step in developing such people for promotion.

As a principle, however, everyone who has to give some form of instruction or coaching during the normal working day should have or should develop some training skills. This applies particularly to every manager and supervisor. A trainer once trained is going to be able to:

1 Know what performance is expected of the staff
2 Recognize training opportunities and make use of them
3 Make training opportunities
4 Know which tasks and critical points need to be learned by trainees
5 Recognize shortcomings in performance
6 Analyse tasks
7 Plan training
8 Prepare and give instruction
9 Produce training aids
10 Keep records
11 Review training.

What is to be taught?

Training in a business context is concerned with bridging the gap between an individual's capabilities and the employer's requirements. This gap is a *training need*. Put this way it sounds simple but in practice it can be quite difficult. This is because what a person needs to bring to a job is a mixture of:

General knowledge
Technical knowledge
Aptitudes
Attitudes
Skills.

Training needs, apart from consisting of knowledge, skills and attitudes, occur at different times in the working life of employees and organizations. For example when:

A new employee starts
Changes take place
Things go wrong.

When a new employee starts

Of course a whole range of things need to be known. You should include items from each of the following:

Relationships between staff and departments
Hours and other conditions
Safety and security practices
Rules and regulations
Methods of work.

When changes take place

A person needs training when the following occur:

Changes in methods, products or standards of performance
Changes in equipment
Transfers and promotions.

When things go wrong (remedial training)

A person may need training when any of the following occur:

Unsatisfactory trading results or standards
Customer complaints
Breakages, waste.

What can be taught?

Some things, such as knowledge and skill, can be transferred to most reasonable trainees quite easily given adequate training expertise on the part of the trainer.

Attitudes, on the other hand, are very difficult and in many respects it is better to aim to select people with the attitudes you want rather than to attempt to 'instil' attitudes into unwilling employees. If, for example, a person resents serving others, it is unlikely that you will have the time and psychological expertise to change his attitudes. Much better to avoid recruiting him in the first place. It is apparent therefore that most training should be concerned with transferring knowledge and skills. To do this the trainer will need to examine his own knowledge and skill and break it down so that he is completely aware of what he has to put over.

This process – job analysis – can be vital, because most skilled people take for granted large parts of their own knowledge and skill.

The managers' responsibility

These different activities have to be set in motion and monitored constantly by management. And as with most other management processes it is a cyclical one starting and finishing with the planning stage.

Figure A4.1 *The manager's responsibilities*

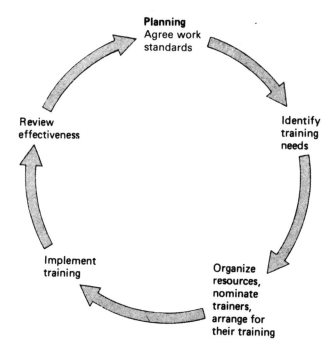

The manager responsible for training must:

1 Set training objectives. To do this, job descriptions may be needed and these will, so far as possible, set standards of performance. For example, if a person is expected to attend to twenty people in an hour, then the trainer should use this standard as his training objective and set progressively more difficult targets during the programme.
2 Select trainers and, where appropriate, he will arrange for them to be trained in training skills. May be he should be the first to attend such a course.
3 Delegate training responsibilities.
4 Provide training facilities such as rooms, equipment and training aids.
5 Inform staff of any changes and any training to be given to cope with changes.
6 Show that he really believes in training by participating in it himself.
7 Review the effectiveness of training by checking upon the work of people who have finished their training and occasionally by interviewing some or all of them or having informal chats with them to obtain their views on the training they received.

What is to be taught?

What has to be taught?

The types of factors staff may have to learn have been listed. One of the problems, however, of teaching others is that the experienced person automatically (even subconsciously) does many things which the trainee is going to have to learn step-by-step. A good example is the difference between a novice driver, who consciously thinks about each element of driving, and the expert who integrates each element unconsciously into the total driving process. Consequently, to be sure that all points are taught the trainer needs to use a systematic process for listing everything that is going to be taught.

If this is not done, many points, sometimes essential or even vital, may be overlooked in training. The omission will then only be highlighted when the trainee (or ex-trainee) does something wrong – possibly with expensive consequences for the employer. Unfortunately in these circumstances the trainee and not the inadequate training is usually blamed.

Here is a simple job broken down into duties.

A room-maid's duties:

1 Collection of guest departure list, and early morning tea and breakfast lists and keys from head housekeeper's office
2 Service of early morning tea and breakfasts in bedroom
3 Preparation of trolley for servicing rooms
4 Servicing of bedrooms
5 Servicing of bathrooms
6 Checking of all appliances

7   Checking of all literature
8   Final room check
9   Reporting back to housekeeper.

Task analysis

After this the duties may be broken down into tasks. Some tasks may be very simple to learn and they may not need to be broken down further. Such tasks usually draw upon a person's knowledge and skills which have been acquired in every day life (the life skills).

Servicing a bathroom

1   Check quantity and take out dirty linen, leave outside bathroom on floor.
2   Check, empty and clean bin and ashtray, remove dirty soap.
3   Wash bath, tiles, clean all chrome fittings, mirrors and lights.
4   Wash toilet bowl, 'U' bend, seat and lid, wash tiles behind toilet and air vent.
5   Put toilet cleanser in bowl and leave.
6   Clean basin and top of vanitory unit then wash and dry drinking glasses after washing hands.
7   Replenish soap, towels, bathmat, disposal bags and toilet paper according to room quantities list.
8   Wash bathroom floor and door, wipe bath and wash basin pipes.
9   Replace bin also checking that shave socket is off.
10 Quickly check around and take out dirty linen to maid's trolley.

More difficult tasks, however, will need to be analysed into the various steps in order to identify exactly what a person has to learn and what he has to avoid. This is called 'task analysis'.

Task analysis – the main elements

Task analysis consists of:

1 *Listing WHAT is done*	This should be one word or a brief phrase describing each distinct step: Greet guest Take glass
2 *Describe HOW the action is performed*	This should be a brief description of how each step is carried out starting with: by taking . . ., by saying . . .,

Figure A4.2 *Task analysis sheet*

What	How	Critical point	Additional information
List each key step or stage, using short phrases starting with words such as:	Describe concisely the method to be used; start sentences with words such as:	Describe the critical signs which indicate that the operation is proceeding satisfactorily or otherwise. Use words which encourage a trainee to use his senses; look for, feel, taste. This column includes elements which involve using the senses in order to make judgements.	Add any additional information which may be necessary for the satisfactory performance of the task or to enhance a normal performance.
write, greet, cut, dispense	by writing by greeting by cutting by dispensing		This column is omitted in some task analyses.
For example, take a glass	For example, by taking a 6 oz Paris goblet by the stem	For example, check that the glass is clean and undamaged	——

Effective staff training 309

Figure A4.3   Task analysis work sheet preparing grapefruit segments

What is done?	How is it done?	Critical points (see/feel/smell/listen/taste)	Additional information
Select a grapefruit	By handling.	Feel for firmness — weight. Look for bruising.	
Cut off ends	By cutting downwards, on to a board with an 8 inch stainless steel knife across growing end, judging thickness of skin.	See the flesh is exposed. See and feel the fingers are bent away from knife.	Safety. Effect of acid on steel.
Cut off skin	By placing the fruit on end and cutting downwards, using all the blade of the knife, following the shape of the fruit. Turn after each cut.	See and feel the knife is cutting between the flesh and the pith.	Wastage.
Remove remaining pith	By lightly cutting downwards, using tip of knife.	See no pith remains on fruit. See any over-ripe patches are removed.	Bitter taste of pith.
Clear the waste	By scraping into bowl with hand.		Tidy work place. Safety
Segment grapefruit	By gently cutting between the membranes, with a stainless steel paring knife, using a 'V' cut for the first two large segments, then an in-out cut for the remainder and pulling the membrane out of the way with the thumb of the hand holding the fruit. Remove any pips while cutting to aid removal of unbroken segments.	Feel tough pith in centre. See all pips are removed.	
Remove excess juice	By hand squeezing what juice is left into bowl.	Feel 'skeleton' free from juice. See no pips fall into bowl.	

Reproduced by permission of the HCTB.

3 *Describing CRITICAL points*   This should describe signs which inform the person carrying out the task that it is going well or otherwise. Such points should consist of sentences or phrases such as:
Check that totals cross-cast
See that the sauce has not curdled

4 *Adding any additional points that should be taken into account*, such as security, safety, sales promotion.

NOTE: This is omitted in some task analyses.

Lesson plans

Once the job has been broken down into the key words or phrases which list all the tasks, and once complicated tasks have been broken down into analysed tasks – the next step is to put all this knowledge and skill into a planned training session.

Not only does the trainer have to analyse and then organize what he is to transfer, but also he has to consider how he is going to:

1 Motivate his trainees to learn.
2 Present the knowledge and skill so that it is assimilated.
3 Give his trainees the opportunity to 'cement in' or consolidate the new knowledge and skills.
4 Ensure that what he has been attempting to transfer has been transferred permanently.
5 Motivate his trainees to use what they have learned.

These processes are incorporated into what is generally called a lesson plan. A lesson plan consists of:

Introduction – motivate to learn
Development – transfer knowledge
Consolidation – make it permanent
Close – motivate to use it

The introduction

The introduction is concerned primarily with motivating the person to want to learn. It should be used to:

1 Establish a personal contact with trainees.
2 Reduce their nervousness.

3   Overcome any particular worries they may have, such as: when the training finishes, what it covers, what will be expected of them.

Unless the introduction is effective the trainee may not be receptive to what is to follow. To help in preparing the introductory phase a useful mnemonic or memory aid has been used by people for many years. It is:

I   interest
N   need
T   title
R   range
O   objective.

Interest

The first thing anyone communicating with others has to do is to attract their attention. This can be done in one of many ways, including:

Making a personal connection between the trainee and the subject, for example, giving a taste or sample, and giving them useful information or news.
Telling a funny story.
Referring to something topical.
Referring to (or inventing) something relevant from one's own personal experience.
Stating something with an apparent contradiction, for example coffee is more important than caviar.
Asking questions.
Giving a demonstration or showing something relevant.

Whatever method is used, however, it should be relevant to the trainee and what is being taught.

Need

The need for the training session should be explained. This should be in two parts, from the employer's point of view and the employee's, but it is essential to emphasize why the trainee needs the training and what benefits he or she will receive.

Title

Obviously the trainee will need to know what is to be taught – usually this is incorporated early on and can be linked with one of the other elements of the INTRO.

Range

The trainee needs to know what is to be covered in the training session and sometimes it is equally important, in order to keep his attention or to reduce his anxiety, to tell him what is not to be covered. It is useful to link back to previous training sessions in order to check, to build confidence and to build on known material.

Objective

Finally the trainee needs to know what he will know or what he should be able to do as a result of the session.

While these five separate elements should be in an introduction, they may be combined skilfully into one or two sentences or, if the training is a long course, the introduction could take thirty minutes or more.

Development

The development stage is the main part of any training session and contains everything to be learned during the session. This should be organized so that:

1 Everything is in a logical sequence.
2 The trainer starts with a quick review of what the trainee knows so that the trainee starts from the known – and therefore feels confident – moving on to the new, the unfamiliar, material.
3 Essential material is picked out ensuring that it is covered, and desirable material is identified – to be covered if the time or opportunity presents itself.

The development stage is concerned with transferring the instructor's knowledge and skills to the trainee. It is, however, rather like serving a meal. The food has to be treated in certain ways to make it appetizing and digestible. In the same way any knowledge and skills to be transferred have to be presented so that they interest the trainee and are retained permanently by him.

There are a number of important rules which will help the trainer to prepare and present his material so that this happens, and these are covered in more depth on pages 314–18.

Consolidation and close

Throughout a training session the trainer must use various means of assisting his or her trainee to learn. One major technique is the correct use of questions and this is covered on pages 316–17. It is vital, however, that at the end of a session the trainer:

1 Tests that the training objectives have been achieved by questioning, testing or observing.

Figure A4.4 *Lesson plan*

Subject:	Aim:	Time:
Preparation and use of a room-maid's trolley	At the end of this session trainees will be able to: 1 Prepare their trolley for use 2 Recognize and know the use of all the contents of the trolley	30 minutes

Key point	Detail	Aids
Cleanliness of trolley	Emphasize that a clean trolley is necessary in order to ensure that clean linen is not made dirty	The actual items Questions
Linen	Show the different types of linen and how the number of each is arrived at, to include: towels sheets pillow cases	The actual items Questions
Cleaning	Show the different cleaning materials and explain what each is used for, to include: lavatory cleaner bath and basin cleaner floor polish	The actual items Questions

2   Reinforces the instruction by recapitulating and questioning so that key points will not be forgotten.

In addition to testing the effectiveness and reinforcing the instruction the instructor should also make quite clear what is now expected of the trainee in work terms and he will also arouse interest in the next session by explaining:

1   What it is about.
2   When it will be.
3   What the objective is.

A useful form for planning a lesson is shown in Table A4.3.

The learning 'sandwich'

Every piece of instruction should be a sandwich consisting of:

a slice of motivation; motivating to want *to learn*; the filling; the main body of the instruction; a slice of motivation; motivating to want *to use* what has been learned.

How do we learn?

The ability of people to learn is dependent to a great extent upon their reasons for wanting to learn something. If someone is very keen to learn, he will apply himself. On the other hand, if he is not keen to learn, he will almost certainly bring little enthusiasm to the learning process.

Why do people learn?

Obviously there are many reasons for people wanting to learn and in a work setting these will be closely linked to why people work. If the trainer knows and understands why each individual wants to learn, he or she should be able to use this to motivate the person – and keep his or her interest. To attempt to treat all people in the same way is certainly not the way to being a successful trainer or supervisor. A key supervisory and training skill therefore is to discover what motivates each of his or her subordinates or trainees.

If a generalization is to be made, however, the main reasons are likely to be one or more of the following:

1   To obtain rewards such as pay, promotion, esteem.
2   To avoid punishment such as dismissal, reprimand, loss of esteem.
3   Interest.
4   Curiosity.

How do people learn?

Learning is the process of acquiring knowledge, skills and attitudes. It occurs when knowledge, skills and attitudes are transferred to the learner from other people or situations. The transfer is through five primary senses and is best when as many senses as possible are used – particularly in combination. For example, in teaching a person to cook it is possible merely to give him detailed recipes but the results are not likely to be edible! In addition to the recipes, however, the trainee would watch demonstrations and the results are likely to be an improvement. But to involve the trainee fully so that he sees, hears, smells, touches and tastes, is the best and only effective way of teaching cookery.

We learn: 1 per cent with our sense of TASTE
1.5 per cent with our sense of TOUCH
3.5 per cent with our sense of SMELL
11 per cent with our sense of HEARING
33 per cent with our sense of SIGHT.

(SOURCE: Industrial Audiovisual Association, USA)

The transfer is made more effective by ensuring that:

1 The amount and type of material is suited to the person being trained. Frequent, short sessions are much more effective than infrequent long ones.
2 It is transferred in logical, progressive steps, building on the known.
3 The methods and choice of words used must suit the capabilities of the trainees.

How do we remember?

We remember: 10 per cent of what we READ
20 per cent of what we HEAR
50 per cent of what we SEE and HEAR
80 per cent of what we SAY
90 per cent of what we SAY and DO simultaneously

(SOURCE: Industrial Audiovisual Association, USA)

In addition, trainers must recognize that there are many factors which inhibit a person's ability or desire to learn and consequently a trainee will have difficulty learning if he is:

1 Nervous, tired or frightened.
2 Worried about his or her job, money, family.
3 Distracted by noise, interruptions.
4 Uncomfortable, too cold, too hot.

So far as the training session itself is concerned people will not get the most out of it if they are bored by:

1 The trainer's style, tone and language
2 The length of the session
3 The content.

The rate at which people learn varies from person to person but most people learn in steps – sometimes making rapid progress and sometimes appearing to make very little progress at all. This is quite natural and a good trainer will recognize this and he will know when a trainee is stuck and needs sympathy and help rather than badgering. A trainer's main duty is to build up confidence and this will only be achieved by sympathy and understanding. Criticism and lack of patience reduce confidence and only slow down the learning process.

Question technique

A trainer can make use of questions in three main ways. These are, to test a person's level of attainment (test question), to stimulate a person to 'learn for himself or herself' (a teaching or extension question), and thirdly to generate understanding and exchange of information and attitudes between members of a group by tossing questions and answers back and forth (bonding questions).

Questions may be used principally for:

1 Testing the level of attainment before a 'training' session.
2 Testing the effectiveness of training.
3 Helping people to work out answers for themselves, thus teaching themselves.
4 Encouraging an exchange of knowledge and information, in a group.
5 Obtaining or focusing interest.
6 Maintaining interest.
7 Creating understanding between the group, and between the group and the instructor.

Question structure

Questions generally are more effective when they are 'open-ended'. This encourages a person to think for the answer. Where questions give simple alternatives or anticipate yes or no, less thought is required by the trainee and the question consequently is less effective both in testing and in consolidating learning. Most questions should contain why, where, when, what, who or how.

Questions, particularly teaching questions, should be planned beforehand – and should relate particularly to the 'critical points' identified in the 'task analysis' stage.

Where questions are not answered satisfactorily by the trainee, the trainer must consider first if the question was properly framed and understood. If not the question should be rephrased and put again. If the question still remains unanswered the trainer must consider whether the training he has given is satisfactory or not.

Putting questions (the three Ps)

When questions are put to a group of people this should be done in a way which encourages everyone in the group to participate. This is achieved by:

1 Putting the question – *without naming* anyone to answer it.
2 Pausing so that everyone thinks about the question and answer.
3 Pointing out who is to answer the question.

Aids to training

Because people learn most easily by using a variety of their senses and their different faculties, trainers should always attempt to support their own instruction with training aids. These include visual aids such as blackboards and film slides and audio aids such as tape recorders. They should only be used to:

Support but not substitute
Simplify complex instruction
Emphasize
Interest
Aid memory.

Training aids ideally should be the real thing, but in some cases the equipment or procedures may be too complex for a clear explanation, so a diagram may help. The preparation of training aids should be carefully planned to support the instruction given.
Training aids include:

Actual equipment or equipment specially modified for training purposes
Drawings and diagrams
Films, slides, recordings
Graphs and charts.

Recently, for various reasons, the need for job descriptions and similar documents has grown considerably with the result that many employers – even small ones – now use such documents as an essential tool of effective management. Unfortunately these documents are rarely used for training purposes although with a little forethought they can be designed to serve the purpose of:

1 Job descriptions
2 Instructor's training programme and checklist
3 Trainee's training programme and checklist
4 Work manual.

Job aids

Many jobs can be made easier with descriptions of the methods or procedures to be employed. Such descriptions may be called job aids.

Job aids can be of value to the experienced worker as a reference, and to the trainee as a learning aid. As such, they can substitute for parts or all of certain training sessions because they enable trainees to teach themselves and they can relieve the trainees from having to attempt to memorize unnecessarily.

Job aids can be used:

1   Where supervision is minimal.
2   Where procedures are changed.
3   Where company standards need to be adhered to.
4   Where mistakes cannot be risked.
5   When memory needs assistance because of the complexity of a procedure, or the infrequency of its use.
6   Where staff may speak limited English but where a drawing or design will describe what is required.

Job aids include:

1   Diagrams
2   Photographs
3   Price lists, menus
4   Procedural instructions, recipes.

Introducing staff to a new employer

How do people feel?

Most people approach a new job feeling nervous and worried. Sometimes this is quite apparent. In other cases, however, it is well-concealed. But whether it is obvious or not, until people have settled into an organization they will be nervous or worried and this will influence their ability to learn their job – to do it effectively and in particular to get on with their colleagues, supervisors and customers. They will not have the feeling of confidence which is essential to their being able to do a good job.

Success during the first few days in a new job is vital and while most managers admit this, less than 10 per cent of managers in some industries actually carry out a formal induction of new employees.

What a job consists of

Induction is not something that takes place on the first morning of a new job, it can be a relatively long process, with some people taking many weeks to settle in. This is because every job has two parts to it. First, there is the work itself and secondly, there are all the peripherals to the job including conditions and social contacts.

Figure A4.5 *The main elements of a job*

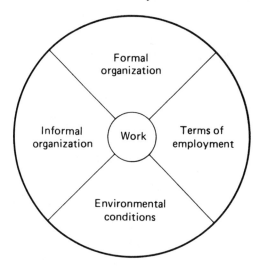

People will not be able to cope with the work part of their job unless they understand and are reasonably happy with the surrounding elements. These include:

1 Location and physical layout
2 Conditions of employment and contracts
3 Company and house rules
4 Customers
5 Management, supervision and formal relationship
6 Colleagues and informal relationships.

The induction process is concerned with introducing an employee to all these elements as quickly as possible so that he or she need not worry about them any more. This enables the trainee to concentrate on the work which is the main purpose of the job rather than having to learn and worry about all the elements surrounding the work.

Benefits of induction

The employer benefits from effective induction by:

1 Reducing staff turnover
2 Improving staff efficiency and work standards
3 Improving staff morale.

The employees benefit by:

1 Fitting in and feeling a part of the team.

2 Being accepted as part of the team.
3 Becoming competent and hence confident in the shortest possible time.

Every organization will need to induct its employees in its own particular conditions, rules and methods, so no example can cover all circumstances. However, the checklist below shows the type of subjects that need to be covered. This, however, shows only the formal aspects of induction, and managers and supervisors should ensure that newcomers are inducted into the informal aspects as well. By definition, however, this can rarely be done by managers or supervisors. Instead, what they need to do is to put a newcomer under the wing of a 'sponsor', that is someone who 'knows the ropes'. This person may well be the newcomer's trainer also.

Checklist for induction programmes:

1 *Documentation*
   Are the following
   points covered?

   Name   Address   Tel. no.
   Next of kin   Name   Address
   Tel. no.   National Insurance no.
   P45   Bank address

2 *Information*
   Are the following
   departments informed?

   Wages/Pensions/Insurance/
   Personnel/Training/etc.

3 *Terms of employment*
   Are the following
   explained and
   understood?

   Hours of duty/Meal breaks/Days off/
   Method of calculating pay/Holiday
   arrangements/Sick leave/Pension
   scheme. Grievance procedures.
   Rights regarding trade unions and Staff
   Association
   Additional benefits such as Group
   Insurance rates or other discounts.

4 *History and organization*
   Are the following
   explained and understood?

   Origin and development of the
   organization. Present situation/
   objectives.

5 *Establishment
   Organization*
   Are the following
   explained and
   understood?

   Layout of establishment including toilets,
   showers, etc.
   Names of relevant supervisors and
   colleagues, introduction where necessary,
   to supervisor, shop steward, etc.

6 *Rules and regulations*
   Are the following
   explained and
   understood?

   (a) Statutory; licensing laws and hours,
       food hygiene, Innkeepers Liability
       Act, etc.
   (b) Company rules; punctuality,
       drinking, smoking, appearance, per-
       sonal business, use of employer's
       property, etc.

7 *The job*
   Are the following
   explained and
   understood?

   Purpose/methods/training needs

When things go wrong, who can help?

Frequently, when things go wrong, management and supervisors jump to quick conclusions regarding the cause. Quick conclusions are often wrong conclusions which lead to wrong solutions. Wrong solutions obviously do not solve the problem and frequently they do the reverse by aggravating people who recognize what is the real cause and just how ineffective is the solution.

Correcting errors depends upon the correct diagnosis of what causes things to go wrong. The correct procedure for putting things right consists of:

1 Identifying a fault as a variation or departure from a standard of perform-ance which may be either specified verbally, in writing or by custom and practice.
2 Identifying the cause or causes.
3 Identifying the person or persons responsible. The person committing the error may not be at fault, but rather the person who issued the order or trained the person responsible.
4 Deciding what action to take, how to communicate this action and how to motivate the person who may take the new instructions as a criticism.
5 Deciding how to prevent a repetition.

Heads of departments and other senior staff are responsible for the prevention and correction of faults. They should, therefore, pay particular attention during training to 'critical points', that is, the points at which things could go wrong.

This book* is designed to assist managers and heads of departments to understand more clearly the knowledge and skills they need to bring to their responsibility in training their staff. The book, however, cannot substitute for thorough practical and theoretical training in the techniques of training because, as the book itself says, effective training makes use of various methods to transfer and consolidate knowledge and skill. Consequently the best way to become an effective trainer and supervisor, having attended a proper course on the subject, is to practise and to be critical always of one's own performance.

'There are no bad staff, only bad managers'

*How to get the Best from Your Staff.

Technology and employment in hotels and catering

by Marian Whitaker, Brighton Polytechnic

According to HCITB statistics, employment in the industry generally increased rapidly up to 1980 before falling back in 1981–82. Certain sectors, e.g. industrial catering, have slumped badly with the onset of recession, while others, most notably fast food, have continued to grow and provide more jobs. There is a marked tendency, however, for new job opportunities to be of the part-time variety, even in the more 'permanent' clerical occupations.

There are, of course, major problems in trying to separate the impact of technology on employment from the impact of the recession. It is particularly difficult when the use of technology appears to be recession driven.

If the predicted growth of the leisure and entertainment sector proves well founded, the hotel and catering industry should expand overall with a corresponding increase in employment levels as the demand for their services grows.

This expansion may be partially facilitated by the use of information technology where it enables companies to provide new services, e.g. video conferencing, fast counter services, and to use the new wealth of management information to plan and market existing services more effectively. This employment-generating aspect of the technology is known as the 'product effect'. The use of information technology may also be an important factor in maintaining competitiveness in international markets – particularly in the hotel conference business. However, there will be some technological impact on the employment of clerical and administrative staff; this will be referred to as the 'process effect'.

It would be useful to the industry's manpower planners to know which of these effects will dominate. Table A5.1 presents the results of research so far into potential job losses and gains which may be directly or indirectly attributed to the use of information technology.

Smaller firms clearly have fewer opportunities to reduce staff numbers, so job losses have been concentrated in larger firms and the public sector.

Much depends, however, on the firm's trading position and their attitude towards information technology. Firms who have suffered heavily in the recession may look towards information technology as a labour-saving device offering opportunities for direct cost reductions. Given the degree of labour

Figure A5.1   *Potential job losses/gains by occupation*

Occupation	No significant change	Significant losses	Significant gains	Increase in part-time ratio
Senior managers	*			
Administrative staff				
Typists		*		*
Secretaries		*		*
Accounts clerks				*
Payroll clerks		* (1)		
Stock clerks				*
Junior managers		*		
Sales staff			*	
Operational staff				
Cashiers				* ⎫
Receptionists				* ⎬(2)
Reservationists				* ⎭
Telephonists		*		,
Supervisors		*		
Chefs	*			
Other kitchen staff	*			
Waiters				* ⎱(3)
Bar staff				* ⎰
Housekeepers	*			
Cleaning staff	*			
Porters	*			
Storekeepers				*
Technical staff				
Systems managers			*	
Programmers			*	
Analysts			*	
Maintenance staff			*	
Technical trainers			*	

(1)   Very significant job loss. Payroll clerks are apparently an endangered species.
(2)   These front office functions frequently merged to form one full-time or several part-time jobs.
(3)   Traditionally part-time jobs anyway, computer provides trading information which allows hours of waiters and bar staff to be scheduled to reflect more accurately peaks and troughs in customer traffic.

turnover in the industry there have been very few notified redundancies, the reductions can usually be achieved by natural wastage.

There has been very little collective employee resistance to the introduction of computer systems. The only negotiated new technology agreements have been in the public sector, but they are rarely implemented. However, that does not mean that managers can or should introduce new equipment and methods without consulting their staff. The efficient use of a computer system can only be realistically achieved by involving employees in the decision to computerize and obtaining their commitment from the outset.

The use of information technology can lead to dramatic improvements in productivity, particularly in administrative/clerical areas. In expanding firms all or part of that increased capacity can be absorbed or redeployed in the provision of new and better services. In addition, a number of new jobs have been created for technical specialists and support staff.

Across the industry the number of jobs for information technology specialists is really quite small – they are expensive to recruit and difficult to retain. Hence there is now a trend towards recruitment of a few highly skilled specialists, supported by a layer of internally trained 'computer literate' administrators (often accounts staff). This trend has also been noted in other industries. Given the degree to which computer systems are now 'user-friendly', it is anticipated that the need for specialist workers will gradually diminish (MSC, 1985, p. 88).

The quality of employment: skills and job satisfaction

In the past, clerical workers were usually considered to be more skilled than shopfloor workers in terms of status, responsibility and the less repetitive nature of their work (Lockwood, 1958). But later Braverman argued that the use of technology would inevitably lead to the conversion of office work into a high speed industrial process. The effect would be to de-skill and reduce levels of autonomy and responsibility among white collar workers (Braverman, 1974).

More recently, Crompton and Reid (1982) have argued that substantial changes in the size and nature of the white collar labour force (including feminization) during the post-war years really meant that the majority of clerical workers were semi-skilled at the most and enjoyed very little autonomy and responsibility in their jobs even before the impact of new technology. They conclude that information technology may be one more factor in a long process of de-skilling that has taken place since the 1950s.

Research into the hotel and catering industry has indicated that the technology can have a de-skilling effect in the lower-grade, clerical occupations; however, in many cases there has been some compensating skill enhancement. It would be wrong therefore to take a deterministic stance on the potential impact of technology on skills.

Typists have clearly lost many of their layout skills to the word processor, so that it is now possible for anybody familiar with a keyboard to produce 'professional' documents. Some companies have eliminated the traditional typing pool altogether; managers and other administrators produce their own letters and documents using word processors.

Secretarial staff have also lost out to the word processor – shorthand skills in particular are less in demand. However, the removal of routine work such as typing and filing should mean that secretaries now have more time to attend to the more interesting and varied PA aspects of their work, and even to enter into decision-making roles. Very often the secretary is a great source of informal knowledge and takes on an important intermediary role which would be difficult to automate (Silverstone and Towler, 1982).

Accounts staff may find that the computer takes away most of the complex calculative routines that they were trained to carry out, and book-keeping now involves a lot of keyboard work. This leaves the field open for less skilled people familiar with keyboards to carry out this work. But again this should give accounts staff more time to spend on the production of summary reports, and the actual interpretation of results.

The roles of receptionists, cashiers and booking clerks are increasingly being merged into a single front office function. It is now important for hotel front office staff to have experience of computerized reservations systems. People without this experience may find themselves at a disadvantage in the job market. There is a noticeable decline in the use of numerical skills; all ledger work can be performed by the computer and/or shifted to back office. There is now a trend towards removing administrative duties from the reception area and increasing the personal service element, placing greater emphasis on communications and social skills.

Supervisors or junior managers in large organizations have occasionally been upgraded to the role of data processing manager. It is usually only supervisory staff that become totally competent with the computer system, hence their ability to move into these positions. At the same time, the need for direct supervision and checking of clerical work is reduced since the computer performs most of the calculation work. However, the importance of accuracy at point of data entry is now doubled, given that input errors can have far-reaching consequences.

On the catering side, use of EPOS equipment has virtually solved this problem in restaurants with pre-set keys and PLU facilities for each menu item. The cashier does not need to know the price of any item. However, the use of similar systems in bars has brought problems. Bar staff are generally very good at mental arithmetic and find the new systems slow and awkward to use. At peak times, the system can prove too restrictive and staff will take shortcuts (which of course throws the stock out).

The solution to this may be found in microprocessor controlled dispensing equipment, which coupled with EPOS equipment can, in theory, provide a total stock and cash control system. It would involve a certain amount of reorganization however. In a large bar, several terminals would be installed with bar staff restricted to serving in a particular area. This is said greatly to improve efficiency. The advertising literature for one company supplying these systems explains:

Our design staff provides each location with blueprints for a compact, five-foot work area built around the computer bar station. Work motion studies have confirmed a 20% or greater increase in the number of drinks a bartender can serve using the computer bar and this 'cockpit efficiency'.

However, this option is still very expensive and technically troublesome.

This is perhaps an example of technology that is ergonomically unsound! The solution favoured by one major firm has been to recruit all new, inexperienced staff when introducing EPOS equipment.

Storekeepers can suffer a major reduction in job satisfaction with the introduction of a computerized stock control system. Their work would normally involve constant checking, counting, recording and updating, and a great deal of book work. The computer can take on most of the book work leaving the storekeeper with little else to do other than physically count the stock. In one case a storekeeper argued that he had been reduced to the status of an unskilled manual worker, and spent most of his time loading and unloading pallets.

This de-skilling effect of computer technology can sometimes be extremely wasteful for the employer as well as the individual concerned. Why pay a semi-skilled man to do an unskilled job in the first place? It can only really be justified in cases of labour shortage where it is necessary to dilute the labour force allowing skilled labour to be redeployed more effectively in tasks that cannot be computerized. De-skilling also has a poor effect on staff morale, and it is then a difficult task for management to gain commitment of employees towards the use of new methods, machinery, and techniques.

The role of the manager

The most significant impact of the technology is likely to be on the role of the manager. Some junior managerial/supervisory posts have been cut by larger organizations, and there is more potential for job loss among regional/area managers where network systems are in use. The role of the manager as an information provider must soon give way to the more significant role of information user. Less managers are required but those that remain will need to be more highly skilled in the use of information and the management of innovation itself.

Initially it is the management who are responsible for choosing and implementing the computer system. Industry-wide lack of experience and knowledge in this area has led to slow rates of technological diffusion. To define information requirements and specify the size and scope of the system is something that most managers are unable to do unaided at present. If the use of information technology is to diffuse widely across the industry, managers will probably have to become involved in the process of design and development of computer systems. Clearly then the technically minded manager will be an important asset for hotel and catering organizations.

Given the degree of staff turnover in the industry, managers and supervisory staff will need to be fully competent with the computer system to ensure continuity in staff training.

The most important shift in emphasis will be away from routine processing work towards the application of interpretative skills. There is little point in having a computer system that will provide accurate, up-to-date information if people do not have the skills to use it. Information management is generally neglected as part of the hotel and catering manager's training. This must surely change if computer systems are to be used effectively as management tools instead of simple electronic clerks.

Conclusions

Given the slow rate of technological diffusion the impact of information technology on employment levels has so far been quite small. However, its use can be positively associated with job loss amongst clerical and administrative staff.

The use of computerized tills also permits precise monitoring of labour productivity in relation to sales and covers per hour. With this information management can arrange staff rotas to reflect more accurately peaks and troughs in customer traffic. The result has been an increase in numbers of part-time staff at the expense of full timers.

There have been some increases in employment associated with the use of new technology particularly among technical specialists, programmers and maintenance staff. However, across the industry their numbers are small and likely to decline.

Higher rates of productivity in clerical and administrative areas have allowed firms to expand without increasing employment. Overall the impact of technology on white collar employment in the industry will be negative, though far less significant than the general impact of recession.

As important as the impact on employment levels are the qualitative effects of information technology on skills, status and job satisfaction. The 'mechanization' of a number of clerical tasks now means less tedious paperwork, which can leave people free to spend more time on interpretative work. This is most likely to occur where companies are expanding. However, the use of information technology sometimes means the removal of some quite satisfying and hard-earned skills, e.g. secretarial shorthand and ledger work. New skills mainly involve the use of computer keyboards.

Most of the jobs affected in this way are traditionally performed by women and most of those likely to disappear have been traditionally performed by women. Most of the technical posts created have been filled by men. In short, the scope for women to obtain 'good jobs' in the hotel and catering industry is narrowing.

The disappearance of jobs and the erosion of some skills may be all the more rapid for the absence of formal industrial relations practices and procedures in the hotel and catering industry.

The service sector, as a whole, is expected to provide the focus for future employment growth in the United Kingdom. The research so far has shown that things are likely to be less straightforward than this suggests. The current pattern of employment changes clearly limits the scope for job creation. Those jobs likely to be created are restricted to certain occupational groups, namely cooking, cleaning and waitressing; jobs which are generally considered to be menial and certainly low paid. If we are relying on the hotel and catering sector to provide new jobs for the future, we need to look closely at the quality of employment in addition to the quantitative aspect.

However, it has been suggested that information technology could be used as an expansionary tool, particularly when closely linked to the marketing function. A significant change in emphasis in management training will be required before that potential is realized.

Bibliography

See also chapter reading lists.

Armstrong, M., *A Handbook of Human Resource Management Practice*, 2nd ed.,
London: Kogan Page, 1984

Boella, M., *Personnel Management in the Hotel and Catering Industry*, 4th ed.,
London: Hutchinson, 1987

Bowey, Angela M., *The Sociology of Organisations*, London: Hodder and Stoughton,
1976

British Hotel, Restaurant and Caterers Association, *Manpower Problems in the Hotel
and Catering Industry*, London: BHRCA, 1975

Commission on Industrial Relations, U.K. *Hotel and Catering Industry. Part I. Hotels
and Restaurants*, (Report No. 23) Cmnd. 4789, London: HMSO, 1971

Commission on Industrial Relations, U.K. *Hotel and Catering Industry. Part II.
Industrial Catering*, (Report No. 27) London: HMSO, 1972

Department of Employment, U.K. *Hotels*. (Manpower Studies No. 10). London:
HMSO, 1971

Department of Employment, U.K. *Catering*. (Manpower Studies No. 11) London:
HMSO, 1972

Doswell, R., and Nailon, P., *Case Studies in Hotel Management*, 2nd ed., London:
Barrie and Jenkins, 1973

Gershuny, J. and Miles, I., *The New Service Economy*, London: Frances Pinter, 1983

Handy, C., *The Future of Work*, London: Blackwell, 1984

Handy, C., *Understanding Organizations*, London: Penguin, 1985

Jones, P., and Lockwood, A., *Management of Hotel Operations*, London: Cassell,
1989

Hill, J. M. M., *Labour Turnover in the Hotel and Catering Industry*, TIHR Doc. No.
CASR 123, London: Tavistock Institute of Human Relations, 1968 (Restricted
document)

Hill, J. M. M., and Menzies, Isabel E. P., *Productivity Measurement in the Hotel and
Catering Industry*, TIHR Doc. No. CASR 30, London: Tavistock Institute of
Human Relations, 1967 (Restricted document)

Hornsey, T., and Dann, D., *Manpower Management in the Hotel and Catering
Industry*, London: Batsford Academic and Educational, 1984

Knight, I. B., *Patterns of Labour Mobility in the Hotel and Catering Industry*, London:
HCITB, 1971

Kotas, R., *Labour Costs in Restaurants: a Study of Labour Costs in Catering
Establishments in the Greater London Area*. London: Intext, 1970

Lockwood, A., and Jones. P., *People in the Hotel and Catering Industry*, Eastbourne:
Holt Saunders, 1984

Magurn, J. P., *A Manual of Staff Management in the Hotel and Catering Industry*,
London: Heinemann, 1977

Mars, G., Hotel pilferage: a case study in occupational theft. In: Warner, M. (ed.), *The Sociology of the Workplace*, London: Allen & Unwin, 1973, pp. 200–10

Mars, G., Some implications of 'fiddling' at work. In: *The Social Psychologist in Industry*. Proceedings of the British Psychological Society Conference at Loughborough University, March 1977. Department of Social Sciences, Loughborough University, Loughborough 1977

Mars, G., and Mitchell, P., *Room for Reform? A Case Study of Industrial Relations in the Hotel Industry*, Unit 6, Industrial Relations Course, p. 881, Milton Keynes: The Open University Press, 1976

Mars, G., and Mitchell, P., *Catering for the Low Paid: Invisible Earnings*, Low Pay Unit Bulletin No. 15, June 1977, London: HMSO

Medlik, S., *The Business of Hotels*, London: Heinemann, 1989

Nailon, P., *A Study of Management Activity in Units of an Hotel Group*, Department of Hotel and Catering Industry Research Unit, University of Surrey, London 1968

Nailon, P., *Organisation Climate and Communication. First report on the organisation improvement programme conducted at the Sonesta Tower*, London, 1970

Nailon, P., *Organisation Climate and Communication. Second report on the organisation improvement programme conducted at the Sonesta Tower*, London, 1970

National Economic Development Office, U.K., Hotel and Catering EDC: *Staff Turnover*, (Chairman: Sir W. Swalllow), London: HMSO, 1969

National Economic Development Office, U.K. Economic Development Committee for Hotels and Catering, *Your Manpower: a Practical Guide to the Manpower Statistics of the Hotel and Catering Industry*, (Chairman: Sir W. Swallow), London: HMSO, 1967

National Economic Development Office, U.K. Hotel and Catering EDC. *Why Tipping?* London: NEDO, 1969

National Economic Development Office, U.K. Economic Development Committee for Hotels and Catering. *Manpower Policy in the Hotels and Restaurant Industry – Research Findings*, London: NEDO, 1975

National Economic Development Office, U.K. Economic Development Committee for Hotels and Catering, *Manpower Policy in the Hotels and Restaurant Industry – Summary and Recommendations*, London: NEDO, 1975

Orwell, G., *Down and Out in Paris and London*, Harmondsworth, Mdx: Penguin Books, 1969

Pratt, K., and Bennett, S., *Elements of Personnel Management*, 3rd ed., Wokingham: GEE, 1989

Pugh, D., and Hickson, D., *Writers on Organizations*, 4th ed., London: Penguin, 1989

Saunders, C., *Social Stigma of Occupations*, London: Gower, 1981

Shames, G., and Glover, W., *World Class Service*, Yarmouth USA: International Press, 1989

Sisson, K. (Ed.), *Personnel Management in Britain*, Oxford: Blackwell, 1989

Thomason, G., *A Textbook of Human Resources Management*, London: Institute of Personnel Management, 1988

Torrington, D., and Hall, L., *Personnel Management, A New Approach*, London: Prentice-Hall, 1987

Whyte, W. F., *Human Relations in the Restaurant Industry*, New York: McGraw-Hill, 1948

Index

Italicized figures indicate pages on which figures appear.